Insubordinate Co…

Insubordinate Costume: Inspiring Performance presents a comprehensive study of historical and contemporary examples of scenographic costume – the type of costume that creates an almost complete stage environment by itself, simultaneously acting as costume, set and performance.

This book provides readers with an overview of the costumes, designers, context and theory that have contributed to the emerging field of 'costume as performance'. Focusing on artists and their creative approach to space, form, materials and movement, the book looks at iconic figures such as Loïe Fuller, Oskar Schlemmer and Leigh Bowery, amongst contemporary examples of practitioners that are blurring disciplinary boundaries between fashion, dance, performance and theatre. The book includes chapters by Dr Sofia Pantouvaki, who focuses on performance costume as a means of research; Christina Lindgren, who presents the findings of the four-year *Costume Agency* project at Oslo National Academy of the Arts in Norway; Charlotte Østergaard, who discusses the implications of 'Listening with costume' and Felix Choong, writing on 'Contemporary Runways, Contemporary Costumes'. The final part of the volume, 'The Practitioners' Voice', examines current practice through interviews and contributions from key practitioners with an afterword by Dr Rachel Hann.

Insubordinate Costume will appeal to professional costume designers, performance artists, dancers, directors, choreographers, fashion designers and theorists, teachers and students of these subjects. With its interdisciplinary focus and unique and dynamic content, this publication is relevant to a range of art, design and performance courses.

Susan Marshall is a costume designer, adjunct professor of Twentieth Century Fashion at FIT in Milan, Politecnico di Milano and lecturer in costume design at AFOL Moda Milan. *Insubordinate Costume* is based on her doctoral research at Goldsmiths University of London, which explored the pivotal role of costume in performance and the fundamental importance of play in the performers' creative approach to the costumes.

Insubordinate Costume
Inspiring Performance

Edited by Susan Marshall

NEW YORK AND LONDON

Designed cover image: Susan Marshall, *Tilde Knudsen as The Queen of Hearts*, 2020.
Photograph Emile Carlsen © Susan Marshall & Tilde Knudsen

First published 2025
by Routledge
605 Third Avenue, New York, NY 10158

and by Routledge
4 Park Square, Milton Park, Abingdon, Oxon, OX14 4RN

Routledge is an imprint of the Taylor & Francis Group, an informa business

© 2025 selection and editorial matter, Susan Marshall; individual chapters, the contributors

The right of Susan Marshall to be identified as the author of the editorial material, and of the authors for their individual chapters, has been asserted in accordance with sections 77 and 78 of the Copyright, Designs and Patents Act 1988.

All rights reserved. No part of this book may be reprinted or reproduced or utilised in any form or by any electronic, mechanical, or other means, now known or hereafter invented, including photocopying and recording, or in any information storage or retrieval system, without permission in writing from the publishers.

Trademark notice: Product or corporate names may be trademarks or registered trademarks, and are used only for identification and explanation without intent to infringe.

ISBN: 978-1-032-37598-4 (hbk)
ISBN: 978-1-032-37597-7 (pbk)
ISBN: 978-1-003-34100-0 (ebk)

DOI: 10.4324/9781003341000

Typeset in Univers
by Deanta Global Publishing Services, Chennai, India

Contents

List of Contributors   vii
Preface   ix
Acknowledgements   x
Introduction   xi

PART 1 INSUBORDINATE BEGINNINGS   1

    1 Insubordinate Beginnings   3
    Susan Marshall

    2 Dance, Performance Art and Insubordinate Costume   31
    Susan Marshall

PART 2 BLURRING THE BOUNDARIES BETWEEN THEATRE, DANCE, PERFORMANCE ART AND FASHION   51

    3 Blurring the Boundaries between Theatre, Dance, Performance Art and Fashion   53
    Susan Marshall

    4 Contemporary Runway, Contemporary Costume   83
    Felix Choong

PART 3 THE INSUBORDINATE HERE AND NOW   95

    5 The Insubordinate Here and Now   97
    Susan Marshall

    6 On Creating Costume Generated Performances   106
    Christina Lindgren

    7 Listening with Costume – A Material-Discursive Listening Practice   119
    Charlotte Østergaard

    8 Researching with and through Costume: Proposition for a Research Framework   129
    Sofia Pantouvaki

■ **Contents**

PART 4   THE PRACTITIONERS' VOICE   **141**

     9   **The Practitioners' Voice – Edited Interviews and Contributions**   **143**
           Susan Marshall et al.

Afterword – Can Bad Costumes Do Good Things?   213
Rachel Hann

Index   216

Contributors

Felix Choong
Felix Choong is a curator and the editor of *Nice Outfit*, an exhibition catalogue and theoretical journal. He lives and works in London.

Christina Lindgren
Christina Lindgren teaches costume design at Oslo National Academy of the Arts KHIO (from 2013) and Stockholm University of the Arts SKH (from 2022). Together with dramaturge Dr Sodja Lotker, she led the artistic research project Costume Agency. At KHiO, she has initiated extensive cross-departmental collaborations such as the laboratory Clothes for Dance. She also works as a costume designer/scenographer. As artistic director of the performing arts company *Babyopera* (www.babyopera.no) she has co-created performances for children 0–3 years old, where the starting point has often been costume and scenography. Lindgren is responsible for costume, as well as for the direction of the productions. Together with the performance artist Liv Kristin Holmberg, she leads the experimental project *Nattens Lys* (The Light of the Night) with a wide range of artistic outputs (www.nattenslys.no).

Charlotte Østergaard
Charlotte Østergaard is an independent Danish visual artist/designer, educator, and artistic researcher. Charlotte has received several grants from the Danish Art Foundation, has exhibited her artworks at curated national and international exhibitions and has designed costumes for more than 65 performances. Charlotte's costume-driven performances have been shown at Gylleboverket's performance festival (2023), Prague Quadrennial for Performance Design and Space (2019 in collaboration with Sally E. Dean & 2023), SWOP – International Dance Festival for Young Audiences (2022), the Metropolis festival Wa(l)king Copenhagen (2020) and the Up Close performance festival (2020).

Sofia Pantouvaki
Sofia Pantouvaki is a scenographer and Professor of Costume Design at Aalto University, Finland. She is an awarded practising designer with over 90 credits in major European venues, and curator of international projects, including the Finnish Student exhibits at PQ2015 (Gold Medal) and PQ2023 (awarded 'Most

■ Contributors

Imaginative and Inventive Design'). She is Chair of *Critical Costume*, a founding Editor of *Studies in Costume and Performance*, and OISTAT Executive Committee member. She led the research project 'Costume Methodologies' (Academy of Finland, 2014–2018) and is lead editor of *Performance Costume: New Perspectives and Methods* (Bloomsbury, 2021).

AFTERWORD

Rachel Hann

Rachel Hann is Assistant Professor in Performance and Design at Northumbria University, Newcastle (UK). She researches material cultures of scenography, transness, and climate crisis. Rachel is the author of *Beyond Scenography* (Routledge 2019) and co-founder of the research network Critical Costume.

Preface

This book evolved from my doctoral thesis awarded by Goldsmiths University of London in 2021. *Insubordinate Costume* presents a comprehensive study of historical and contemporary examples of scenographic costume, the type of costume that creates an almost complete stage environment by itself, simultaneously acting as costume, set and performance. It provides readers with an overview of the costumes, designers, context and theory that have contributed to the emerging field of 'costume as performance'. Focusing on artists and their creative approach to space, form, materials and movement, the book looks at iconic figures such as Loïe Fuller, Oskar Schlemmer and Leigh Bowery, amongst contemporary examples of practitioners that are blurring disciplinary boundaries between fashion, dance, performance and theatre. The book includes chapters by Sofia Pantouvaki who focuses on performance costume as a means of research in 'Researching with and through Costume: Proposition for a Research Framework', Christina Lindgren who presents the findings of the four-year *Costume Agency* project at Oslo National Academy of the Arts in Norway, Charlotte Østergaard who discusses the implications of 'Listening with Costume' and Felix Choong writing on 'Contemporary Runways, Contemporary Costumes'. The final part of the volume is dedicated to 'The Practitioners' Voice' and examines current practice through interviews and contributions from key practitioners.

Acknowledgements

I would like to express my sincere thanks and gratitude to the many writers, practitioners and photographers who have contributed to this book and to Professor Emeritus Anna Furse for her invaluable help and constant encouragement that made my PhD at Goldsmiths University of London such a pleasure to undertake. Many thanks to Lucia Accorsi and Stacey Walker, my editors at Routledge for their guidance and patience and, last but not least, I would like to Sergio, Daisy and Joshua and all my family and friends who never stop believing in me and dedicate my book to the memory of my Mum and our frequent trips to the theatre.

Introduction

Susan Marshall

Insubordinate Costume provides the reader with an overview of the costumes, designers, context and theories that have contributed to the emerging field of 'costume as performance'. Focusing on artists and their creative approach to space, form, materials and movement, the book will include iconic figures such as Loïe Fuller, Oskar Schlemmer and Leigh Bowery, amongst contemporary examples of practitioners that are blurring disciplinary boundaries between fashion, dance, performance and theatre. The introduction outlines the concept of Insubordinate Costume as an instigator of performance and introduces the different parts of the book which bring together historical and contemporary examples of performance-defining costumes for the first time and include contributions from key practitioners and theorists. Insubordinate Costume is a unique anomaly which takes many forms - costume, object, scenography, sculpture, fashion - and defies precise definition. However, all instances have a common factor: the costumes are the primary driving elements of the performance. Insubordinate Costumes contravene norms, expectations and preconceived ideas, they cannot be ignored or disassociated from the performance to which they are integral.

INTRODUCTION

Within the traditional hierarchies of the theatre the costume designer/maker is typically required to dress an actor according to the script, taking into consideration historical accuracy and semiotics as a visual aid to understanding characterisation. The requests of the director or choreographer need to be accommodated and practical concerns such as freedom of movement and rapid costume changes need to be taken into consideration. In recent years, however, the agency of costume has been acknowledged as a vital aspect of performance and there has been a noticeable development in the areas of both practical and theoretical costume research and its performative possibilities. As noted by editors Sofia Pantouvaki and Peter McNeil in the introduction to their book *Performance Costume: New Perspectives and Methods*, costume is not

> seen anymore as being 'in service of' performance in a subordinate role, but rather as a central contributor to an often-renewed sense of collective practice, proposing new directions in turn, to the making of performance itself. There,

■ Introduction

> costume becomes a catalyst as well as a subject and object of study [where] costume as a field and disciplinary practice is finding new theoretical tools and investigative frameworks.
>
> (Pantouvaki and McNeil 2021: 2)

Insubordinate Costume provides the reader with an overview of the costumes, designers, context and theory that have contributed to the emerging field of costume as performance. While acknowledging that all costume has an important role in performance, the examples given in this book concentrate on a specific anomaly that had its beginnings in Modernism at the turn of the twentieth century in Europe and Russia: costume as performance, costume that instigates performance, costume as an art form in itself. Focusing on artists and their creative approach to space, form, materials and movement, iconic figures such as Loïe Fuller, Oskar Schlemmer and Leigh Bowery are included amongst contemporary examples of practitioners that are blurring disciplinary boundaries between fashion, dance, performance and theatre and exploring new meanings of creativity.

Defining Insubordinate Costume

The term Insubordinate Costume evolved from my doctoral research at Goldsmiths University of London and is used to reflect 'the defiant, rebellious and unruly nature of costume when it flouts practicalities and textual confines to embrace the role of protagonist' (Marshall 2021a: 283). Insubordinate Costumes are 'insubordinate' because they are not subordinate to the text or choreography, which are instead developed by experimenting and playing with the costume. Insubordinate Costumes 'contravene norms, expectations and preconceived ideas, they cannot be ignored or disassociated from the performance to which they are integral' (Marshall 2021b, 29). Performance theorist Patrice Pavis defines this type of costume as constituting 'a kind of travelling scenography, a set reduced to a human scale that moves with the actor' (Pavis 2003: 177). An Insubordinate Costume generates an almost complete stage environment by itself, simultaneously acting as costume, set and performance. It has the ability to transform the performing body by disguising or emphasising the human form and modifying or constricting natural movement to create, what costume theorist Donatella Barbieri describes as, a 'three-dimensional world for the body in movement that tells a story' (Barbieri 2012).

Insubordinate Costume is an artform in its own right. It has been experimented with, and continues to be experimented with, by artists, designers and choreographers striving towards new modes of artistic and corporeal expression. While at times they may appear frivolous, looking closely at the context in which the costumes were produced and their conceptual reasoning, they frequently reveal their subversive nature, a form of activism using costume as a visual protest. Materiality is a prominent feature, as the costumes are often crafted from materials not usually associated with traditional tailoring techniques: papier-mâché, cardboard, metal, wood, plastic, rubber - as well as from a wide variety of textiles and textures. The technological innovations of the nineteenth and early twentieth centuries led to huge changes in weaving, sewing and dyeing techniques but, while many things are now taken for granted, it is important to remember that before Elias Howe invented the sewing machine in 1845, garments and costumes were sewn by hand, before bright synthetic dyes were introduced in the mid-1850s, natural dyes were used, which were either muted or very expensive, and before the advent of Bakelite in 1907, plastic did not exist. Creative possibilities in the twenty-first century have been augmented by technological advancements such as 3D printing, laser-cutting, led lighting and innovative materials.

Loïe Fuller's *Serpentine Dance*, which she developed during the 1890s, was an early example of costume as performance, and the first example to be discussed in chapter one. Since Loïe Fuller, it has been a 'phenomenon that has continued to appear sporadically in different forms throughout the twentieth and twenty-first centuries, with the principal focus being on experiment and enquiry' (Marshall 2021b: 29). Used as a research tool or to make a strong artistic statement, there 'is frequently a conceptual component to their design that illustrates a social or political comment or questions bodily and gender norms' (29). Insubordinate Costume can be observed in different disciplines with examples visible in all the avant-garde art movements of the early twentieth century, in experimental dance, in performance art, in fashion and in contemporary costume research. It can take many different forms but 'historical and contemporary examples all have a common factor: the costumes are the primary driving elements of the performance' (29). Although the use of Insubordinate Costume was, until recently, unusual in verbal theatre there has always been a certain affinity between Insubordinate Costume and dance, as dance is closely associated to movement, the body and space. Pablo Picasso's costumes for *Parade*, 1917, Oskar Schlemmer's *Triadic ballet*, 1922, Martha Graham's *Lamentation*, 1935, Alwin Nikolais' *Allegory*, 1959, Robert Rauschenberg's *Pelican*, 1963 and Michael Clark's *No Fire Escape in Hell*, 1986, all pushed the limits of costume design and dance to new experimental levels and paved the way for contemporary designers and choreographers.

Research Parameters

As already noted, the examples given in this book refer to a particular timespan, from Loïe Fuller in the 1890s onwards, and to a specific genre of costume as artistic practice and research. Although it might be argued that some late sixteenth and early seventeenth century masque costumes, folkloric and traditional Asian and African costumes could also be considered to be performance-defining, these will not be discussed here, partly as the topic is so vast it deserves a separate volume and partly because they do not completely fulfil the prerequisites of Insubordinate Costume as defined in this book. Rather than being a provocative artistic statement they are predominantly scenographic in a decorative, allegorical, narrative or traditional sense. Narrative costume differs from Insubordinate Costume as the former fulfils a requirement of the script rather than reflecting an artistic concept as the basis for a performance. 'It is a question of characterisation rather than style' write Kirby and Kirby in their book *Futurist Performance* citing Fortunato Depero's 1924 production of *Macchina del 3000*: 'the appearance of actors pretending to be robots should not be mistaken for a significant innovation in acting or costuming' (Kirby and Kirby 1986: 92). Although Depero's costumes can be seen to transform the human body and alter the movement of the actors, they are a narrative requirement rather than an example of Futurist style.

Insubordinate costumes are performative, they tell stories, they explore pertinent questions, artistic styles, they push boundaries, in many cases they reflect the era in which they were produced. Why examples of Insubordinate Costume appear to be more prevalent in certain countries than others could be due to the political, social and cultural dynamics of a country at a particular point in history and/or the awareness of other artists working in this field, the knowledge of which has naturally broadened since the advent of internet. Spurred on by societal changes, artistic and theatrical trends, 'the growing influence of today's Character culture in Fashion' (Granata et al. 2011) and the increasing interest in the agency of costume, the number of examples has grown significantly since the end of the twentieth century. Social and political change, new waves of feminism and queer rights have had a notable impact on the freedom of expression in many countries and the exploration of gender and bodily norms. Both the rise of conceptual art, where the concept is fundamental to the work, and post-dramatic theatre, which focuses on the effect of the performance rather than the text, have opened the way for designers to experiment with new media. Leigh Bowery's self-created alternative personae have been highly influential in the emergence of 'radical characters' (Granata et al. 2011), striking individual figures seen both in performance art and on the runway. 'Avant-garde fashion, like art, is increasingly becoming a reflection of the repressed tensions and discrepancies that mark contemporary culture' (Teunissen 2011, 18).

The Philosophy of Costume

In recent years 'a new emphasis has been placed on the importance of costume' (Marshall 2020: 166), with costume analysis an ever expanding area of interest. Much has changed since 2010 when Aiofe Monks suggested in her book *The Actor in Costume* that the reason so few books had been written on the subject of theatre costume was that it was considered 'far too trivial or playful for serious scholarship' (Monks 2010: 10). Costume research is now developing its own theoretical framework many years after Elizabeth Goepp called for it in 'An essay toward a philosophy of costume' written in 1928:

> Books in plenty have been written on the costume of the stage, of course; on its history, its construction, its traditions, its contribution to and dependence on pictorial art. But few deal with that quality of costume which makes it theatrical material, the stuff of which drama is made. Costume has, or should have, a philosophy of its own, as certainly as architecture has; and theatrical costume more particularly than social costume, although the social tendencies influence both (Goepp 1928: 396).

For the first volume of the *Studies in Costume and Performance* journal in 2016, Donatella Barbieri and Sofia Pantouvaki wrote in their editorial 'Towards a philosophy of costume' that the philosophical and scholarly attention that costume deserves [is] finally emerging as a vibrant area of research [although] still in the early stages of development [ ] being often subsumed into others' work and dissolved into a range of other different scholarly priorities (Barbieri and Pantouvaki 2016: 3-5).

In 2024, only eight years later, the study of performance costume is an established area of research with both practitioners and theorists investigating many different themes. Important literature such as Donatella Barbieri's book *Costume in Performance: Materiality, Culture, and the Body*, published in 2017, and Sofia Pantouvaki and Peter McNeil's aforementioned book *Performance Costume: New Perspectives and Methods*, published in 2021, as well as the *Studies in Costume and Performance* journal [1] and the biennial *Critical Costume* conference and exhibition [2], demonstrate the wide interest in costume and the varied research undertaken in recent years which has helped to establish and consolidate the philosophy of costume. Current research interests look at many different aspects of costume and the relationship between theory and practice. These include concepts and theories surrounding theatre making and dramaturgy, socio, cultural, political and historical context, the body and embodiment, performer experience, cognition, phenomenology and somatics, New Materialism, play and creativity, collaboration, gender studies, aesthetics and ecological questions. Four areas of research that are particularly relevant to the study of historical and contemporary examples of Insubordinate Costume are costume and the body, play and playfulness, New Materialism theories which look at the agency of things, and the agency of costume. While it could be argued that all costume has agency, not all costume can be categorised as 'insubordinate' and the examples given in this volume concentrate on experimental costume which, along with instigating performance, could be considered as wearable art/wearable sculpture in performance.

Book sections and chapters

The volume is divided into four parts and nine chapters that bring together historical and contemporary examples of Insubordinate Costume for the first time and include contributions from key practitioners and theorists. The first part of the book, 'Insubordinate Beginnings' examines the emergence of costume as performance, with the first chapter looking at historical examples from Loïe Fuller's 1895 *Serpentine Dance* and the Ballets Russes to the experiments of the avant-garde art movements. Insubordinate Costume in this period was emblematic of the rapidly changing society at the beginning of the twentieth century and was frequently used as 'a research tool to question aspects of modernity, industrialisation and the role of humankind in the new mechanised world as well as to explore form, movement and emotion' (Marshall 2021b: 30). In 1909, Diaghilev's Ballets Russes took Paris by storm with its many artistic collaborations and its innovative approach to dance, choreography, composition and design which was grounded in the concept of *Gesamtkunstwerk* [3]. The company was highly influential in Europe as artists such as Picasso, Matisse and Sonia Delaunay brought their artistic concepts to stage costume and Léon Bakst's explosion of pattern and colour inspired Paul Poiret's new fashions. The historical avant-garde movements

Introduction

spanned cultural, literary and artistic interests which led to experimentation in various medium including performance and costume. Examples of Insubordinate Costume can be seen in the work of Russian avant-garde artists Alexandra Exter and Kazimir Malevich, Dadaists Hugo Ball and Sophie Taeuber-Arp, Oskar Schlemmer's Triadic Ballet for the Bauhaus, the expressionistic designs of Lavinia Schulz and Walter Holdt who were inspired by Norse mythology, the Italian Futurists Fortunato Depero, Ivo Pannaggi and Giacomo Balla and the Surrealism of Salvador Dalí and Elsa Schiaparelli.

The second chapter 'Dance, Performance Art and Insubordinate Costume' concentrates on instances of Insubordinate Costume in dance and performance art between 1930 and 1980. Martha Graham's *Lamentation*, 1935, Alwin Nikolais' Allegory, 1959 and *Sanctum*, 1964 and Robert Rauschenberg's *Pelican*, 1963, are examples of work by designers and choreographers that have pushed the limits of costume design and dance to new and experimental levels in this period. Since the 1960s there has also been a significant association between Insubordinate Costume and performance art, where artists such as Louise Bourgeois and Rebecca Horn have used costume in order to explore questions of the body and identity.

The second part, 'Blurring the Boundaries between Theatre, Dance, Performance Art and Fashion' discusses the increasingly indistinct boundaries between these disciplines since the nineteen-eighties and gives examples of Insubordinate Costume being used in all fields. In the nineteen-eighties and early nineteen-nineties the inimitable Leigh Bowery transcended precise categorisation with his radical characterisations which have since exerted an enormous influence on experimental costume design, performance art and fashion. There has always been a perceptible link between fashion and the theatre for, as Aoife Monks writes in her book *The Actor in Costume* 'Actors have been (and still are) particularly important figures for the display of fashion…and have played a key role in the promotion and invention of fashion' (Monks 2010: 36). Many fashion designers such as BodyMap, Rei Kawakubo, Issey Miyake, Walter Van Beirendonck and Hussein Chalayan, have designed costumes for dance productions where the costumes exert an enormous influence on the dancers' movements. In recent years fashion shows have become ever more theatrical, often showing concept pieces alongside the main collection in order to grab the attention of the press and the public. Moncler, Gareth Pugh, Iris van Herpen, Viktor & Rolf, Junya Watanabe and Thom Browne are a few of the many examples where runway collections have included at least one conceptual costume. This section also includes a contribution from curator and fashion writer Felix Choong entitled 'Contemporary Runways, Contemporary Costumes'. With reference to conceptual showpieces presented on the runway by Jonathan Anderson for Loewe, Matty Bovan and Craig Green, Choong looks beyond fashion's initial function and purpose as a commodity and locates it within the parameters of costume as artwork and performance.

Costume as performance is an exciting and fervent field of practical and theoretical research at present. The third part, 'The Insubordinate Here and Now', examines the development in the areas of both practical and theoretical costume research as the agency of costume becomes increasingly recognised as a fundamental aspect of performance with its own discipline, no longer 'subsumed into others' work and dissolved into a range of other different scholarly priorities (Barbieri and Pantouvaki 2016: 3-5). Looking at contemporary ideas surrounding theories of agency, materiality, New Materialism, performativity and phenomenology in relation to costume, this section includes a general introduction and essays from key practitioners and theorists. In 'On creating costume generated performances' Christina Lindgren presents the findings of the four-year *Costume Agency* project at Oslo National Academy of the Arts in Norway and discusses some themes that emerged with two of the participants, Signe Becker and Zofia Jakubiec. Designer and researcher Charlotte Østergaard discusses the implications of listening with costume and the relationship between human and non-human companions in 'Listening with costume – a material-discursive listening practice' and Sofia Pantouvaki, scenographer and professor of Costume Design at Aalto University, focuses on insubordinate performance costume as a means of research and on the processes of costume creation which generate new research methodologies in 'Researching with and through Costume: Proposition for a Research Framework'.

The final part of the volume is dedicated to 'The practitioners' Voice' and examines current practice through interviews and contributions from key practitioners. Contemporary designers working in the field of costume as performance include, among others, Hungarian costume designer Fruzsina Nagy, Dutch visual artists Daphne Karstens and Iris Woutera, Japanese-German artist Yuka Oyama, Danish designer and researcher Charlotte Østergaard, Indian designer Debashish Paul and Mexican scenographer Laura Marnezti. Fruzsina Nagy's costumes are playful with a social-political undertone. She describes them as 'the whole performance…the main characters, and the most important elements' (Nagy 2020). Daphne Karstens' wearable sculptures are made from unconventional materials and experiment with shape and structure. Iris Woutera and Yuka Oyama, both create 'playworlds' for their performers. Iris Woutera *Deform* costumes are created by sewing long strips of vinyl plastic onto stretch fabric resulting in an 'extraordinarily mesmeric writhing living organism in constant metamorphosis' (Marshall 2020). For Yuka Oyama's project *Helpers – Changing homes* she interviewed different participants to understand which objects helped them feel at home then created giant cardboard costumes of these items for them to wear. Charlotte Østergaard's artistic work looks at connections and co-creation and includes textile landscapes as a collective bodily experience. Debashish Paul creates costumes made of paper pasted on cloth and filled with drawings intimately connected to his personal memories in order to explore questions of gender and identity. In *Inhabiting Noise and Silence* Laura Marnezti uses giant honeycomb pleated white plastic costumes to create a sound landscape as the performers move.

Contemporary designers are using costume to upend the traditional hierarchies of the theatre and experiment with new forms of performance. Whereas instances of Insubordinate Costume were a rarity throughout most of the twentieth century, in recent years these have become much more prolific, driven by conferences, recent publications, and specific costume for performance courses, such as the degree and master's courses at the London College of Fashion. Exhibitions

■ Introduction

such as *Extreme Costume*, curated by Czech costume designer Simona Rybáková at the Prague Quadrennial in 2011, *Innovative Costume of the 21st century the Next Generation* curated by Igor Roussanoff and Susan Tsu in Moscow in 2019 and the *World of Wearable Art* international competition held every year in New Zealand demonstrate the growing interest in performative costume. *Critical Costume*, originally founded by Dr. Rachel Hann, Sidsel Bech and Prof. Sofia Pantouvaki in 2013 to 'promote research and practice on the interdisciplinary study of costume' (Hann, 2019) has been a major game-changer in the world of costume design as it brings together practitioners and scholars from around the world to present their latest work and research. *Critical Costume 2020* focused on the agency of costume in performance, costume as the main performer and the costume designer as the initiator of performance, major themes that were also prevalent at *The Prague Quadrennial* in 2019 and 2023. The contemporary use of costume as performance proves that costume has agency, the ability to generate performance and the capacity to be defiant, rebellious and insubordinate. Designs are not based purely on aesthetic choices, they are also 'being employed to explore and research pertinent themes and fears, personal, universal, old and new innovative technologies and materials, recycling, climate change and ecology, mental health, diversity, equality, gender, bodily norms and aesthetics - the possibilities are endless' (Marshall 2020: 179).

NOTES

1 https://www.intellectbooks.com/studies-in-costume-performance
2 https://www.criticalcostume.com/
3 The term Gesamtkunstwerk, translated as 'total work of art', was introduced by Karl Friedrich Eusebius Trahndorff in his 1827 essay 'Ästhetik oder Lehre von Weltanschauung und Kunst'. Wagner used the term in his 1849 essays 'Art and Revolution' and 'The Artwork of the Future' to advocate the synthesis of all elements of performance.

REFERENCES

Barbieri, Donatella. 2012. 'Costume Re-Considered', In *Costume Endyesthai (To Dress): Historical, Sociological and Methodological Approaches*, 147–152. Athens.

Barbieri, Donatella. 2017. *Costume in Performance: Materiality, Culture, and the Body.* London: Bloomsbury Academic. https://doi.org/10.5040/9781474285353

Barbieri, Donatella, and Sofia Pantouvaki. 2016. 'Towards a Philosophy of Costume', *Studies in Costume & Performance* 1 (1): 3–7.

Goepp, Elizabeth. 1928. 'An Essay toward a Philosophy of Costume', *The Quarterly Journal of Speech* 14 (3): 396–411. https://doi.org/10.1080/00335632809379754

Granata, Francesca. 2017. *Experimental Fashion Performance Art, Carnival and the Grotesque Body.* London, New York: I.B. Tauris & Co. Ltd. https://doi.org/10.5040/9781350986312

Hann, Rachel. 2019. 'Debating Critical Costume: Negotiating Ideologies of Appearance, Performance and Disciplinarity', *Studies in Theatre and Performance* 39 (4): 1–17. https://doi.org/10.1080/14682761.2017.1333831

Kirby, Michael, and Victoria Nes Kirby. (1986). *Futurist Performance.* New York: PAJ Publications.

Marshall, Susan. 2018. 'Following the Threads of Scenographic Costume at PQ19', *Theatre and Performance Design* 6 (1–2): 165–81. https://doi.org/10.1080/23322551.2020.1785229.

Marshall, Susan. 2021a. 'Insubordinate Costume', *Studies in Costume & Performance*, 6:2, pp. 283–304. https://doi.org/10.1386/scp_00052_3

Marshall, Susan. 2021b. *Insubordinate Costume*. Doctoral thesis, Goldsmiths, University of London. https://doi.org/10.25602/GOLD.00031204

Monks, Aoife. 2010. *The Actor in Costume*. London: Palgrave Macmillan.

Nagy, Fruzsina. 2020. 'Fruzsina Nagy – Costume Agency.' 2020. https://exhibition.costumeagency.com/project/fruzsina-nagy/ accessed [10/10/20]

Pantouvaki, Sofia, and Peter McNeil. 2021. 'Introduction: Activating Costume: A New Approach to Costume for Performance', in *Performance Costume: New Perspectives and Methods*, edited by Sofia Pantouvaki and Peter McNeil, 1–4. London: Bloomsbury Visual Arts. http://dx.doi.org/10.5040/9781350098831.ch-00I

Pavis, Patrice. 2003. *Analyzing Performance: Theater, Dance, and Film*. Michigan: University of Michigan Press. https://doi.org/10.3998/mpub.10924

PART 1

INSUBORDINATE BEGINNINGS

1 Insubordinate Beginnings

Susan Marshall

INTRODUCTION

Insubordinate Costume is a phenomenon that had its beginnings in Modernism at the turn of the twentieth century in Europe and Russia. It then appeared sporadically throughout the 1900s before gaining momentum in the twenty-first century with the growing interest in the agency of costume and costume as a research tool. Insubordinate Costume flouts practicalities and the confines of text, it is the starting point of a performance, it is the protagonist, it is the performance. This chapter looks at 'Insubordinate Beginnings', early examples of this genre of costume from Loïe Fuller to the avant-garde art movements that used costume as a tool for research and experimentation. Although frequently seen as part of a total stage picture rather than as a unique entity in this period, the costumes described in this chapter defined the performance, the choreography and the movement of the performers through the constrictions they imposed.

The turn of the twentieth century was a period of great change which greatly influenced the advent of Modernism and the early twentieth-century avant-garde movements. *La Belle Epoque* in Europe, named in retrospect to describe the years from the end of the Franco-Prussian war in 1871 to the beginning of the First World War, was a time of optimism, peace, technological advances, scientific discoveries and economic prosperity, albeit for the upper and middle classes. Industrialisation had revolutionised the textile industry in the nineteenth century with the development of power looms, the first sewing machines and bright, colourful synthetic dyes. Although many technological advances in this period developed from previous experiments, inventions such as Alexander Graham Bell's telephone, 1876, Edison's electric light bulb, 1879, the first Kodak camera which used photographic film instead of plates, 1888, Carl Benz's first practical modern automobile, 1886, Emil Berliner's gramophone, 1887, the Lumière brothers' first films, 1895, the Wright brothers first flight, 1903, and the Model T Ford, the first mass-produced assembly-line car, 1908, had a profound impact on society as did the considerable growth in urban populations. The focus on machinery, speed and technology was reflected in artistic experimentation as the popularity of Art Nouveau waned. Behind the gilded façade of the era, however, were underlying problems including discontent among the working classes, militarism and political tensions between nation-states.

Scientific discoveries had a growing influence on philosophical thought which emphasised individual experience and the study of consciousness and the subconscious. Political and social instability in the early twentieth century which led to two World Wars, as well as the emergence of philosophical movements such as existentialism and nihilism, gave rise to numerous avant-garde literary and artistic movements, many of which proclaimed their own manifesto for change: the Futurists, the Dada Movement, Surrealism, Russian Constructivism, the Bauhaus. In 1936, M.F. Agha wrote in a Vogue article about Surrealism:

> periods of trouble are notoriously a fertile ground for the movements which, in one way or the other, enable people to forget the exterior world. These 'escape' movements are responsible for some of the greatest achievements in the field of arts and letters.
>
> (Agha 1936: 129)

Emblematic of the rapidly changing society at the beginning of the century, the avant-garde movements experimented with many different art forms including theatre, film, dance and costume, exploring new ideas surrounding the body, form and materiality. Materiality was a prominent feature of Insubordinate Costumes in this period as they were often crafted from materials not usually associated with traditional tailoring techniques – papier-mâché, cardboard, metal, wood, plastic, rubber – as well as from a wide variety of textiles and textures. Early examples of Insubordinate Costume mirrored their creator's specific artistic interests as they strove towards new modes of artistic and corporeal expression. The modification of the human shape and the body in movement appear as recurring themes, as does the playfulness of many of the costumes. Nearly all examples of avant-garde performative costume occur in dance productions. Writing in the *Italian Modern Art Journal*, Nell Andrew notes that

> plastic artists from various movements across the European avant-garde, looked to dance as a model for expanding the expressive capabilities of their own mediums. By unifying art's materials with its maker, dance may be seen to communicate directly, as if unmediated. In this way, it achieves the modernist ideal of synthesizing form and content.
>
> (Andrew 2019)

LOÏE FULLER

Loïe Fuller's *Serpentine Dance*, which she developed during the 1890s, was an early example of costume as performance, and the first instance of Insubordinate Costume within the research parameters of this book, as the size and shape of Fuller's costume directly influenced her movements. Born in the United States in 1862, Loïe Fuller began her career in Paris in the late nineteenth century, where she gained recognition for her innovative and mesmerising performances

1.1
Loïe Fuller Dancing.
Photograph, ca. 1900. Gelatin silver print. 10.3 x 13.3 cm (4 x 5 1/4 inches), irregularly trimmed. Recto. Gilman Collection, Purchase, Mrs Walter Annenberg and The Annenberg Foundation Gift, 2005 (2005.100.950) ©The Metropolitan Museum of Art/Art Resource/Scala, Florence.

manipulating flowing silk robes with long wands hidden inside gargantuan, extended sleeves (Figure 1.1). She has been described as 'a progenitor of modern dance' (Garelick 2007: 9) and a pioneer of theatrical lighting; however, she is equally important to the history of costume as an early instance of costume instigating performance. Loïe Fuller's distinctive robes, which paved the way for the experimental costume designs of the twentieth century, evolved from an accidental discovery while preparing her costume for the hypnotism scene of a play called *Quack M.D.* Fuller had been given a white, Indian silk skirt that was much too long and had to be pinned to a bodice rather than worn at the waist. In her book *Fifteen Years of a Dancer's Life*, she describes how, to avoid stepping on the fabric, she 'raised her arms aloft [and] continued to flit around the stage like a winged spirit with the audience exclaiming "It's a butterfly!", "It's an orchid!"' (Fuller 1977: 31). *Quack M.D.* was not successful, but the idea for her *Serpentine Dance* was born from further experiments in manipulating the fabric and playing with different coloured lights in front of a mirror. Fuller experimented with glass plates treated with chemical dyes and phosphorescent salts which shone iridescent colours onto the moving silk cloth.

> I had discovered something unique, but I was far from imagining, even in a daydream, that I had hold of a principle capable of revolutionising a branch of aesthetics. I am astounded when I see the relations that form and colour assume.
>
> (Fuller 1977: 36)

In her article 'Interruptions by Inevitable Petticoats: Skirt Dancing and the Historiographical Problem of Late Nineteenth-Century Dance', Catherine Hindson notes that Skirt Dances first became popular in the 1870s when they were performed at the Gaiety Theatre in London by dancers, such as Kate Vaughan, gracefully manipulating light, accordion-pleated skirts to gentle musical accompaniment. Loïe Fuller was therefore by no means the first skirt dancer but the modifications she made to the genre gave rise to a craze during the 1890s inspired by the 'unprecedented popularity of the American performer' (Hindson 2008: 48). The light, voluminous fabrics, complex arm movements and coloured lighting effects employed by Loïe Fuller inspired other skirt dancers who appeared on stage as an interlude in burlesques and musical comedies where 'skirt and serpentine dancing became interchangeable terms for audiences, critics and promoters' (Hindson 2008: 48).

DIAGHILEV'S BALLETS RUSSES

During the early twentieth century the Ballets Russes played a significant role in shaping the world of dance, fashion and the arts and several examples of performance-defining Insubordinate Costume can be seen in the productions where collaborations with artists from the avant-garde art movements pushed the traditional boundaries of dance further. The company was formed in Paris in 1909 by director and impresario Serge Diaghilev who brought together Russian dancers and composers, renowned artists and experimental choreographers to create a completely new style of performance that, like Loïe Fuller, 'revolutionis[ed] a branch of aesthetics' (Fuller 1977: 36). The Ballets Russes made a profound impact and, as Peter Williams notes in *Masterpieces of Ballet Design*, has continued to do so:

> There are probably no persons – choreographers and dancers in any field, composers, painters, designers – working in dance today who do not owe what they are doing, and the way they are doing it, to the achievements of Diaghilev.
> (Williams 1981: 21)

Léon Bakst's exotic, erotic designs for the inaugural season were unlike anything seen before, combining Russian patterns, shapes and colours with an Art Nouveau aesthetic. Their influence on visual arts and fashion was immense and Bakst's designs were the inspiration for Paul Poiret's subsequent fashion designs. By 1920 the Ballets Russes had a sizeable repertoire and commissioned artists from different avant-garde movements who showcased their artistic concepts on the stage. These included Natalia Goncharova's Neo-Primitive designs for *Le Coq d'Or* in *1914* inspired by Russian folk art, Picasso's Cubist designs for *Parade* in 1917, Matisse's stylised, appliquéd costumes for *Le Chant du Rossignol* 1920, reminiscent of his later cut-out work, Giorgio De Chirico's costumes for *Le Bal* in 1929, covered with architectural motifs, and two commissions for designs by Italian Futurist artist Fortunato Depero which were ultimately not produced: *Le Chant du Rossignol*, 1916–17, later designed by Matisse, and the automaton ballet *I Balli Plastici*, 1918. The company worked closely with the Parisian ateliers of Marie Muelle or Maison Jove and the London-based costumier Barbara Karinska to give three-dimensional life to the designs.

The costume designs for the Ballets Russes have an aesthetic quality closely related to art, sculptural form and materiality and are frequently infused with an underlying playfulness. While the Ballets Russes aimed for a total stage picture, costume was a fundamental part of the whole visual image and, in several cases, also had an impact on the movements of the performers through the constrictions they imposed. The following examples of 'insubordinate' costume designs by Picasso, Sonia Delauney and Mikhail Larionov, all exercised a notable influence on the choreography of the productions.

In 1917 Diaghilev invited Picasso to design the sets and costumes for the Ballets Russes production of *Parade* at the Théâtre du Châtelet in Paris which gave him the perfect opportunity to experiment with his Cubist ideas on the stage. Cubism aimed to capture the essence of the subject matter and convey it through geometric shapes and fragmented forms, simultaneously presenting various viewpoints in a single image. Picasso's Cubist costumes explore these ideas three-dimensionally and, just as he added collage pieces to his paintings, he utilised assemblage techniques and employed recognisable, everyday objects in his designs.

Picasso's design for *Parade* was an early example of design dictating the choreography, most noticeable in his costume designs for the two rival managers who announced the acts. The managers wore three-dimensional sculptures personifying America and France. The *American Manager* was a robot with a hat shaped like a ship's funnel, flags, cowboy chaps and Manhattan skyscrapers on his shoulders (Figure 1.2); the *French Manager* had a starched shirtfront, pipe,

1.2
Statkewickz as the American Manager in the first performance of the ballet Parade, Paris, Théâtre du Châtelet, 18 May 1917. Curtain, scenery and costumes by Pablo Picasso. © The Metropolitan Museum of Art/Art Resource/Scala, Florence.

stick and a background of Parisian chestnut trees. The materials used to create the costumes which concealed the actor's body were rigid – wood, metal and papier-mâché – not the traditional soft fabrics normally associated with clothing, and it is therefore inevitable that choreography and movement were affected. These costumes restricted the movement of the two dancers who wore the structures and thus 'Picasso's towering Cubist structure for the two rival managers became virtually the first instance of choreographed sculpture' (Williams 1981: 17), although it should be noted that Picasso's costumes were preceded by Malevich's *Victory over the Sun* in 1913 and experiments for Schlemmer's *Triadic Ballet* which, while first performed in 1922, had begun in 1916.

In the programme notes for the production, French poet Guillaume Apollinaire wrote an introduction which describes the effect of the Cubist settings and costume as 'a kind of surrealism', using the word 'surrealism' for the first time, several years before the beginning of the Surrealist Movement:

> The cubist painter Picasso and the most daring of today's choreographers, Léonide Massine have here consummately achieved, for the first time, that alliance between painting and dance, between the plastic and mimetic arts, that is a herald of the more comprehensive art to come … This new alliance-I say new, because until now scenery and costumes were linked only by factitious bonds-has given rise, in Parade, to a kind of surrealism … The costumes and scenery in Parade show clearly that its chief aim has been to draw the greatest possible amount of aesthetic emotion from objects … Here the aim is, above all, to express reality. However, the motif is not reproduced but represented-more precisely, it is not represented but rather suggested by means of an analytic synthesis that embraces all the visible elements of an object and, if possible, something else as well: an integral schematization that aims to reconcile contradictions by deliberately renouncing any attempt to render the immediate appearance of an object. Massine has adapted himself astonishingly well to the discipline of Picasso's art. He has identified himself with it, and his art has become enriched with delightful inventions … The fantastic constructions representing the gigantic and surprising features of The Managers, far from presenting an obstacle to Massine's imagination, have, one might say, served to give it a liberating impetus.
>
> (Doyle 2005: 66–7)

Robert Delaunay was commissioned to design the sets and Sonia Delaunay to design costumes for a 1918 revival of the Ballets Russes production of *Cléopâtre*, which had first been designed by Léon Bakst in 1909. Ukrainian-born artist Sonia Delaunay was a pioneer of abstract art and a key figure in the development of the avant-garde although, as for many women who have been marginalised by the priority given to male artists throughout history, her work was, for many years, overshadowed by that of her husband Robert with whom she co-founded Orphism, an abstract art movement derived from Cubism. In 1912, Sonia and Robert Delaunay had begun to work on the concept of simultaneity: contrasting saturated colours to give the idea of motion. Advocating this concept, Sonia Delaunay worked in many different media from painting to textiles and from fashion to theatre, dance and film costumes believing that, as such, their ideas and theories would reach a broader audience. Fabrice Hergott wrote, in the foreword to the Tate Gallery's exhibition catalogue, that 'she pursued her artistic mission without distinguishing between fine and applied arts [with] a flexibility of vision that allowed her to switch from one technique to another … to achieve a sense of vitality and freshness in every creation' (Hergott 2014: 9).

Photographs of Lubov Tchernicheva wearing Cleopatra's costume illustrate the restrictive nature of the dress which would have constricted and defined the dancer's movements. The modernist costume, which featured striking geometric patterns and concentric circles in different colours and padded conical breasts made from silk, sequins, mirrors and beads, wool yarn, metallic thread braid and lamé, was representative of her artistic style as were her designs for the other characters in the ballet. Together these created a whole stage picture with the Simultanist aesthetics of the set, becoming 'a painting that developed in time' (Bellow 2014: 101). Juliet Bellow notes that the

> 'dance of the veils', presented this concept in microcosm. Cleopatra made her entrance wrapped tightly in several layers of multicoloured draperies (designed by Sonia). As servants gradually unveiled Cleopatra, they held the veils behind her, forming a screen-like surface akin to a painted backdrop. Dressed in her simultaneous costume, Cleopatra began to dance, thus creating a composition in a state of constant becoming, never achieving fixed or final form.
>
> (Bellow 2014: 101)

Sonia Delaunay continued to design costumes in the 1920s for productions including Tzara's satirical Dadaist play *Le Coeur à Gaz* in 1923 where her two-dimensional, trapezoid costumes for *Le Coeur à Gaz*, made from thick cardboard, constricted the performers' movements completely and were integral to the performance as they gave 'a visual clue to [the characters'] one-dimensionality' (Nicholls 1991: 338). Delaunay also designed performative 'dress-poems', based on the work of avant-garde poets such as Tristan Tzara, Philippe Soupault, Vicente Huidobro and Joseph Delteil, which featured bold, graphic shapes and painted words across sleeves, waistlines and hems.

Russian avant-garde artist Mikhail Larionov was also invited to design for the Ballets Russes. His brightly coloured costumes for the 1921 production of *Chout, The Tale of the Buffoon who Outwits Seven Other Buffoons*, were inspired by his interest in Cubo-Futurism and Neo-Primitivism and transformed the dancers into living sculptures. Aside from the set and costumes, Larionov devised much of the choreography to emphasise the constricted movements of the dancers. Writing in *Ballets Russes The Stockholm Collection*, Erik Näslund notes that the 'method of depersonalising and mechanising the dancers through the structure of their costumes and settings' (Näslund 2009: 249) draws parallels to Fernand Léger's slightly later designs for *Skating Rink* and *La Crèation du Monde* by the more experimental Ballets Suédois. However, neither the dancers, who found the costumes heavy and cumbersome, nor the critics were positive about the production's experimental style with reviewer C.W. Beaumont writing:

Larionov's settings, inspired, as usual by Russian peasant art, interpreted in the spirit of Cubism, were brilliantly conceived, but the colour contrasts accentuated by the angular shapes composing design was so vivid and so dazzling that it was almost painful to look at the stage, and the position was not improved when brilliantly clad figures were set in movement against such a background. I would say that the effect on the eyes was almost as irritating as those flickering streaks of coloured light so characteristic of early colour films. Again, some of the costumes exceeded the limits of fantasy, for instance, certain of the women wore high-heeled satin shoes with their peasant dresses.

(Beaumont in Näslund 2009: 249)

Interesting that, of Larionov's colourful designs with cubist extensions protruding at different angles from the costumes, any of which could have contravened the expectations of the theatre critic, the example C.W. Beaumont gave as exceeding the limits of fantasy was the women wearing high-heeled satin shoes with their peasant dresses.

BALLETS SUÉDOIS

The aforementioned experimental Ballets Suédois company was founded by Swedish art collector Rolf de Maré in the autumn of 1920 with Jean Börlin as lead dancer and choreographer. In the five years before its closure in 1925, the company performed twenty-four different productions in twelve countries, seeking to bring a new, more modern and expressive form of dance to the stage. Writing in *Paris Modern: The Swedish Ballet, 1920–1925*, Nancy Van Norman Baer states that by 'combining dance, drama, painting, poetry, and music with acrobatics, circus, film, and pantomime, the company developed a unique production style in which dance was the binding element in the creation of three-dimensional stage pictures' (Baer et al. 1995: 11). Like the Ballets Russes, visual design was fundamental to the Ballets Suédois ethos, as they too aimed to create *Gesamtkunstwerk*, total works of art that achieved a synthesis between the different creative aspects of a production: costume, sets, choreography, lighting and music. Van Norman Baer notes the influence that the designs exerted on the stage directions and choreography:

> Not only did the company venture further into the realm of experimental dance and total theatrical spectacle, it willingly ceded control of production aspects to the visual artists it employed. For example, the design conceptions of Jean Cocteau, Fernand Léger and Francis Picabia extended beyond a ballet's costumes and sets to include stage directions and choreographic elements … Because movement was often subordinated to stage design, one might argue that the Ballets Suédois was not really a dance company in any traditional sense but rather a group dedicated to performance and installation art.
>
> (Baer et al. 1995: 11–12)

The Ballets Suédois productions were inspired by avant-garde artistic styles, most notably in the cubist designs by Fernand Léger and Serge Gladsky and the Dadaist designs of Francis Picabia. Costumes formed part of a total stage picture rather than being seen as separate entities but there are several examples where the costumes dictate the movements of the dancers and therefore the choreography. Productions such as *Les Mariés de la Tour Eiffel*, with costumes by Jean Hugo, 'made use of gigantic masks, so the characteristics of the types in the ballet were stressed and magnified by the dancers' wearing special masks and padded costumes' (C.W. Beaumont in Hager 1990: 151). Three of the most experimental costume design ideas were for the productions of *Skating Rink, La Creation du Monde* and *Offerlunden*. Fernand Léger designed the sets and costumes for the production of *Skating Rink*, 1922, which was based on a prose poem by Ricciotto Canudo who used the rink as a metaphor for contemporary life. Like Picasso's earlier designs for *Parade*, Léger's designs were inspired by his own artistic interests in Cubism. Maurice Raynal wrote a review in *Der Querschnitt* in 1922: 'Leger does away with the dancer as a representation of human elements. The dancer, in his view, should become an integral part of the décor; a plastic element that will be a moving part of the décor's plastic elements' (Hager 1990: 163). The concave backdrop, which mimicked the shape of a skating rink, was painted with brightly coloured geometric shapes and the dancers wore roller skates and costumes that 'formed a kaleidoscope sequence of images, which changed according to the evolutions of the dance' creating 'a big abstract tableau, whose lower section was engaged in a constant process of transformation' (35). As often occurs with anything new and experimental, the production was not without its critics as Léger noted in *Les Ballets Suedois*, Paris, 1932: 'The innovativeness of the production inevitably caused some ructions with the public, prompting one wit to remark that he saw no need whatsoever for an orchestra, given the racket that was unleashed in the auditorium' (163). Maurice Bex was even less favourable in the *Revue Hebdomadaire* on 25 February 1922, describing it as

> A poem with noble philosophical tendencies disappears beneath the systematically debauched garb of a freakish costume designer, and a curtain which so thoroughly creates the effect of movement that it becomes a substitute for the dancers themselves, who appear not to move at all, so little variation is there in their aimless revolutions.
>
> (163)

Léger also designed the sets and costumes for *La Creation du Monde* in 1923 which was based on African folk mythology and told the story of the creation of the world, from the creation of the sun and moon to the emergence of humanity. The music, by Darius Milhaud, was a fusion of jazz and African rhythms, and the choreography, by Jean Börlin, incorporated elements of African dance and modern movement. Léger's costumes were inspired by African masks and sculptures and frequently constrained the movement of the dancers, some of whom were on stilts, others on all-fours. He describes his concept as:

> Figures (dancers) heavily disguised, wearing carapaces, with the result that no dancers will have human proportions. By this means, we will achieve a grandiose, dramatic ballet.
>
> (191)

In the same year, Gunnar Hallstrom designed the sets and costumes for *Offerlunden*, a tale of sacred fire and sacrifice. Hallstrom was inspired by Viking mythology and archaeological findings for some of the costumes, particularly the helmets, whereas others appear more abstract: wide cone-shaped dresses painted with bold primitive designs, paired with large hoop earrings, metal collars, bracelets and anklets. Described as set 'in the cardboard age rather than in the bronze age' (Vuillermoz 1923) with 'strange costumes that have an element of the grotesque about them (fat white beans!): the creation Dadaist of Gunnar Hallstrom' (Du Moulin 1923), neither critics nor de Maré liked the ballet and it was only performed five times. It is probable that the more experimental costumes of the Ballets Suédois repertoire contravened the expectations of audience and critics alike, leading to these somewhat negative reviews, although many other productions received much higher praise from critics, particularly those for the more conservative first season in 1920.

LAVINIA SCHULZ AND WALTER HOLDT

In 1986, twenty avant-garde costumes, created by the mask dancers Lavinia Schulz and Walter Holdt in the early 1920s, were rediscovered in boxes stored in the attic of the Museum für Kunst und Gewerbe in Hamburg, together with drawings, personal notes, choreographic notations and photos of the costumed performers, taken by Minya Diez-Dührkoop in 1924 (MK&G 2012; Marshall 2021: 50). The find revealed an extraordinary archive of performative costume which had formed part of a memorial exhibition organised in 1925 by the museum director and art historian, Max Sauerlandt, one year after the violent, untimely deaths of Schulz and Holdt by the hand of Schulz, and were then placed, uncategorised, into storage where they remained until 1986, untouched and undiscovered and thus saved from being classified as degenerate art by the Third Reich (Jockel & Stöckemann 1989: 56; Marshall 2021: 50).

Lavinia Schulz studied painting, music, dance and 'lessons in the expressionistic art of the stage' (Jockel and Stöckemann 1989: 57) at the Kunstschule Der Sturm, founded by Herwarth Walden in Berlin in 1916. Her teacher was Lothar Schreyer, who later ran the stage workshop at the Bauhaus from 1921 to 1923 before Oskar Schlemmer took over. He described Schultz as 'a brilliant person with wild passion, tamed only by the breeding of art' (57). Schulz followed Schreyer to Hamburg in 1919 where she began to experiment with full-body masks and where she met Walter Holdt, who became both her artistic partner and, in 1920, her husband. However, as they became increasingly more eccentric and insular, Schulz and Holdt left Schreyer's theatre company. Borrowing money from her parents, Schulz set up her own workshop, which Sauerlandt described as:

1.3
Lavinia Schulz and Walter Holdt, *Springvieh*. Photograph by Minya Diez-Dührkoop © MKG Hamburg.

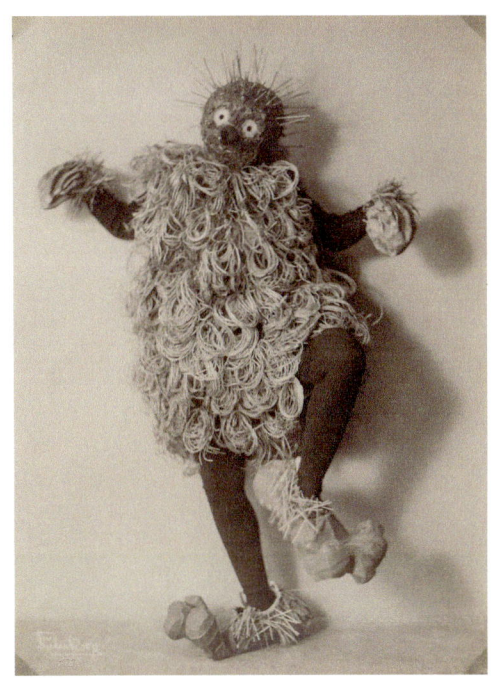

1.4
Lavinia Schulz and Walter Holdt, *Bibo*. Photograph by Minya Diez-Dührkoop © MKG Hamburg.

1.5
Lavinia Schulz and Walter Holdt, *Toboggan Frau*. Photograph by Minya Diez-Dührkoop © MKG Hamburg.

1.6
Lavinia Schulz and Walter Holdt, *Technik*. Photograph by Minya Diez-Dührkoop © MKG Hamburg.

■ **Insubordinate Costume**

1.7
Lavinia Schulz and Walter Holdt, *Springvieh* © MKG Hamburg.

1.8
Lavinia Schulz and Walter Holdt, *Bibo* © MKG Hamburg.

1.9
Lavinia Schulz Walter Holdt, *Toboggan Frau* © MKG Hamburg.

1.10
Lavinia Schulz and Walter Holdt, *Technik* © MKG Hamburg.

> A large room in one of the most despicable lodgings on Lübecker Strasse: a bedroom, a bedroom, and an atelier at the same time, filled with a jumble of colourful cloth, cardboard, paper, rope, and colours, and laying and standing and hanging down from the ceiling all around were the strangest inventions of form and colour, as strange as their names: Springvieh, Bibo, Toboggan.
>
> (Sauerlandt 1925: 23)

It would appear from the signed designs, paper patterns, notes and letters held in the Museum für Kunst und Gewerbe archives, that Schulz was the creative force behind the extraordinary costumes that she and Holdt produced and danced in between 1919 and 1924 (Figures 1.3–1.10). At first sight, the full-body masks, made from papier-mâché, fabric, cardboard, wire and recycled objects, recall both Schlemmer's costumes for the 1922 *Triadic Ballet* and the distorted, highly subjective characteristics of Expressionism (Marshall 2021: 52). Their friend, the musician Hans Heinz Stuckenschmidt described the costumes as 'expressionist primitive animals' (Stuckenschmidt 1979: 36) but Schulz distanced herself from the Expressionism movement, stating: 'Expressionism is no solution; Expressionism works with industry and machines' (Jockel and Stöckemann 1989: 61). Not interested in the new mechanised age, Schulz and Holz were instead inspired by Norse mythology and the mediaeval, Islandic *Poetic Edda* and *Prose Edda* which they treated as their holy scriptures.

Schulz and Holdt lived every aspect of their life dedicated to research into costume and expressive movement, developing an artist/performer *Gesamtkunstwerk* ethos where costume and performance were inextricably linked. According to Jockel and Stöckemann, 'deprivation, pain and heaviness [were] a prerequisite for [their] spiritual-artistic creation' (Jockel and Stöckemann 1989: 64). Living in abject poverty in a basement flat, Schulz and Holdt spent their days wearing 'grey jerseys [and] dancing, practising, working on the masks, putting them on and taking them off' (Stuckenschmidt 1979: 36). When asked by Stuckenschmidt why she didn't use lighter materials, Schulz replied 'Material should not be easy; art is heavy and should work hard, otherwise it's no good' (Stuckenschmidt 1979: 36).

KAZIMIR MALEVICH

As in Europe, the avant-garde art movements in Russia, that emerged in the early twentieth century, were characterised by their radical departure from traditional artistic conventions and by their experimentation with new forms of expression and techniques. The period preceding the Russian Revolution of 1917 saw the emergence of movements, such as Cubo-Futurism, Suprematism, and Constructivism, which were inspired by developments in other fields, such as science, technology, and politics, and which sought to challenge traditional norms and conventions in order to reflect their utopian visions. Costume in the theatre, and later in film, gave artists the opportunity to further their artistic research and express their ideas.

The Russian avant-garde futuristic opera *Victory over the Sun* was performed twice at the Luna Park Theatre in Saint Petersburg in 1913. It was conceived

■ Insubordinate Costume

at the first All-Russian Congress of Futurists which was organised by Kazimir Malevich, Mikhail Matyushin and Alexei Kruchenykh who were the only people to attend. Afterwards, Malevich and Matyushin proclaimed in the St Petersburg newspaper *Day* that: 'The Futurists … want to transform the world into chaos, to smash the established values to pieces and from these pieces create new values' (Kruchenykh et al. 1995: 67). The plot of *Victory over the Sun* involved the capture and domination of the sun in order to destroy time and abolish reason. Malevich, Matyushin and Kruchenykh believed that the play would help create new values for a new utopian world. Mikhail Matyushin wrote the music/soundtrack while the poet Alexei Kruchenykh wrote the libretto in the 'experimental "zaum" language, a kind of primeval Slavic mother-tongue, mixed with birdsong and cosmic utterances' (Wainwright 2014). In *Our Arrival* Kruchenykh described the abstract scenography and enormous sculptural costumes (Figures 1.11 and 1.12) designed by Kazimir Malevich:

> Malevich's sets consisted of large planes – triangles, circles, and parts of machines. The cast was in masks resembling gas masks of the period *Likari* (actors) were like moving machines. The costumes, designed by Malevich again, were cubist in construction: cardboard and wire. This altered the anatomy of a person – the performers moved as if tied together and controlled by the rhythm of the artist and director.
>
> (Kruchenykh et al. 1995: 67)

1.11
Kazimir Malevich, *Enemy, Victory over the Sun*, 1913.

1.12
Kazimir Malevich, *Attentive Labourer, Victory over the Sun*, 1913.

The costumes extended the human body with Cubist planes and angles which affected the movements of the performers leading Kruchenykh to note the influence of the artist on the performance. According to Nina Gourianova, writing in *The Aesthetics of Anarchy: Art and Ideology in the Early Russian Avant-Garde*: 'In the deliberate transcendence of genre and eclectic theatricality of "Victory", there is a touch of variety theatre, the circuslike, buffoonish grotesque' (Gourianova 2012: 127) where 'the sense of absurdity resists the persistent routine of aesthetic, social and ideological dogmas and values by means of parody, of dissonance, of the philosophical "openness" of nihilism' (125). The 'complete disintegration of idea, text, and traditional staging' in 'Victory over the Sun' did not, however, mean that there was 'a complete dissolution of narrative' (125) but rather a new type of theatre.

ALEXANDRA EXTER

The revolution in 1917 had a profound impact on the development of avant-garde art in Russia. After 1922, the Soviet government saw art as a tool for the creation of a new society and for the dissemination of its ideas and values and artists were encouraged to use their works to propagate the ideals of communism and promote the ideals of the new socialist state. Although the film *Aelita: Queen of Mars*[1] is often presumed to be an example of socialist propaganda, *Scifist* argues that it was actually 'a daringly critical and multi-layered satire on the concept of the popular revolution' (Scifist 2014). Based on a Tolstoy novel and directed by Yakov Protazanov in 1924, it was one of the first films to include science fiction elements, three years before Fritz Lang's more famous *Metropolis*. The costumes (Figure 1.13) were designed by the original and eclectic avant-garde Ukrainian artist and theatre designer Alexandra Exter who was inspired by Malevich's Suprematist art, Russian Constructivism, Cubism and Futurist dynamism. Exter's playful designs utilised heavily worked textiles alongside more unusual industrial materials to produce a series of sculptural costumes for the inhabitants of Mars, light years away from the Russian proletariat pictured at the beginning of the film.

THE ITALIAN FUTURISTS

Like other avant-garde movements at the beginning of the twentieth century, the Futurists applied their principles to the fields of poetry, painting and sculpture, as well as all aspects of performance, theatre and cinema. Desiring to destroy the old and embrace new technology, machines and modernity, 'The Futurist Manifesto', published by Filippo Tommaso Marinetti in *Le Figaro* in 1909, advocated a series of actions which are difficult to accept in today's society: aggression, speed, the glorification of war, the destruction of museums and libraries and a fight against moralism and feminism (Marshall 2021: 58). The Futurists are frequently associated with fascism although, in their book *Futurist Performance*, Michael Kirby and Victoria Kirby suggest that Italian Futurist performances have been 'dismissed for political reasons, even though few of them were political in any way and none was explicitly Fascist' (Kirby and Kirby 1986: 5). The Futurists' interest in dynamic

■ Insubordinate Costume

1.13
Alexandra Exter,
Aelita.
Source N.D.
Lobanov-Rostovsky
CC BY-SA 3.0 DEED.

movement and machinery is reflected in their theatrical experimentations in scenography and costume design. 'Theoretical and practical aspects of Futurist costume design and acting primarily focus around two concepts: the integration of the performer with the setting and what could be called the mechanization of the performer' (97). Artist Fortunato Depero noted various objects that could be used to transform the human body into a machine: 'headlight – eyes / megaphone – mouths, funnel – ears / in movement and transformation / mechanical clothes' (210).

Vinicio Paladini and Ivo Pannaggi's *Ballo Meccanico Futurista*, 1922,

> performed by three Russian dancers to the varied noise rhythms of two motorcycles ... dramatized the dilemma of a proletarian worker torn between his attraction for a machine and for a woman. This struggle pitted the values of mechanical virility against 'feminized' tradition and sentiment, although the woman, like the 'machine' and the robot-man, wore a costume made of cardboard, shiny polychrome papers, and other colored and metallic materials.
>
> (Poggi 2008)

Although technically not mechanical, the costumes designed by Ivo Pannaggi satisfy Enrico Prampolini's call for 'unity of action between man and his environment' (Prampolini 1924 quoted in Kirby and Kirby 1986: 113) as they were conceived as part of a *Gesamtkunstwerk* (total artwork) which included scenography, costume and sound. Inspired by Edward Gordon Craig's Über-marionette and his article 'The Artists of the Theatre of the Future' (Craig 1908), Prampolini wrote two manifestos which described his ultimate aim to completely remove performers from the stage. In '*Scenografia e Coreografia Futurista (*Futurist Scenography and Choreography)', written in 1915, and '*Atmosfera scenica futurista* (Futurist Scenic Atmosphere)' 1924, he wrote that 'in the final synthesis, human actors will no longer be tolerated' as 'the intervention of the actor in the theatre as an element of interpretation is one of the most absurd compromises in the art of the theatre' (Prampolini 1915; 1924 quoted in Kirby and Kirby 1986: 91).

Fortunato Depero's theatrical experiments aimed to consolidate his theories of mechanisation and kinetic movement. In 1916, inspired by Loïe Fuller's illuminated stage costumes, he designed the costumes for three dancers in an unfinished project called *Mimismagia* where the dancers were to be subservient to the costumes. Depero called these costumes *vestiti ad apparizione* (apparition clothes). Devices were to be hidden within the draped costumes so the performer could 'release certain springs and open fan-like contrivances, accompanied by bursts of luminous apparitions and rhythms of noise-producing contraptions' (Depero in Berghaus 2019; Passamani 1970b: 59). Later the same year he was commissioned by Diaghilev to design the sets and costumes for *Le Chant du Rossignol*, although this project was later abandoned and, when the production was eventually performed in 1920, it was designed by Matisse. Depero's original designs again show his interest in mechanical movement. He describes the costumes as:

> Rigid costumes, solid in style, mechanical in movement; grotesque enlargements of arms and large, flat legs; hands made of cans or discs or fans with long, pointed and rattling fingers; golden or green masks showing only one nose or a set of eyes or a luminous, smiling mouth made out of a mirror; bell-shaped coats and trousers and shirt-sleeves; all of them polyhedral and asymmetric, all of them detachable and mobile … a stupefying image of the plastic man of a new world.
>
> (Berghaus 2019; Passamani 1970a: 147–51)

Depero envisioned that the costumes would be integrated into the scenery where the 'dancer functioned as a motor that propelled the assemblage into action and turned the whole stage into a unified chromatic, phonetic, and kinetic construction' (Berghaus 2019) In 1918, Depero's aesthetic ideals for a utopian future came to fruition in his *Balli Plastici* (Plastic Dances) as he resolved the problem of the human form by using marionettes in a series of five short performance pieces.

DADA

At the opposite end of the political spectrum from the Futurists, Dada was strongly anti-war and anti-violence. It was formed in Zurich during the First World War, by a diverse group of artists of varying nationalities who had chosen to live

■ Insubordinate Costume

in Switzerland for its neutrality. These included Hugo Ball, Emmy Hennings, Jean Arp, Marcel Janco and Sophie Taeuber-Arp. At a conference held at the Weimar Congress of 1922, poet Tristan Tzara stated: 'The beginnings of Dada were not the beginnings of art, but of disgust'[2] (Rubin 1968). Through its apparently nonsensical art forms, Dada protested against 'nationalist politics, repressive social values, and unquestioning conformity of culture and thought' (MoMA 2018), upending and subverting bourgeois conventionality and traditional aesthetical ideals (Marshall 2021: 59).

The focal point for the artists of the Dada Movement was the Cabaret Voltaire. It was opened by Hugo Ball and Emmy Henning in Zurich in February 1916 'with the object of becoming a centre for artistic entertainment' (Ball 1996: 70). Dressed 'like a magical bishop' (71), Hugo Ball performed his sound poem, *Karawane*, that constricted his movements so much that he had to be carried on and off stage (Figure 1.14). Together with Malevich's *Victory over the Sun*, *Karawane* remains a rare example of the use of Insubordinate Costume in spoken theatre. Hugo Ball describes his costume:

> I had made myself a special costume for it. My legs were in a cylinder of shiny blue cardboard, which came up to my hips so that I looked like an obelisk. Over it I wore a huge coat collar cut out of cardboard, scarlet inside and gold outside. It was fastened at the neck in such a way that I could give the impression of wing-like movement by raising and lowering my elbows, I also wore a high, blue-and-white-striped witch doctor's hat.

(Ball 1996: 70)

1.14
Hugo Ball, Cabaret Voltaire, 1916.
Source: Swiss Literary Archives (SLA), Berne. Literary heritage of Hennings-Ball, SLA-HEN-C-04-a-OP-02-03.

Sophie Taeuber-Arp, one of the founding artists of the Dada Movement, also performed at the Cabaret Voltaire and experimented with costume as well as creating a series of intricately dressed modernist marionettes. In a photo of Taeuber-Arp taken with her sister, both are wearing dance costumes and masks, inspired by Hopi kachina dolls. In another, she wears a white shirt and trousers, an apron made of three overlapping corrugated cardboard shields and a matching hat with streamers. Described by Jonathan Jones in *The Guardian* as being 'one of the most radical – but far from best known – women in modern art' (Jones 2016), Taeuber-Arp's work is playful, moving seamlessly between different artistic disciplines. As well as training in textile design, Taeuber-Arp studied dance with Rudolf von Laban at the Ecole Laban in Zurich 'not as chance improvisation but as a creative game with variable rules that unfolds in time and space as a unique, moving, ephemeral sculpture' (Vachtova 1977).

SURREALISM

Closely associated with the Dada Movement, Surrealism was described by M.F. Agha, in an article entitled 'SURrealism or the Purple Cow' in the November 1936 issue of *American Vogue*, as being 'nothing but Dada with a dash of Freud' (Agha 1936). Like Dada and Futurism before it, Surrealism had its foundations in a literary movement. First used by Apollinaire in 1917 to describe the Ballet Russes production of *Parade*, the word 'surrealism' was later adopted by André Breton and formalised as a movement in his 'Surrealist Manifesto' of 1924 where it was defined as:

> Pure psychic automatism … based on the belief in the superior reality of certain forms of association heretofore neglected, in the omnipotence of dreams, in the undirected play of thought.[3]

(Rubin 1968: 64).

Surrealist artist Salvador Dalí, who was as famous for his own idiosyncratic style of dress as for his artwork, frequently experimented with the absurdities of costume and fashion which he believed were 'equally rooted in fantasy and disdainful of the role of reason as his art' (Radford 1997: 170). Dalí's sense of playfulness and the absurd can be noted in the costume he designed for Charles Henri Ford, photographed by Cecil Beaton for *Vogue* in 1937 where Ford is wearing giant white gloves and a black body suit hung all over with smaller white gloves. His interest in fashion led to a long-term collaboration with Paris-based, Italian fashion designer Elsa Schiaparelli. An article by Steff Yotka in *Vogue* describing the 2017 Dalí Museum's exhibition, *Dalí & Schiaparelli, In Daring Fashion*, is entitled 'Dalí and Schiaparelli Invented the Art-Fashion Collaboration' (Yotka 2017). Citing Dalí and Schiaparelli's 'art-meets-fashion projects', Yotka notes that, eighty years on, artists and fashion houses continue to collaborate and that 'the irony – the mix of high and low materials, and the multimedia promotional materials that they pioneered are still used by artists and designers today' (Yotka 2017).

Dalí, who began designing for the theatre in 1927, was particularly interested in dance and collaborated on two productions with the Ballets Russes de Monte-Carlo, ten years after the death of Diaghilev, when choreographer Léonide Massine commissioned him to write the libretto and design costumes for *Bacchanale* and *Labyrinth* in 1939. The influence of his surrealist art can be seen in his designs for the stage. *Bacchanale* was based on Richard Wagner's opera *Tannhäuser* which told of King Ludwig of Bavaria's descent into madness. Dalí's surreal costume designs included a skirt hung with false teeth, a woman wearing a fish head and men's trousers with lobsters clinging to their thighs. Horst P. Horst's famous photo of the production taken for *Vogue* shows two dancers with their faces in shadow, one wears a long full tulle skirt and is leaning on Dalìesque crutches, often seen in his paintings, while the other has a tulle halo.[4] Rachel Grew writes in her article 'Monstrous Bodies: Theatrical Designs by Salvador Dalí and Leonor Fini', that 'both artists viewed costume as a catalyst for accessing the ambiguous, manifold self' which Dalí believed could reveal 'unknown sides of the fragmented, neurotic self, hidden from the conscious mind' (Grew 2019: 12). Grew believes that Dalí and Fini's costume designs can be read as

> creating new, strange bodies for the dancers, producing a monstrous self that is experienced through the body. The concepts evoked through these costumes may potentially encourage the audience to reflect on the nature of their body ... further enabling an opportunity to critique the "normative" self.
>
> (Grew 2019)

In his essay 'Realizing Dalí's Scenic Designs', George Dunkel, who worked with Salvador Dalí on building the set, describes the difficulty that the costume maker had in executing Dalí's designs for the 'monstrous bodies' in *Bacchanale*:

> Mme. Karinska, the well-known theatrical costumer, got the commission to do the costumes for *Bachannale*. She called us for a consultation, as she could not figure out how some of the dancers would fit into the costumes. Dalí was obviously more interested in visual effect and mood, rather than the dancer being able to dance. The designs were full of amorphic and organic forms, to be made of cellophane, lucite, and other plastic materials, some to be supported by all sorts of surrealistic props. We did some tracing paper overlays for her – showing where and how the figure would fit in, but as we also had our hands full, we suggested she hire a scenic artist who could also sculpt the many crutches, rocks, sticks, branches, and other paraphernalia typical in a Dalí design. Most of the costumes were built, rather than sewn and hardly any have survived because of their limited appeal. Many dancers are still out of condition because they had to work once in a Dalí costume.
>
> (Dunkel 2000: 27–8)

MARCHESA LUISA CASATI

As seen in many of the previous examples, Insubordinate Costume has a strong aesthetic element to it which may at times appear frivolous. Looking closely at the context in which they were produced and their conceptual reasoning, however, they frequently reveal their subversive nature' (Marshall 2021: 75). Like Dalí, the extraordinary and eccentric Marchesa Luisa Casati was famous for her own idiosyncratic style as she played with costume and dress in her quest to be 'a living work of art' (Ryersson and Yaccarino 2004: ix). Although neither artist nor artiste, the Marchesa was a patron to the arts, spending most of her vast, inherited fortune on preserving her image for posterity by commissioning artwork by artists such as Augustus John, Giovanni Boldini, Fortunato Depero, Léon Bakst and Man Ray. She hosted masked balls and, when they were performing in Italy, the Ballets Russes, at the Palazzo Venier dei Leoni, on the Grand Canal in Venice, now home to the Peggy Guggenheim Collection and, while she was never a performer in the traditional sense, she was unfailingly performative, like an early twentieth-century Leigh Bowery or Lady Gaga.

> For her dressing up was the chief embodiment of her creative vision, a type of living theatre, where there was no discernible difference between costumes and clothes. In her own way, she anticipated Lady Gaga. She transformed her body and her face in a never-ending process, creating meaning somewhere between playfulness and artistic research.
>
> (Serafini 2015)

Wearing heavy black eye makeup, Casati dyed her hair red and took belladonna to dilate her pupils. She dressed with theatrical flamboyance and extravagance with a penchant for unusual garments designed by Paul Poiret, Mariano Fortuny and Léon Bakst, completing her looks by wearing her pet boa constrictor draped around her neck as a scarf. Photos show her dressed as the 'Queen of the Night' (Figure 1.15), in a design attributed to Bakst and produced by House of Worth, covered entirely in diamonds and in Poiret's 'Fountain Dress' with cascades of pearls (Figure 1.16). Casati led an unconventional lifestyle for the time, flouting the social, moral and sexual norms of the period, questioning 'stable identities, gender codes, and standards of beauty [as well as] the boundaries between art and life, reality and make-believe' (Ryersson and Yaccarino 2004: 253).

THE BAUHAUS *TRIADIC BALLET*

The Bauhaus was probably the most influential modernist arts and crafts school of the twentieth century. It was founded by architect Walter Gropius in Weimar in 1919 in order to reform both fine arts and design education in all artistic media, including fine art, industrial design and architecture. Adopting an interdisciplinary approach, students studied many subjects such as colour theory, metalwork, furniture making, weaving, pottery, typography and theatre. In 1925, the Bauhaus moved from Weimar to Dessau then, in 1930, to Berlin before finally closing in 1933 after Hitler's rise to power.

Although Oskar Schlemmer conceived the initial idea many years earlier, the *Triadic Ballet* (*Das Triadisches Ballett*, Figure 1.17), which was premiered at the Stuttgart Landestheater in 1922, was very much associated with his time at the Bauhaus. Schlemmer had joined the Bauhaus in 1920 to run the sculpture

■ **Insubordinate Costume**

1.15
The Marchesa Luisa Casati dressed as the Queen of the Night. Photographer unknown, 1922. (Images of the Marchesa Casati courtesy of Ryersson/Yaccarino –The Casati Archives – marchesacasati.com).

1.16
The Marchesa Luisa Casati in fountain costume designed by Paul Poiret. Photographer unknown, ca. 1920s (Images of the Marchesa Casati courtesy of Ryersson/Yaccarino – The Casati Archives – marchesacasati.com).

1.17
Oskar Schlemmer, *Das Triadische Ballett* costumes and costume variations in a revue 1927. Photograph Atelier Schneider. © Bauhaus-Archiv Berlin.

and mural painting departments before taking over the theatre stagecraft workshop from Lothar Schreyer in 1923. The *Triadic Ballet* was based on a trinity in three acts, with three dancers, twelve choreographies and eighteen costumes. Schlemmer's costume designs defined the choreography completely, abstracting the human shape and reducing forms to symbolise types of human character – serene, tragic, funny, serious. Schlemmer pronounced the emblems of the 1920s to be abstraction and mechanisation, technology and invention, and stated:

> One of the emblems of our time is mechanization, the inexorable process which now lays claim to every sphere of life and art. Everything which can be mechanized is mechanized. The result our recognition of that which cannot be mechanized … The theatre, which should be the image of our time and perhaps the one art form most peculiarly conditioned by it, must not ignore these signs.
>
> (Schlemmer 1961a: 17–18)

It is important to note, however, that Schlemmer did not consider the costumed figures of the *Triadic Ballet* to be an attempt at mechanisation or dehumanisation but rather, as Anna Kisselgoff wrote in 1982 in the New York Times, as 'an abstraction of man' (Kisselgoff 1982: 11). Although the figures, wearing padded cloth and papier-mâché costumes coated with metallic or coloured paint, were completely disguised they retained a recognisably human, gendered form, albeit exaggerated. In his work with the Bauhaus, Schlemmer strove to free the performer from physical limitations. While noting that 'the endeavour to free man from his physical bondage and to heighten his freedom of movement beyond his native potential resulted in substituting for the organism the mechanical kunstfigur: the automaton and the marionette', he proposed

> the possibility of relating the figure of natural naked Man to the abstract figure, both of which experience, through this confrontation, an intensification of their peculiar natures. Endless perspectives are opened up: from the supernatural to the nonsensical, from the sublime to the comic.
>
> (Schlemmer 1961a: 28–9)

The characteristic quality of the Bauhaus Theatre was space, the concentration on, and theory of, the figure moving in space. In 'Man and Art Figure', Schlemmer writes about the performer in space:

> Man the human organism, stands in the cubical, abstract space of the stage. Man and space. Each has different laws of order. Whose shall prevail? Either the abstract space is adapted in deference to natural man and transformed back into nature or the imitation of nature. This happens in the theatre of illusionistic realism. Or natural man in deference to abstract space is recast to fit its mould. This happens on the abstract stage.
>
> (Schlemmer 1961a: 22–3)

■ Insubordinate Costume

The costume designs for the *Triadic Ballet* dictated how the figures moved in space. With rigid padding the costumes restricted the dancers to purely upright movement, performers were forced into a marionette-like dance by the constraining shapes of their garments, the human form became a moving structure, a sculptural perception of motion.

American architect Howard Dearstyne studied at the Bauhaus under Mies van der Rohe, Wassily Kandinsky, and Josef Albers from 1928 to 1933 and subsequently wrote a book entitled *Inside the Bauhaus*. Chapter 14 is dedicated to the Bauhaus Theatre. Although Dearstyne was not involved in the theatre workshop, he did attend Schlemmer's performances, which he described in detail, and which give a clear idea of the experience:

> No word was spoken, no story suggested by sign or gesture, no human emotion communicated to the audience The performances consisted solely of bodily movements synchronized with music, a form of the dance. The movements were abrupt, staccato, angular – more mannequins ... divested of their human identity and wholly of their individuality by being encased in costumes which converted them into assemblages of geometric shapes such as cylinders, cones, spheres, or disks. Schlemmer did not believe in total abstraction, the elimination of all reference to the human being. His continuing objective was to 'place the human figure in space', to create compositions, whether moving or static, or half-human, half-geometrized forms put in just relation to each other and to the real or imaging space in which they existed or seemed to exist.
>
> (Dearstyne 1986: 174–5).

A newspaper review by critic of the *Triadic Balle*t noted that the fundamental aspect of the performance was play and that any deeper meaning should not be sought:

> He who seeks 'something' behind all this finds nothing, because there is nothing behind it. Everything is in what one perceives with his senses! No feelings are 'expressed' but rather, feelings are aroused ... The whole thing is play, emancipated and emancipating play ... pure absolute form, just as in music.
>
> ('dt' review in Dearstyne 1986: 178–9)

Schlemmer acknowledged the importance of play to his work. In speaking about the Bauhaus Theatre in a lecture-demonstration at the Bauhaus in 1927, later published as an essay under the title 'Theater' (*Bühne*) in the book *The Theater of the Bauhaus*, Oskar Schlemmer said:

> From the first day of its existence, the Bauhaus sensed the impulse for creative theater; for from that first day the play instinct [der Spieltrieb] was present. The play instinct, which Schiller ... calls the source of man's real creative values, is the unselfconscious and naive pleasure in shaping and producing, without asking questions about use or uselessness, sense or nonsense, good or bad.
>
> (Schlemmer 1961b: 82)

Costume became a focal point at the Bauhaus, not only for the stagecraft workshop but also for the numerous events and costume parties held there. In 1925 Farkas Molnár wrote a description of life at the Bauhaus, describing the elaborate costumes created:

> our costumes are truly original. Everyone prepares his or her own. Never a one that has been seen before. Inhuman, or humanoid, but always new. You may see monstrously tall shapes stumbling about, colorful mechanical figures that yield not the slightest clue as to where the head is. Sweet girls inside a red cube. Here comes a winch and they are hoisted high up into the air; lights flash and scents are sprayed … Kandinsky prefers to appear decked out as an antenna, Itten as an amorphous monster, Feininger as two right triangles … Klee as the song of the blue tree. A rather grotesque menagerie …
>
> (Molnár 2002, 465)

The cultural and political upheaval in Europe acted as an impetus to choreographers and designers at the beginning of the century. But with the rise of fascism in Germany, and the closing and abolition thereby of the Bauhaus by the National Socialists, German theatre and dance were separated from their revolutionary heritage until the 1960s and the experimental Dance Theatre of Wuppertal.

The original *Triadic Ballet* was performed for the last time in Paris in 1932 before the National Socialists banned Schlemmer's work in the theatre in 1937, categorising it as *Entartete Kunst*, degenerate art.

This chapter has looked at the phenomenon of Insubordinate Costume within the avant-garde art movements at the beginning of the twentieth century in Europe and Russia where it was used by artists, designers and choreographers striving to find new modes of artistic and corporeal expression, frequently with an underlying social or political agenda. Since then Insubordinate Costume has continued to be used as a platform for social, cultural and political comment and as a way to subvert norms and conventions. Most of the avant-garde costumes reflected the artistic styles and interests of their designers. The Russian Constructivists, the Cubists, the Futurists and the Bauhaus were all interested in the possibilities of costume as it offered the opportunity to experiment with, and question, the new age of Modernism and industrialisation. By altering the natural shape of the body, the performer took on a wholly different, more mechanical, appearance which, in turn, transformed their movements in the surrounding space. As often happens with anything new and innovative, these experiments were not always appreciated at the time by the public and theatre critics but they offer a fascinating insight into the period, both historically and artistically, and paved the way for future experiments with Insubordinate Costume in the twentieth century and beyond.

NOTES

1 https://www.youtube.com/watch?v=yoROo4Ur49c&ab_channel=OpenCulture

2 'Conference sur Dada', delivered at the Weimar Congress of 1922, published in Men (Hanover), January 1924, pp. 68–70; English translation, 'Lecture on Dada', in Robert Motherwell (ed.), *The Dada Painters and Poets* (New York, 1951), pp. 246–51
3 From André Breton's 'Le Manifeste du Surréalisme', 1924, quoted in Rubin 1968.
4 https://emuseum.mfah.org/objects/76181/costumes-by-salvador-dali-for-leonide-massines-ballet-bacc

REFERENCES

Agha, M. F. 1936. 'SURrealism or the Purple Cow', *Vogue* 88 (9): 60–61. 129–131, 146.

Andrew, Nell. 2019. 'Fortunato Depero and Avant-Gard Dance', *Fortunato Depero*, monographic issue of *Italian Modern Art*, 1 (January 2019). https://www.italianmodernart.org/journal/articles/fortunato-depero-and-avant-garde-dance/ accessed [05/04/21].

Baer, Norman, Nancy Van, J. T. Ahlstrand, and Marion Koogler. 1995. *Paris Modern: The Swedish Ballet, 1920–1925*. San Francisco: Fine Arts Museums of San Francisco.

Ball, Hugo. 1996. *Flight Out of Time: A Dada Diary*. Elderfield. Berkeley; Los Angeles and London: University of California Press. https://doi.org/10.1525/9780520354388.

Bellow, Juliet. 2014. 'On Time: Sonia Delaunay's Sequential Simultanism', In Sonia Delaunay. London: Tate Publishing.

Berghaus, Günter. 2019. 'Fortunato Depero and the Theatre', Fortunato Depero, monographic issue of Italian Modern Art, 1. https://www.italianmodernart.org/journal/articles/fortunato-depero-and-the-theatre/ accessed [10/01/23].

Dearstyne, Howard. 1986. *Inside the Bauhaus*. London: Elsevier Science & Technology. https://doi.org/10.1016/B978-0-85139-863-1.50020-3.

Doyle, Tracy A. 2005. 'Erik Satie's Ballet Parade: An Arrangement for Woodwind Quintet and Percussion with Historical Summery', https://doi.org/10.31390/gradschool_dissertations.3389.

Du Moulin, Albert. 1923. 'Mise en Scene, Costumes', *Bonsoir*, Paris, May 27, 1923.

Dunkel, George. 2000. 'Realizing Dalí's Scenic Designs', *Dali and the Ballet: Set and Costumes for The Three-Cornered Hat,* edited by Curtis Carter. Milwaukee: Haggerty Museum, Marquette University.

Fuller, Loïe. 1977. *Fifteen Years of a Dancer's Life, with Some Account of Her Distinguished Friends*. New York: Dance Horizons Inc

Garelick, Rhonda K. 2007. *Electric Salome: Loïe Fuller's Performance of Modernism*. Princeton, NJ: Princeton University Press. https://doi.org/10.1515/9781400832774.

Gill, Michael. 1990. *Image of the Body: Aspects of the Nude*. New York: Doubleday.

Gordon Craig, Edward. 1908. 'The Artists of the Theatre of the Future', *The Mask* I (3 and 4): 57. Florence: Arena Goldoni.

Gourianova, Nina. 2012. *Aesthetics of Anarchy: Art and Ideology in the Early Russian Avant-Garde*. Berkeley: University of California Press. https://doi.org/10.1525/9780520951730.

Grew, Rachael. 2019. 'Monstrous Bodies: Theatrical Designs by Salvador Dalí and Leonor Fini', *Studies in Costume & Performance* 4 (1): 9–24. https://hdl.handle.net/2134/37409 doi:10.1386/scp.4.1.9_1.

Hager, Bengt. 1990. *Ballets Suedois*. London: Thames and Hudson.

Hergott, Fabrice. 2014. 'Foreword', in *Sonia Delaunay*. London: Tate Publishing.

Hindson, Catherine. 2008. 'Interruptions by Inevitable Petticoats: Skirt Dancing and the Historiographical Problem of Late Nineteenth-Century Dance', *Nineteenth Century Theatre and Film* 35 (2): 48–64. https://doi.org/10.7227/NCTF.35.2.5.

Jockel, Nils, and Patricia Stöckemann. 1989. 'Flugkraft in Goldene Ferne…Bühnentanz in Hamburg Seit 1900.' Hamburg: Museum für Kunst und Gewerbe.

Jones, Jonathan. 2016. 'Sophie Taeuber-Arp: It's about Time the Radical Dada Star Got a Google Doodle', *The Guardian*. 2016. https://www.theguardian.com/artanddesign/jonathanjonesblog/2016/jan/19/sophie-taeuber-arp-google-doodle-dada-art.

Kirby, Michael, and Victoria Nes Kirby. 1986. *Futurist Performance*. New York: PAJ Publications.

Kisselgoff, Anna. 1982. 'The Dance: 6 Works based on Schlemmer's Art', *New York Times*, November 1, 1982. https://www.nytimes.com/1982/11/01/arts/the-dance-6-works-based-on-schlemmer-s-art.html accessed [10/12/20].

Kruchenykh, Alexei, Vasily Rakitin, Andrei Sarabianov, and Rudolf Duganov. 1995. Translation into English by Alan Myers. *Our Arrival: From the History of Russian Futurism*. Archive of Russian Avantgarde. Moscow: RA.

Lanchner, Carolyn. 1981. *Sophie Taeuber-Arp*. New York: The Museum of Modern Art. https://www.moma.org/documents/moma_catalogue_2261_300062660.pdf accessed [20/12/20].

Marshall, Susan. 2021. *Insubordinate Costume*. Doctoral thesis, Goldsmiths, University of London. https://doi.org/10.25602/GOLD.00031204.

Molnár, Farkas. 1925. 'Life at the Bauhaus', in *Between Two Worlds: A Sourcebook of Central European Avant-Gardes, 1910-1930*. Cambridge: The MIT Press, 2002. https://thecharnelhouse.org/2013/06/02/oskar-schlemmers-bauhaus-costume-parties-1924-1926/ accessed [04/04/21].

MoMA. 2018. 'Dada.' Moma.Org. https://www.moma.org/learn/moma_learning/themes/dada/ accessed [10/12/20].

MK&G. 2012. 'Lavinia Schulz.' MK&G Collection Online. http://sammlungonline.mkg-hamburg.de/en/search?s=Lavinia Schulz&h=undefined&sort=scoreDesc.

Näslund, Erik. 2009. *Ballets Russes the Stockholm Collection*. Stockholm: Dansmuseet.

Nicholls, Peter. 1991. 'Anti-Oedipus? Dada and Surrealist Theatre, 1916–35', *New Theatre Quarterly* 7 (28): 331–347. Cambridge: Cambridge University Press. https://doi:10.1017/S0266464X00006035.

Molnár, Farkas. 2002. 'Life at the Bauhaus.' Translated by John Bátki. In *Between worlds: a sourcebook of Central European avant-gardes, 1910-1930* pp 462-465. Cambridge, MA: The MIT Press.

Passamani, Bruno, ed. 1970a. *Fortunato Depero 1892–1960. Exhibition Catalogue. Bassano del Grappa Palazzo Sturm e Museo Civico*. Bassano del Grappa: Minchio.

Passamani, Bruno, ed. 1970b. *Depero e la scena: Da "Colori" alla scena mobile, 1916–1930*. Torino: Martano.

Poggi, Christine. 2008. *Inventing Futurism: The Art and Politics of Artificial Optimism*. New Jersey: Princeton University Press.

Radford, Robert. 1997. *Dalí*. London: Phaidon Press.

Rubin, William S. 1968. *Dada, Surrealism, and Their Heritage*. New York: The Museum of Modern Art. https://www.moma.org/documents/moma_catalogue_1884_300299023.pdf accessed [10/03/20].

Ryersson, Scot D., and Michael Orlando Yaccarino. 2004. *Infinite Variety*. Minneapolis: University of Minnesota Press.

Sauerlandt, Max. 1925. 'Lavinia Schulz Und Walter Holdt.' Hamburg: Der Kreis, Zeitschrift Für Künstlerische Kultur. Offizielles Organ Der Hamburger Bühne.

Schlemmer, Oskar. 1961a. 'Man and Art Figure', in *The Theater of the Bauhaus*, edited by Walter Gropius and Arthur S. Wensinger, 17–48. Middletown, CT: Wesleyan University Press.

Schlemmer, Oskar. 1961b. 'Theater (Bühne)', in *The Theater of the Bauhaus*, edited by Walter Gropius and Arthur S. Wensinger, 81–104. Middletown, CT: Wesleyan University Press.

Scifist. 2014. 'Aelita: Queen of Mars', *Scifist*. 2014. https://scifist.wordpress.com/2014/09/11/aelita-queen-of-mars/ accessed [15/05/21].

Serafini, Paolo. 2015. 'An Italian Fashion Legend: The Marchesa Luisa Casati.' http://paoloserafini.com/fine-arts/luisa-casati/ accessed [10/11/20].

Stuckenschmidt, Hans H. 1979. *Zum Hören Geboren: Ein Leben Mit Der Musik Unserer Zeit*. Munich: Piper.

Vachtova, Ludmila. 1977. 'Taeuber- Arp Im Winterthurer Kunstmuseum', *Neue Zürcher Zeitung*, January 29, 1977. Zürich: NZZ.

Vuillermoz, Emile. 1923. 'Les premières: Théâtre des Champs-Elysées', *Excelsior,* May 30, 1923 Paris.

Wainwright, Oliver. 2014. 'Russia's Stage Revolution: When Theatre was a Hotbed for Impossibly Space-age Design', *The Guardian,* October 15, 2014. https://www.theguardian.com/artanddesign/2014/oct/15/russian-theatre-design-revolution-avant-garde-v-and-a accessed [02/01/21].

Williams, Peter. 1981. *Masterpieces of Ballet Design*. London: Phaidon Press Ltd.

Yotka, Steff. 2017. 'Dalí & Schiaparelli, In Daring Fashion Proves They Were the Best at Art-Fashion Collaborations', Vogue. 2017. https://www.vogue.com/article/dali-schiaparlli-in-daring-fashion-exhibit-dali-museum accessed [09/04/21].

2 Dance, Performance Art and Insubordinate Costume

Susan Marshall

At the beginning of the twentieth century, notable examples of Insubordinate Costume design were predominantly linked to the avant-garde modernist art movements, as artists and designers strove to find new means of expression. Many of these experimental costumes were sculptural and restricted natural movement, forcing the performers to find alternative ways to interact with the imposed constrictions. These restrictive costumes were the antithesis of the costumes worn by the forerunners of modern dance, such as Isadora Duncan, Mary Wigman, Ruth St Denis and Ted Shawn, or the unitard favoured by Merce Cunningham, whose choreography emphasised freedom of movement and corporeal expression and revealed the contours of the body rather than hiding or constricting it. There are fewer examples of costume instigating performance in this period than there were within the avant-garde art movements earlier in the century, perhaps due to the aesthetic preferences of the modern dance movement and the impact of the Second World War, or perhaps due to a natural evolution of interests and ideas where each generation of practitioners rebels against the previous. Although less common in this period, there are still instances of work by dancers, choreographers and artists that pushed the limits of costume design in dance and performance art to new and experimental levels.

DANCE

Dance is closely associated with movement and experimentation between body and space and does not necessitate the spoken word to portray ideas or emotions. For these reasons, a particular affinity can be noted between dance and the use of costume as an instigator of performance, from the first examples of Insubordinate Costume to the present day. With the threat of impending war already present in the early 1930s the focus on experimental costume in performance saw a significant shift away from the European and Russian avant-garde artists and dance companies towards primarily American dancers/choreographers. The examples pinpointed in this chapter demonstrate how costume can influence a dancer's movements through constriction, thereby defining the choreography and becoming fundamental to the creation of the performance.

DOI: 10.4324/9781003341000-3

■ Insubordinate Costume

MARTHA GRAHAM (1894–1991)

Dancer and choreographer Martha Graham revolutionised American dance and American dance education with her techniques based on 'a vocabulary of movement that would "increase the emotional activity of the dancer's body"' (Martha Graham Dance Company 2023). She believed that 'dance became a collective memory that could communicate the emotions universal to all civilizations' (Kisselgoff 1991), and she explored questions of emotion and constriction through her choreography and use of costume:

> Unlike classical ballet and many modern dance companies who prefer no imposed restrictions, sets and costumes designed for Martha Graham often provided obstacles for her and her dancers to overcome. Graham said: 'I refuse to admit that dance has limitations … Dance décor can, I believe, serve as a means of enhancing movement and gesture to the point of revelation of content'.
>
> (Brown and Woodford 1998: 52)

After 1935, Martha Graham chose to work mainly with the Japanese American artist Isamu Noguchi (1904–88) and the pioneer lighting designer Jean Rosenthal. Noguchi's abstract sculptures of wood, bone, stone and twisted metal inspired Graham's choreography, as did the costumes she designed herself. Graham's use of costume in/as performance was notably different from the cumbersome sculptural costumes of avant-garde performances such as Malevich's *Victory Over the Sun*, 1913, or Schlemmer's *Triadic Ballet*, 1922, but the link between constriction and movement can also be seen in her work. In his book *Martha Graham: Portrait of an Artist*, LeRoy Leatherman wrote of Graham's use of costume constriction to add meaning and significance to the performance:

> the more complex, and dramatically more meaningful costumes are designed against the movement. She has put herself and her dancers into tubes of cloth like cocoons; in voluminous robes, weighty and unyielding; in cloaks and capes made of yards of material.
>
> (Leatherman 1967: 140)

In the four-minute solo performance entitled *Lamentation*, choreographed and first performed in 1930, Graham wore a shroud of stretch jersey (Figure 2.1), which she stretched and twisted into different shapes; her body emblematic of sorrow, the choreography inextricably entwined with her use of the costume as an expressive tool (Marshall 2021). Describing this negotiation between body and costume in Graham's work, Rachel Hann writes:

> To watch *Lamentation* is to watch an ongoing negotiation [with] costume as an active and reactive performance agent … costume shapes movement through an affective reciprocal exchange between body and costume: where the immediacy of the costumed act affects both the worn and the wearer.
>
> (Hann 2017: 15)

2.1
Martha Graham, *Lamentation (Oblique)*. Photograph by Barbara Morgan. © Barbara and Willard Morgan photographs and papers, UCLA Library Special Collections.

Graham wrote in her autobiography about the symbolic significance of the costume:

> I wear a long tube of material to indicate the tragedy that obsesses the body, the ability to stretch inside your own skin, to witness and test the perimeters and boundaries of grief.
>
> (Graham 1992: 117)

Kisselgoff called it

> an iconic embodiment of grief distilled to its essence, all the more powerful because it abstracts an emotion rather than depicts a character experiencing grief … Graham's program note called the solo a dance of sorrows, 'not the sorrow of specific person, time or place but the personification of grief itself.
>
> (Kisselgoff 2001)

RUTH PAGE (1899–1991)

American ballerina and choreographer Ruth Page was inspired by her eclectic studies with Adolph Bolm and expressionist modern dancers Harald Kreutzberg and Mary Wigman as well as her experience dancing with Anna Pavlova's classical ballet company and Diaghilev's Ballets Russes. In her chapter '"Gone Modern":

Skyscrapers, Sacks, and Sticks', Joellen A. Meglin describes how Page's collaborations with international visual artists Nikolai Remizov, Isamu Noguchi and Pavel Tchelitchew

> pushed her toward international, modernist currents in a variety of modes: Constructivism, neo-primitivism, abstractionism, and Futurism [and led her to explore] the materiality of motion – the dynamic-functional architecture of the body as it moved in space and could be elaborated through portable sculptures, sculpted fabric, extensional props, or multifaceted masks, In the collaborative works that resulted, motion transformed the figurative possibilities of material and material transformed the figurative possibilities of motion.
>
> (Meglin 2022: C3.P25)

Meglin notes that a cutting saved by Ruth Page in a choreography scrapbook of a *New York Times Magazine* article entitled 'Newest Ballets Scorn the Merely Human Form', demonstrates that she was already interested in Oscar Schlemmer's work at the Bauhaus as early as 1926 (C3.P75). Photos of Ruth Page wearing Remisoff's costume for *Ballet Scaffolding*, 1928, show a constructivist design which is somewhat reminiscent of Schlemmer's *Triadic Ballet* costumes or Picasso's Cubist American Manager in *Parade*. Although Page can seemingly move her legs freely under the short tubular crinoline, she has three-dimensional constructions attached to her back and head which influence her movements. The performance programme notes that:

> This dance is a stylized interpretation of the foundation steps upon which the classical ballet is built. The structural nature of the movement is emphasized by the costume.
>
> (C3.P21)

Page met Isamu Noguchi three years before he began collaborating with Martha Graham in 1935. They began a year-long personal and creative relationship during which Noguchi designed two blue wool jersey sack costumes for her. The first dress, a closed sack with an elastic waistband and only one opening at the neck, is depicted in his sculpture *Miss Expanding Universe*, 1932. The second, a rectangular shape with one opening at the neck and two at the bottom with stirrups for the feet, inspired Page's solo dance *Expanding Universe*, 1932, later renamed *Figure in Space No. 1* and *Figure in Space No. 2*, 1933. The sack dress hid Page's body as she twisted and stretched the fabric into extended abstract forms.

> Noguchi's sack costume stretched and folded with Page's moving body – constraint and confinement produced her expansion. But the jersey fabric was no straitjacket. Page took the sack as far as her body could go. Noguchi's sack was more freeing than an elaborate dance costume, or the simple leotard and tights worn to reveal dynamic bodily movement. Noguchi's sacks offered Page a similar dynamism but without baring the body's exact features.
>
> (Olsen 2021)

Page described *Figure in Space No. 1* in programme notes:

> To those who are plastically-minded the dance will seem to be a series of startling poses – new inventions in design and ever-remindful of Twentieth Century sculpture in its most abstract and fourth-dimensional imagery. To those who are philosophically-minded the dance will seem to be the continuous struggle of mankind, through calmness and strife, to expand into new ideas and new forms ending in the complete mystery which is the universe. But for this dance each must make his own interpretation.
>
> (Hart 2013: 4–5)

As Noguchi's half-sister Ailes was dancing in Martha Graham's company at this time and their mother Leonie Gilmour helped to sew Graham's costumes (Olsen 2021), it is likely that Noguchi was aware of Graham's costume for *Lamentation*, 1930. Although, as Dakin Hart, Senior Curator at The Noguchi Museum, wrote in the 1913–14 exhibition guide to *Space, Choreographed: Noguchi and Ruth Page*:

> The conception and intent of Noguchi's second dress however turn Graham's inside out. Where *Lamentation* dramatizes an internal struggle with a universe of grief conducted within the confines of the self, Page's dance *Expanding Universe* is an extroversion of human aspiration on a cosmic scale.
>
> (Hart 2013: 4)

Page's *Variations on Euclid*, which premiered in 1933, also showed the influence of modernist aesthetics, her interest in Schlemmer's theories of the body in space, and her studies with Harald Kreutzberg. Wielding two sticks in the first *Variation*, Page's dance recalls Schlemmer's *Triadic Ballet*, 1922, or the 1928 *Stäbetanz* (Stick Dance). Photos of the second *Variation* show the dancer in black wearing three long white elastic bands at different points on each arm, which stretch down to a stirrup under each foot. Both *Variations* transformed the dancing figure into abstract geometric formations which the programme notes described as creating 'an abstract arithmetical problem quite devoid of human emotionalism' (Meglin 2022: C3.P77). A black-and-white film entitled *Variations on Euclid*, probably filmed in Paris in 1950 with *Les Ballets Américains*, shows a composite version of three of Page's solo dances: the two *Variations* and *Expanding Universe*. The five-minute ballet shows Dorothy Hill dancing in the centre, wearing the Noguchi sack costume and ballet pointe shoes rather than barefoot as in the original. The company, dressed in black unitards as a contrast to the sticks and elastic, danced the two *Variations of Euclid* as a duet using sticks and a quartet wearing the elastic bands.[1]

ALWIN NIKOLAIS (1910–93)

Alwin Nikolais' artistic vision was shaped by his early years studying drama, music, and puppetry. The American choreographer, designer, and composer was inspired to dance after seeing Mary Wigman perform in the early 1930s and later

■ Insubordinate Costume

trained under Truda Kaschmann, Hanya Holm, Martha Graham, Doris Humphrey, and Charles Weidman, learning both American modern dance techniques and 'the German modernists' tradition of space awareness and an analytical approach to the body' (Jowitt 1989: 354).

After becoming co-director of the Henry Street Playhouse in New York in 1948–9, Nikolais began to develop his philosophy of 'decentralisation' where the dancer was to become 'a fellow traveller with the total universal mechanism rather than the god from which all things flowed' (Nikolais, quoted in Jowitt 1989: 354). He believed in group action, whereby the focus was on the overall effect of the performance rather than on one individual dancer, and used costume to depersonalise the performers and create repetitive abstract forms. Nikolais believed in the importance of *Gesamtkunstwerk*, a total work of art, and 'mixed light, sound, and dance for years before the term "mixed media" occurred to anyone' (Benson 1970). Aside from the dancing, he oversaw and undertook all aspects of a production. A *New York Times* article in 1970, entitled 'Choreography, Music, Costumes, Sets, Etc., Etc.', wrote of his work:

> Music is by Alwin Nikolais. The sets are by Alwin Nikolais. The costumes are by Alwin Nikolais. The lighting effects are by Alwin Nikolais. The projections are by Alwin Nikolais. The dancers are members of the Alwin Nikolais Dance Theater.
>
> (Schonberg and Nikolais 1970)

Looking at Nikolais's costume designs, it is possible to draw similarities with Schlemmer's *Triadic Ballet* costumes. Although, according to Nikolais's assistant for forty years, Ruth E. Grauert, in her essay 'Nikolais and the Bauhaus': 'Nikolais was adamant that he was not a Bauhaus product' (Grauert 2000). In the age of

2.2 Alwin Nikolais, *Imago (The City Curious)*, five dancers connected by arm extensions, 1963. Photograph by Tom Caravaglia. © Nikolais/Louis Foundation for Dance. Alwin Nikolais and Murray Louis Papers. MSS181 Ohio University Libraries.

the internet and constant image sharing, it is somewhat difficult to believe that designers were not aware of each other's work, but *The Theater of the Bauhaus*, originally published in German in 1924 with a collection of now-famous essays by Gropius, Schlemmer, Moholy-Nagy and Farkas Molnar, was only translated and published in English in 1961, two years after the first performance of Nikolais's *Allegory*. However, as Nikolais had studied dance in his youth under Hanya Holm and Truda Kaschmann, both former students of Mary Wigman, it was probable that he had encountered Bauhaus notions and may have been subconsciously, if not consciously, inspired by them (Grauert 2000).

In the 1950s Nikolais named his first company The Theater of Sound, Light and Motion, subsequently changing it to Total Theater before settling on the eponymous The Alwin Nikolais Dance Theater (Grauert 2000). Here similarities can again be noted between Nikolais's work and the Bauhaus Theatre as Nikolais's idea of 'Total Theater' finds a parallel in Moholy-Nagy's 'Theatre of Totality', described in his essay 'Theater, Circus, Variety' (Marshall 2021). Grauert suggests that 'the coincidence of labels is perhaps just that because both Moholy-Nagy and Nikolais were describing similar processes' (Grauert 2000). When Nikolais describes his work as 'a polygamy of motion, shape, color and sound' (Schonberg and Nikolais 1970), it recalls Moholy-Nagy's description:

> The Theater of Totality with its multifarious complexities of light, space, plane, form, motion, sound, man and with all the possibilities for varying and combining these elements – must be an ORGANISM.
>
> (Moholy-Nagy 1961: 61)

Moholy-Nagy's theory of the 'Theater of Totality' being a cohesive organism is also reflected in Nikolais's idea of the performer in costume as being a minor, if important part of the whole production (Marshall 2021):

> My costumes are part of a total stage design, action or painting. The idea is not to see each body separately. My stage designs are a theatrical abstraction of the way I see man – not as an ego, but as part of a socio-economic mechanism, an agreeable but not a central part … I have often been accused of dehumanization of the dancers. It's not that, it's de-egoization … Man has to learn to design himself into the total environment, to see himself as a relatively minor part of the whole universal thing.
>
> (Norell et al. 1967: 136)

In Nikolais's productions, such as *Allegory, Sanctum, Imago* (Figure 2.2) or *Chrysalis* (Figure 2.3) each element forms part of an aesthetic entity where 'everything was used to create patterns in space and time' (Schonberg and Nikolais 1970). Design elements were integral to a performance, and Nikolais frequently formulated the choreography after asking dancers to play and experiment with costumes and props which extended their bodies, and therefore affected movement (Marshall 2021).

■ **Insubordinate Costume**

2.3
Alwin Nikolais, *Chrysalis*, 1973. © Nikolais/Louis Foundation for Dance. Alwin Nikolais and Murray Louis Papers. MSS181 Ohio University Libraries.

One never knows what kind of oddball costume will send Nikolais off. He will try anything out with his dancers. Sometimes it works, sometimes not. 'Get into this costume', he will say, flourishing a tube of plastic or whatever. 'Get into it and see what you can do in it'. He will have his company improvise for hours in the costume ... Closed in their structures, the dancers execute elaborate geometric designs, using the equipment itself as part of their bodies. The structures vibrate with a life of their own ... 'I have tried to make my dancers conscious of their physical, sculptural look', he says. 'For dance is as much visual and sculptural as it is movement alone'.

(Schonberg and Nikolais 1970)

In *Time and the Dancing Image* dance critic Deborah Jowitt describes the 'opulent patterns and dream-country electronic sounds, the metamorphosed bodies in Nikolais' dances [as] a theatre of hallucination that was almost as good as an acid trip' (Jowitt 1989: 356). She notes that watching the costumed dancers perform Nikolais' 'complex vocabulary of movement' (354) is like 'peering into a world of tiny organisms, gaily anthropomorphized; or ... a kaleidoscope' (356).

ROBERT RAUSCHENBERG (1925–2008) AND MERCE CUNNINGHAM (1919–2009)

Choreographer and dancer Merce Cunningham founded his eponymous dance company in 1953 and, in a seventy-year career, created hundreds of dances, performance events and site-specific works, which had a major impact on both modern dance and avant-garde art. He collaborated with many visual artists including, among others, Marcel Duchamp, Isamu Noguchi, Roy Lichtenstein, Jasper Johns, Robert Rauschenberg, Nam June Paik and Andy Warhol, and embraced technology, often using video in his later performances. Cunningham believed that dance needed no explanation, no narrative and no underlying meaning: 'all connotations and perceptions were valid reactions, and none more valid than the other' (Sargeant 2019), 'each spectator may interpret the events in his own way' (Sarathy 2017). Cunningham viewed 'each dancer [as] a separate identity; [where] there is not a chorus along with which there are soloists, but rather [where] each in the company is a soloist, and in a given dance we may act sometimes separately and sometimes together' (Cunningham 1968). He used chance and randomness as a creative tool and changed traditional stage hierarchies, choreographing dance on all parts of the stage rather than centre front.

Unlike Alwin Nikolais' use of elaborate costumes and prosthetics, Cunningham frequently utilised the unitard as a neutral garment which, by making the body's movements highly visible, complied with his visual aesthetic. Carolyn Brown, who danced in Cunningham's company from 1952 to 1972 noted:

> Merce has never cared very much about costumes … Rarely did the dance steps get made with any thought about what the costumes might be. Anyone designing costumes for Merce had to work within very strict limitations; the nearly inflexible rule was: body unencumbered, body visible.
>
> (Brown 2007: 147)

Despite this, Cunningham's creative collaborations led to some interesting experimentation in performance costume, most notably with artist Robert Rauschenberg and haute-couture designer Rei Kawakubo, who designed the costumes for the 1997 production of *Scenario*, which will be discussed in the next chapter.

Rauschenberg is often associated with the Neo-Dada Movement of the 1950s and 1960s, and is renowned for his 'Combines', artwork that combined paint, everyday objects and non-traditional materials. His dance designs reflected his artistic interests, and from 1954 onwards Rauschenberg designed lighting, sets and costumes for over twenty Merce Cunningham Dance Company productions. Rather than making the final decision on musical and artistic choices, Cunningham believed that 'no medium should be subordinate' and that music and design elements should 'function as independent elements as opposed to complementing the choreography' (Sarathy 2017). His chosen artistic process meant that dancers and collaborators worked separately and only came together for the final rehearsals. Rauschenberg described working with Cunningham: 'It was the most excruciating collaboration, but it was the most exciting, and most real, because nobody knew what anybody else was doing until it was too late' (Sarathy 2017).

Cunningham described working with Rauschenberg on *Antic Meet*, 1954, a production with little or no budget:

> He came up with a basic set of black leotards and tights to which he added numerous props, clothes, objects … I remember telling him that in one dance, a duet I did with Carolyn Brown, I wanted to wear a chair strapped to my back. He thought for a moment and then said, 'If you have a chair, can I have a door?' 'Certainly'.
>
> (Cunningham 1983)

■ Insubordinate Costume

A photo shows Cunningham jumping in the air with the aforementioned chair strapped to his back 'like a large mosquito that won't go away' (Vaughan 1997: 105). Interestingly, even given the apparent constriction of wearing a large cumbersome object attached to the body, the body, clothed in a unitard, is wholly visible, and the impression is of complete freedom of movement. Rauschenberg's use of assemblages in his costumes reflected the eclectic nature of his artwork and complemented Cunningham's philosophy of chance and randomness as variations could occur during the performance, with different objects and clothing added to the basic unitard costume. In another section of the dance piece, Cunningham, surrounded by four dancers in giant ruched dresses made from white nylon parachutes, wears a sweater with four sleeves and no neck hole which he designed himself and knitted together with members of the company. The bodies of the dancers are partially hidden; the designs are integral to the performance but, again, do not constrict the dancers' movements.

For their 1977 collaboration on the production of *Travelogue*, Cunningham gave Rauschenberg very minimal information, noting only that the dancers 'were going to travel around the stage at different points and in different ways' (Robert Rauschenberg Foundation 2019a). Rauschenberg designed costumes and sets that were reminiscent of his *Jammer* series of artworks (Robert Rauschenberg Foundation 2019b), sewn from brightly coloured Indian silks. He added colour-wheel fan skirts, a recurring image in his own painting, to the basic unitards, which could be opened by the dancers to create a full circle bisecting the body. 'Manipulated by the dancers from between their legs the fans were also manipulative … transforming the dancers into moving art objects' (Potter 1993: 19). In one scene Rauschenberg plays with the idea of a group costume as a group of eight dancers move slowly across the stage holding two long strips of translucent white silk tightly under their arms, creating a moving wall that concertinas together as they reach the other side. In another vignette a solo dancer wears tin cans attached down the outside of his legs. In her accompanying essay to the MOMA exhibition *Robert Rauschenberg: Among Friends*, Jennifer Harris writes: 'Rauschenberg's collaborations with Cunningham [challenged] the conventions of modern dance through the integration of everyday objects. With Cunningham, Rauschenberg's objects became increasingly cumbersome and interactive, almost equal in their commanding presence to that of the steps themselves' (Harris 2017).

ROBERT RAUSCHENBERG AND THE JUDSON DANCE THEATER

With *Pelican*, 1963, Rauschenberg's first experience as a choreographer, the costume objects commanded even greater presence. Rauschenberg only decided to choreograph this piece after he was accidentally credited as choreographer instead of stage manager in the press release, but he later went on to choreograph a total of thirteen dance performances. The production of *Pelican* formed part of an evening of performances by the highly experimental Judson Dance Theater at the Pop Art Festival in Washington DC and took place in an abandoned roller-skating rink called America on Wheels. Rauschenberg designed, choreographed, danced in and created the soundtrack, 'a collage of sounds ranging from

Dance, Performance Art and Insubordinate Costume

2.4
Robert Rauschenberg, *Pelican*, 1963. Photograph by Peter Moore. © Robert Rauschenberg Foundation/ Northwestern University.

radio, television, and film to music by George Frideric Handel and Franz Joseph Haydn' (Robert Rauschenberg Foundation 2019).

Pelican was performed by Rauschenberg and artist Per Olof Ultvedt on roller skates with Carolyn Brown of Cunningham's dance company *en pointe*. Dressed in grey tracksuits Rauschenberg and Ultvedt also wore giant modified parachutes open on their backs (Figure 2.4) 'forming an architectural environment while simultaneously emphasizing the movements of the two skaters' (Sarathy 2016). Rauschenberg was interested in 'a more spontaneous, unplanned sort of choreography, letting the specific environment in which they find themselves dictate what they do at each performance' (Tomkins 1965: 230). He recounted that: 'since I didn't know much about actually making a dance, I used roller skates as a means of freedom from any kind of inhibitions that I would have' (Sarathy 2016), believing that 'the limitations of the materials as a freedom that would eventually establish the form' (Rauschenberg 1977: 184). Rauschenberg's ethos that 'you work with what's available, and that way the restrictions aren't limitations, they're just what you happen to be working with' (Tomkins 1965: 226), influenced the Judson Dance Theater who broke with conventions incorporating the ordinary everyday into their productions.

PERFORMANCE ART

Rauschenberg and Judson Dance Theater's performances blurred the boundaries between dance and performance art. Performance art as a genre emerged within the experimental avant-garde art movements of the early twentieth century as a way to challenge the conventions of traditional art and theatre. The Dada Cabaret Voltaire and Futurist productions are early examples of performance art, although the actual term was not widely used until the 1970s. Taking place in unconventional settings, the genre includes, amongst others, happenings, events, artistic action and conceptual performances, which may be live or filmed. The body is central to performance art as the artistic medium. Since the late 1950s there have been significant examples of visual artists using Insubordinate Costume in their performances in order to explore questions of changing society and identity.

ATSUKO TANAKA AND THE GUTAI ART ASSOCIATION

The Gutai Art Association was a Japanese avant-garde group of artists founded in 1954 and led by Jiro Yoshihara. Gutai translates as 'concrete' or 'embodiment', which reflects the group's focus on materiality and process in art-making. Its fifty-nine members produced a wide range of works across a variety of media, including painting, sculpture, performance, and installation until the group disbanded in 1972 after the death of Yoshihara. The Gutai Art Association rejected traditional artistic techniques and forms and explored new methods of expression, anticipating the later happenings and conceptual art of the 1960s and 1970s. They sought to challenge the boundaries between art and life, creating works that were interactive, dynamic and constantly evolving. Their manifesto stated that:

> Gutai art does not transform material but brings it to life. Gutai art does not falsify the material. In Gutai art, the human spirit and the material take each other by the hand, even though they are diametrically opposed. The material is not subjugated by the spirit.
>
> (Yoshihara 1956: 202–4)

Atsuko Tanaka played a crucial role in the formation of the Gutai Art Association. One of her most famous works was the *Denkifuku* (Electric Dress, Figure 2.5), which was first exhibited in the inaugural Gutai exhibition in Tokyo in 1956. The dress covered her body and head, leaving only her face free. Electric wires and nearly two-hundred dangling neon lightbulbs, hand-painted with brightly coloured synthetic resin enamel paints, were attached to a traditional Japanese kimono. During a performance at the exhibition Tanaka wore the dress, which was suspended from the ceiling, activating the light bulbs that flashed sequentially, creating a sense of pulsating movement and energy. Although Tanaka stated at a symposium at the University of California in 1998 that: 'My works have nothing to do with politics ... neither do they have anything to do with gender. It doesn't matter whether I am a man or a woman' (Kunimoto 2013: 481). Namiko Kunimoto believes that the performance 'owed its captivating quality in no small measure to the tension it generated between the sphere of cyborg spectacle and the vulnerable female body' (465).

Electric dresses featured again as part of her performance piece *Stage Clothes,* which formed part of the 1957 *Gutai Art on the Stage* show at Sankei Kaikan in Osaka, this time worn by male performers. Costume is the basis of the whole performance, as Ming Tiampo describes in 'Electrifying Art: Atsuko Tanaka, 1954–1968':

Dance, Performance Art and Insubordinate Costume

2.5
Tanaka Atsuko wearing Electric Dress at the second Gutai Art Exhibition, Ohara Kaikan, Tokyo, 1956. © Kanayama Akira and Tanaka Atsuko Association courtesy Museum of Osaka University.

> The backdrop of the performance was an enormous red dress ... Tanaka emerged wearing a shiny, loose-fitting bottle green dress in organza, with one yellow sock and one green sock. In a series of quick changes that lasted no more than a few seconds each, Tanaka removed the sleeves of her green dress, then the midsection to reveal a yellow dress that was instantly transformed into a fuchsia chiffon evening gown that unrolled from the hem of the yellow dress. Seconds later, she removed the fuchsia dress to reveal the yellow dress again, which she transformed into a yellow and black striped dress by peeling off pieces of the yellow dress, the way one would peel an orange. Down to her black leotard and tights, the performance seemed over, but then Tanaka revealed yet another costume, which she removed from her gloves ... the artist disappeared back under the large red dress, and two figures dressed in costumes made of coloured flashing light bulbs came on stage against the backdrop of a large cross, also covered in lights.
>
> (Tiampo 2004: 73)

Through the use of the specially constructed costume pieces, Tanaka's body became a site of constant change and metamorphosis.

LOUISE BOURGEOIS

The rise of second-wave feminism in the 1960s and the appropriation by women artists of the themes of identity, sexuality and the body led to a new era of

■ Insubordinate Costume

2.6
Louise Bourgeois, in 1975, wearing her latex sculpture *Avenza* which became part of *Confrontation*, 1978. Photograpgh by Mark Setteducati. ©The Easton Foundation/ Licenced by VAGA, New York and SIAE.

experimentation (Marshall 2021). Louise Bourgeois was a prolific artist who worked in all artistic mediums, from textiles to sculptures in marble or iron, to drawing and print.

> Bourgeois almost always focused on the human form, whether supine, oversized, realistic or abstract. Sometimes it was the whole figure; sometimes just a foot. But all of her work was deeply personal.
>
> (Ferrier 2016)

Her multi-breasted *Avenza* costume (Figure 2.6) was made from a latex mould that Bourgeois took from a sculpture in plaster she had made in Avenza, Italy, in 1968. Reminiscent of an ancient Cycladic sculpture, *Avenza*, like much of her work, has distinctly sexual/maternal overtones (Marshall 2021). Bourgeois's friend and assistant, Jerry Gorovoy, maintains, however, that:

> To call her a 'female artist' or a 'feminist artist' is reductive. It was simply autobiographical – she was dealing with universal emotions: jealousy, rejection, and so on. These are pre-gender.
>
> (Ferrier 2016)

The Avenza costume later formed part of a one-off performance piece entitled *A Banquet/A Fashion Show of Body Parts* that she created for the opening of her installation entitled *Confrontation*, 1978, at the Hamilton Gallery of Contemporary Art in New York City. The mock fashion show saw male performers parading in long translucent white tunics hung with bulbous latex body parts, which mirrored the 'flesh-like protuberances' (Wye 1982) laid out on the long dining table at the centre of the installation. The performance could be seen as a comment on gender and objectification, but Bourgeois maintained that 'it was all a joke … The humor is black. Despair is always black' (quoted in Garner 1980).

GENERAL IDEA

Canadian art collective *General Idea* also used a fashion show format to critique the fashion industry and its influence on popular culture, creating a series of surreal beauty pageants between 1970 and 1978 entitled the *Miss General Idea Pageant*. The collective was founded in Toronto, Canada, in 1969 by A.A. Bronson, Felix Partz and Jorge Zontal, and together they explored themes related to media, popular culture, and queer identity. In the exhibition catalogue to *The Search for the Spirit: General Idea 1968–1975*, curator and art historian Fern Bayer writes:

> The beauty pageant format provided General Idea with a basic vocabulary of contemporary cultural clichés and allowed them to express their ideas about glamour, borderline cases, culture/nature interfaces, the role of the artist as an inspiration[al] cultural device, the body of myths surrounding the art world, and the relationship of the artist to the media and the public.
>
> (Bayer 1997: 23)

In 1975 they filmed a mock rehearsal for the *General Idea Beauty Pageant* in front of a live audience with a contestant being given directions on what to do and where to go by a voice off-stage. Entitled *Going Thru the Motions*, it also saw the introduction of the collective's VB (Venetian Blind) gowns for the first time, worn by contestants in the beauty pageant. The VB gowns, came in different versions and were made of baked aluminium venetian-blind slats held together with chains (Figure 2.7). Calling the gowns architectural studies for the 1984 *Miss General Idea Pavillion*, they were a parody of complicated haute-couture fashions and were comprised of two or three large, ziggurat shaped, three-dimensional forms which covered the head and body of the performer, hiding their identity. Various photos exist of the VB gowns, at the pageant rehearsal, outside City Hall in Toronto, and even skiing down the Lake Louise ski slope in Alberta.

■ Insubordinate Costume

2.7
General Idea, VB gown from the 1984 Miss General Idea Pageant, Urban Armour for the Future, 1975, Gelatin silver print, 25.4 x 20.3 cm. Image courtesy of General Idea and Esther Schipper, Berlin. © General Idea.

REBECCA HORN

German artist Rebecca Horn has an interdisciplinary approach to her work, which combines sculpture, installation, film and performance, and frequently uses mechanical devices to create works that are dynamic and interact with the body. She explores the relationship between the body, space and the environment, often using natural elements such as feathers in her creations and filming her performances outside. Recovering from lung poisoning in a sanatorium in the 1960s, Rebecca Horn started to create prosthetic body-extensions from her hospital bed in order to combat her sense of isolation and to reach out, both metaphorically and literally (Marshall 2021). These body-sculptures, made of fabric and wood, extend and constrict various parts of the body and explore the concept of loneliness and 'the equilibrium between body and space' (Tate 2016; Horn 2017). While the prostheses 'seem to offer an "improvement" of human capability, the results are often debilitating or grotesque, serving only to highlight the fragility and helplessness of the human body' (Watling 2012). The two themes of constriction and extension can be seen both simultaneously and separately in Horn's work.

The theme of body extension, which intrigued and inspired Horn, led to a series of structures that expanded the body into space. These included *Unicorn*, *Head Extension* and *Shoulder Extensions*. In 1970, *Unicorn* was the first of many short performance films she produced. A naked woman walks through a path in a shady wood and through a crop field with a long horn attached to her head, held in place by white straps all down her torso. *Head Extension*, two years later in 1972,

Dance, Performance Art and Insubordinate Costume

again uses a horn-like structure, this time with an appendage that is so tall the performer needs help to balance it on his head.

With *Finger Gloves*, 1972, Horn explores the sensory feeling of reaching out once more. The 'gloves' are five metre-long fingers on each hand made from wood and fabric, attached to the wrists and controlled by the performer. Horn noted:

> The finger gloves are made from such a light material, that I can move my fingers without effort. I feel, touch, grasp with them, yet keep a certain distance from the objects that I touch. The lever action of the lengthened fingers intensifies the sense of touch in the hand. I feel myself touching, see myself grasping, and control the distance between myself and the objects.
>
> (Quoted in Haenlein 1997: 58)

The *White Bodyfan*, 1972, and *Mechanical Bodyfan*, 1974 (Figure 2.8), are further examples of Horn's interest in extending the body into space. Made of fabric and metal, the two giant fans are both nearly 3 metres in diameter and, in both instances, can be manoeuvred and rotated to form different combinations between circle and semi-circle.

Other works investigate 'confinement – cocoons, swaddling, bondage, prostheses' (Hughs 1993). Talking about one of her first prosthetic sculptures, *Arm Extensions*, 1968, Horn described the constrictions of the costume:

2.8
Rebecca Horn, *Mechanical Bodyfan*, 1973–4. Photography by Achim Thode. © Rebecca Horn by SIAE 2024.

■ Insubordinate Costume

> Her body is bandaged crosswise from the chest down to the feet, like a mummy. Movement becomes impossible. Both her arms are stuck in thickly padded red stumps that serve as supports for her body. In the course of the action, the performer feels that arms, despite her upright posture, begin to touch the ground, fuse with it, become 'insulating pillars' of her own body.
>
> (Horn 1997)

Constriction is a recurrent theme in works such as *Overflowing Blood Machine*, 1970, where a naked performer is confined by a series of vertical transparent tubes pumping blood; *Paradise Widow*, 1975, a 240-cm high structure covered with black feathers which open to reveal different parts of the body; and *The Feathered Prison Fan*, 1978, which features in her film *Die Eintänzer*.

As can be seen in the examples given in this chapter, from the late 1950s and throughout the 1960s and 1970s, an overlapping of boundaries between dance and performance art became more noticeable, with both genres focusing on the body as a central theme. Choreographers such as Merce Cunningham, who integrated everyday objects into his work, and Alwin Nikolais, who incorporated design elements to extend the dancers' bodies, challenged traditional notions of movement and expression, while performance artists furthered the exploration of socio-political themes through the costumed body. Although there are fewer examples of Insubordinate Costume in this period than within the avant-garde art movements of the early twentieth century, designers, choreographers and performance artists continued to investigate the potential of Insubordinate Costume as a means to challenge conventions and explore questions of society and identity. The following chapter will look at how, from the 1980s and 1990s, the blurring of boundaries increased further to include fashion.

NOTE

1 https://www.chicagofilmarchives.org/collections/index.php/Detail/Object/Show/object_id/16845

REFERENCES

Bayer, Fern. 1997. 'Uncovering the Roots of General Idea: A Documentation and Description of Early Projects, 1968–1975', in *Exhibition Catalogue: The Search for the Spirit: General Idea 1968–1975*. Toronto: Art Gallery of Ontario.

Benson, Harry. 1970. 'Space Follies: The Alwin Nikolais Dance Theatre 1970, New York', *Vogue* 155 (3): 192–93.

Brown, Carolyn. 2007. *Chance and Circumstance. Twenty Years with Cage and Cunningham*. New York: Knopf.

Brown, Jean Morrison, and Charles Woodford. 1998. *The Vision of Modern Dance: In the Words of Its Creators*. Trenton, NJ: Princeton Book Company.

Cunningham, Merce. 1968. 'Characteristics of Dancers', *Dance Perspectives* No. 34, Summer 1968. https://www.mercecunningham.org/the-work/writings/characteristics-of-dancers/ accessed [10/10/23].

Cunningham, Merce. 1983. 'Collaborating with Visual Artists.' Merce Cunningham Trust. https://www.mercecunningham.org/the-work/writings/collaborating-with-visual-artists/ accessed [10/10/23].

Ferrier, Morwenna. 2016. 'Louise Bourgeois – the Reluctant Hero of Feminist Art', *The Guardian*. https://www.theguardian.com/lifeandstyle/2016/mar/14/louise-bourgeois-feminist-art-sculptor-bilbao-guggenheim-women accessed [12/11/19].

Garner, Paul. 1980. 'The Discreet Charm of Louise Bourgeois', *Art News* Vol. 79.

Graham, Martha. 1992. *Blood Memory: An Autobiography*. Washington: Washington Square Press.

Grauert, Ruth E. 2000. 'Nikolais and the Bauhaus', *Bearnstow Journal*. http://bearnstowjournal.org/bauhaus.htm accessed [05/09/19].

Hann, Rachel. 2017. 'Debating Critical Costume: Negotiating Ideologies of Appearance, Performance and Disciplinarity', *Studies in Theatre and Performance* 39 (4): 1–17. https://doi.org/10.1080/14682761.2017.1333831.

Harris, Jennifer. 2017. 'Dance among Friends Robert Rauschenberg's Collaborations with Paul Taylor, Merce Cunningham, and Trisha Brown.' MOMA. https://www.moma.org/calendar/events/3441 accessed [05/05/21].

Hart, Dakin. 2013. 'Space, Choreographed: Noguchi and Ruth Page.' The Isamu Noguchi Foundation and Garden Museum. https://www.noguchi.org/wp-content/uploads/2019/09/Space-Choreographed-Noguchi-and-Ruth-Page-Exhibition-Brochure.pdf accessed [10/09/23].

Haenlein, Carl (ed.) 1997. *Rebecca Horn: The Glance of Infinity*. Zurich; Berlin; New York: Scalo.

Horn, Rebecca. 1997. *Rebecca Horn: The Glance of Infinity*. Edited by Carl Haenlein. Zurich; Berlin; New York: Scalo.

Horn, Rebecca. 2017. 'Rebecca Horn.' http://www.rebecca-horn.de/pages-en/biography.html accessed [10/10/20].

Jowitt, Deborah. 1989. *Time and the Dancing Image*. Berkeley: University of California Press.

Kisselgoff, Anna. 1991. 'Martha Graham Dies at 96; A Revolutionary in Dance.' *The New York Times*. https://www.nytimes.com/1991/04/02/obituaries/martha-graham-dies-at-96-a-revolutionary-in-dance.html accessed [10/10/20].

Kisselgoff, Anna. 2001. 'DANCE; Powerful Emotions Distilled', *The New York Times*. 2001. https://www.nytimes.com/2001/09/13/arts/dance-powerful-emotions-distilled.html accessed [10/10/20].

Kunimoto, Namiko. 2013. 'Tanaka Atsuko's "Electric Dress" and the Circuits of Subjectivity', *The Art Bulletin* 95, no. 3. http://www.jstor.org/stable/43188842 accessed [17/09/23].

Leatherman, Leroy. 1967. *Martha Graham; Portrait of the Lady as an Artist*. London: Faber & Faber.

Marshall, Susan. 2021. *Insubordinate Costume*. Doctoral thesis, Goldsmiths, University of London. https://doi.org/10.25602/GOLD.00031204.

Martha Graham Dance Company. 2023. 'Martha Graham.' https://marthagraham.org/history/ accessed [07/03/23].

Meglin, Joellen A. 2022. '"Gone Modern": Skyscrapers, Sacks, and Sticks', *Ruth Page: The Woman in the Work*. New York: online edn, Oxford Academic. https://academic.oup.com/book/41562/chapter-abstract/353035116?redirectedFrom=fulltext accessed [12/04/23]. https://doi.org/10.1093/oso/9780190205164.003.0003.

Moholy-Nagy, László. 1961. 'Theater, Circus, Variety', in *The Theater of the Bauhaus*, edited by Walter Gropius and Arhur S. Wensinger, 49–70. Middleton, CT: Wesleyan University Press. https://monoskop.org/images/a/a7/Gropius_Walter_ed_The_Theater_of_the_Bauhaus.pdf accessed [11/03/20].

Norell, Norman, Louise Nevelson, Irene Sharaff, Alwin Nikolais, Andre Courreges, and Priscilla Tucker. 1967. 'Is Fashion an Art?' *The Metropolitan Museum of Art Bulletin* 26 (3): 129–40. https://www.jstor.org/stable/3258881 accessed [18/03/21]. https://doi.org/10.2307/3258881

Olsen, Liesl. 2021. 'Flicker of an Eyelid: Isamu Noguchi, Ruth Page, and the Universe of Chicago.' The Isamu Noguchi Foundation and Garden Museum. https://www.noguchi.org/isamu-noguchi/digital-features/flicker-of-an-eyelid-isamu-noguchi-ruth-page-and-the-universe-of-chicago/ accessed [07/03/23].

Potter, Michelle. 1993. '"A License to Do Anything": Robert Rauschenberg and the Merce Cunningham Dance Company.' *Dance Chronicle* 16 (1): 1–43. http://www.jstor.org/stable/1567909 accessed [19/01/21].

Rauschenberg, Robert. 1977. *Robert Rauschenberg Exhibition Catalogue*. Washington: The Smithsonian Institution.

Robert Rauschenberg Foundation. 2019a. 'Chronology 1970-79.' https://www.rauschenbergfoundation.org/artist/chronology/1970-79/all accessed [19/01/21].

Robert Rauschenberg Foundation. 2019b. 'Robert Rauschenberg.' https://www.rauschenbergfoundation.org/art/art-context/mirage-jammer accessed [19/01/21].

Sarathy, Jennifer. 2016. 'Rauschenberg as Choreographer.' Robert Rauschenberg Foundation. https://www.rauschenbergfoundation.org/art/lightboxes/rauschenberg-choreographer accessed [19/01/21].

Sarathy, Jennifer. 2017. 'Rauschenberg and Cunningham.' Robert Rauschenberg Foundation. https://www.rauschenbergfoundation.org/art/lightboxes/rauschenberg-and-cunningham accessed [19/01/21].

Sargeant, Hannah. 2019. 'How Merce Cunningham Reinvented the Way the World Saw Dance.' https://www.dazeddigital.com/art-photography/article/44033/1/merce-cunningham-reinvented-radical-chance-technique-john-cage-dance accessed [30/01/21].

Schonberg, Harold C., and Alwin Nikolais. 1970. 'Choreography, Music, Costumes, Sets, Etc., Etc.', *New York Times*, December 6, 1970. www.nytimes.com/1970/12/06/archives/choreography-music-costumes-sets-etc-etc-by-alwin-nikolais-alwin.html accessed [19/01/20].

Tate. 2016. 'Rebecca Horn – Body Extensions and Isolation | Fresh Perspectives.' https://www.youtube.com/watch?v=6uEkq3IBIf0 accessed [14/03/21].

Tiampo, Ming. 2004. 'Electrifying Art: Atsuko Tanaka, 1954-1968.' Morris and Helen Belkin Art Gallery. https://www.academia.edu/871149/Electrifying_Art_Atsuko_Tanaka_1954_1968 accessed [19/06/23].

Tomkins, Calvin. 1965. *The Bride and The Bachelors*. New York: Viking Press.

Vaughan, David. 1997. *Merce Cunningham. Fifty Years*. New York: Aperture.

Watling, Lucy. 2012. '"Arm Extensions", Rebecca Horn, 1968.' Tate. https://www.tate.org.uk/art/artworks/horn-arm-extensions-t07857 accessed [14/03/21].

Wye, Deborah. 1982. 'Louise Bourgeois.' The Museum of Modern Art. New York. https://www.moma.org/documents/moma_catalogue_2243_300296411.pdf accessed [14/01/21].

Yoshihara, Jiro. 1956. 'Gutai bijutsu sengen.' *Geijutsu Shinchō* 7 (12). https://www.shozoshimamoto.org/en/critical_essays/the-gutai-manifesto-jiro-yoshihara/ accessed [09/09/23].

PART 2

BLURRING THE BOUNDARIES BETWEEN THEATRE, DANCE, PERFORMANCE ART AND FASHION

3 Blurring the Boundaries between Theatre, Dance, Performance Art and Fashion

Susan Marshall

INTRODUCTION

There are 'multiple ways in which costume works' (Maclaurin and Monks 2015: 2), as Aoife Monks observes in the introduction to *Costume: Readings in Theatre Practice*, noting that costume is not used just to dress the performers or provide visual pleasure, but that it 'plays an intricate role in organising the relationship between the actor's body and the character's body' (4). Costume can create social or historical identity, present power structures, play with stereotypes, 'situate performers within a series of aesthetic and spatial structures' (1) and 'offer new visions of embodiment' (4). In his critical essay, 'The Diseases of Costume', written in 1955, philosopher and semiotician Roland Barthes gives his opinion on what constitutes a 'good or bad, healthy or sick' costume (Barthes 1972: 41), judging it on its function within a play as an aid to understanding what Brecht termed as social gestus. Brecht uses the term *gestus* to mean 'both gist and gesture; an attitude … expressible in words or actions' (Brecht and Willett 1964: 42) with the ability to convey a social comment while Barthes expands the idea to include costume which he believes 'must constantly link the work's meaning to its "exteriority"' (Barthes 1972: 41). For Barthes the 'costume has a powerful semantic value … not there only to be seen' but also to be read, to communicate ideas, information or sentiments (Barthes 1972: 46). The costume, according to Barthes, must be purely functional, it 'must be an argument' (46), it should not become an 'esthetic avatar of costume' (44) and distract the spectator from the action (42), it 'must serve the human proportions … make [the actor's] silhouette natural' (48).

> 'When costume becomes an end in itself … it becomes condemnable' (42) … The costume 'must renounce every egotism … it must pass unnoticed in itself yet must also exist … we must see it but not look at it.
>
> (50)

At first sight Barthes' notion of costume appears diametrically opposed to the concept of Insubordinate Costume which never passes unnoticed, does not create a natural silhouette and often has aesthetical elements (50, 48, 44). On closer analysis, however, Insubordinate Costume can often be seen to fulfil certain of his criteria as 'an argument', with 'a powerful semantic value' linking 'the work's meaning to its "exteriority"' (46, 41).

While this type of costume may not immediately be understood through more conventional social semiotics, as examples frequently transgress social norms, new methods of communicating meaning are explored and the audience is able to perceive the meaning. At the centre of the performance, the costume is not 'an end in itself' as it is fundamental to the action. Insubordinate Costume is a very specific area of costume design, with an emphasis on individuality, originality and experimentation. Infused with an underlying playfulness it has an aesthetic quality closely related to art, sculptural form and materiality. While at times they may appear frivolous, looking closely at the context in which the costumes were produced and their conceptual reasoning, they frequently reveal their subversive nature, a form of activism using costume as a visual protest.

As seen in the previous chapters, sporadic examples of Insubordinate Costume can be observed throughout the twentieth century. Since the 1980s, however, instances of this type of performative costume have continued to increase exponentially with the distinction between fashion, dance, performance art and theatre less defined than previously. A combination of factors has led to this development. Along with the growing awareness of the power and agency of costume and the relatively recent academic studies developing a philosophy of costume (Barbieri and Pantouvaki 2016: 3–5), a variety of other reasons may have contributed to this rapid growth in numbers. The rise of Postdramatic Theatre at the end of the 1960s saw the narrative development of literary and literal text discarded to be replaced by, what Hans-Thies Lehmann describes as, 'a simultaneous and multi-perspectival form of perceiving' performance (Lehmann 2006: 16). Postdramatic notions led to text playing a less central role and the emergence of 'performer as theme and protagonist' (25), which opened up the potential for performances 'where a costume speaks its own language' (Heiner Goebbels in Lehmann 2006: 86). Second-wave feminism was another factor which may have had an effect on the greater use of experimental costume in performance as costume was developed as an artform to explore questions of identity, sexuality and the politics of the body and these themes have continued to be explored ever since. The London club scene of the 1980s also had a notable impact on costume, fashion and performativity as clubgoers vied for attention and characters such as Leigh Bowery and Trojan took dressing up to new levels of extreme costume and body manipulation.

The relationship between fashion, theatre and performance consolidated during the 1980s although this was nothing new as, at the beginning of the twentieth century, lead actresses would commission their costumes from their personal dressmakers, or couture houses like Lucile, and audiences would go to the theatre to see the latest styles. From the 1980s diverse examples of Insubordinate Costume can be noted in experimental dance collaborations between fashion designers and choreographers, such as BodyMap and the aforementioned Leigh Bowery with Michael Clark, Jean Paul Gaultier with Régine Chopinot, Issey Miyake with William Forsythe and Rei Kawakubo with Merce Cunningham; while, from the late 1990s, runway shows have become ever more theatrical, with concept pieces often shown alongside the general collection as a unique form of marketing. The boundaries between fashion, dance, performance art and theatre began to blur in this period, interest in costume as an artform in its own right grew and the development of specific costume design courses, such as the London College of Fashion's MA in Costume Design for Performance course, have led to a notable increase of practice research in the field.

Contemporary Insubordinate Costume, situated somewhere between, art, performance and fashion, continues to experiment with materiality and form, sometimes conceptually, sometimes aesthetically, sometimes with serious intent and sometimes with seeming frivolity. This chapter will pinpoint a number of key examples of Insubordinate Costume from the 1980s onwards, while the final part of the book presents contemporary practice through interviews with and contributions from artists, designers and practitioners currently working in the field.

WEARABLE SCULPTURE AND ARCHITECTURE FOR THE BODY

The relationship of the costume to the body is fundamental in all costume as it is the body that animates the object. Since the early twentieth century instances of Insubordinate Costume have transformed, hidden and extended the human form with what Sonia Biacchi defines as architecture for the body.

SONIA BIACCHI

After recreating the costumes from Oskar Schlemmer's *Triadic Ballet* for a performance on a barge in Venice, self-taught Italian costume designer and choreographer, Sonia Biacchi, developed an interest in object and form, materiality and movement. In 1982 she founded the Centro Teatrale di Ricerca[1] in Venice, creating a theatre of images and developing a series of costumes, sculptural 'insubordinate' forms (Figure 3.1), 'architecture for bodies' (Biacchi 2015),[2] which simultaneously work with and against the body. The productions she designed and choreographed used poetic imagery without words or narrative plot, relying instead on the costume, the moving body and the musical rhythm. Her early costumes were heavily influenced by Schlemmer's work and were 'geometrically minimalist forms of essential lines and volumes' whereas her later work was defined by 'spontaneous shapes: fluid and indefinite architecture in constant development' (D'Agostino 2015: 84). For these Biacchi worked directly on a mannequin with nylon sailcloth and lightweight boning to create the effect she wanted. When worn, these costumes exude kinetic energy in a 'union of body, costume and space' (85). Biacchi describes the work method she came to use:

> I have dedicated a good part of my life to understanding and analysing theatrical costume, to the study of its forms, the specificity of the materials to be used and the use of colours ... Years of experience as a craftsman have gradually led me to the invention and construction of new materials that have a life of their own ... when moved by the performer ... The plastic processes that come to life in 'doing' are based on ideas, feelings, emotions, atmospheres and gestures: a

■ Insubordinate Costume

3.1
Sonia Biacchi,
Architetture per i Corpi, 2011.
Photograph Kristine Theimann.

union of method and madness. Often, I don't know if it's me or the structure of the material that is leading the game.

(C.T.R 2023)

LEE BUL

South Korean sculptor and performance artist Lee Bul's early work focused on the body and materials, although Bul never reveals the precise meaning behind her work, preferring to leave it open to interpretation as there are often 'layers of meanings':

> I choose what I work with very carefully. Everything has connotations, stories and I utilise them. I borrow the general meanings materials have and embrace them in my work. Many times, things have clashing, conflicting connotations or layers of meanings.
>
> (Bul n.d.)

In the late 1980s, Bul created a series of soft sculptures, entitled *Cravings*, grotesque bulbous fabric constructions formed of deformed body parts and tentacles like the roots of a tree, some embellished with sequins or beads. Lena Fritsch, writing for the Tate website, describes *Untitled (Cravings White)* as a 'manifestation of uninhibited obsession [which] touches upon the human fascination with the wild, grotesque and monstrous' (Fritsch 2013). The soft sculptures were worn as costumes during several performances where she walked or crawled along the ground, experimenting with movement and sound which was amplified with hidden microphones. In 1990 she performed *Sorry for Suffering — You Think I'm a Puppy on a Picnic?* wearing a similar giant mutant body suit with extra limbs, in an epic performance that lasted twelve days and took her from Seoul to Tokyo.

Artists Mari Katayama and Daisy May Collingridge also use their work to explore questions surrounding the body. Born with congenital tibial hemimelia, Katayama opted to have her legs amputated. Using her body as a living sculpture, her photographic self-portraits incorporate mannequin replicas of her own body, painted prosthetics, and a wide variety of objects she crafts, embroiders and decorates with shells, sequins and crystals. In *Bystander #01*, 2016, inspired by Botticelli's *Birth of Venus*, and *Bystander #02*, 2016, Katayama becomes 'a multi-armed, many-handed entity' (Campion 2017). Katayama's work reflects on normative conceptions as she searches for the epitome of beauty. She notes that, while it is not possible to separate her body from her work, her work 'is not about disability rights, it's about the human condition … themes that affect anyone who is human, not just people with disabilities' (Warner 2023). Textile artist Daisy May Collingridge creates heavily padded flesh bodysuits which question the idea of an ideal body type. The suits, which are made from a three-dimensional quilting technique in different hues of pink cotton and jersey stuffed with padding, sand and beans, look like inflated anatomy diagrams although the effect appears more playful than the complex subject matter of Katayama's self-portraits or the disturbing connotations of Lee Bul's work.[3]

LUCY MCRAE

In 2007 visual artists Lucy McRae and Bart Hess began to collaborate as LucyandBart[4] on a series of witty and conceptual photographic images that explored genetic manipulation of the body and questioned beauty norms using themselves as models. Emphasising the aesthetic qualities of the materials and the whole visual impact, they combined aspects of fashion, performance and architecture to construct 'costumes' made from multiples of a single material: paper, foam, balloons, grow bags spouting grass. In an interview with Merel Kokhuis in 2010, they stated:

> It's not fashion. You are not able to wear it on a daily basis … We make something to use on the human body, wear it ourselves and make pictures of it. The creations are not made to last, the pictures are the end result.
> (LucyandBart 2010)

Both cerebral and visually compelling, Lucy McRae's more recent work investigates the interface between technology and the body and the impact this will have on human evolution. Currently exploring 'whether human consciousness can be a form of planetary survival' (Weber 2022), she defines herself as 'an interpreter; picking up on weak signals at the fringes of culture and turning those into art' (Weber 2022). TED curator Bruno Giussani describes her as 'a special kind of storyteller, one that probes hypothetical futures in order to help us prepare for

■ Insubordinate Costume

the real futures to come' (Giussani and McRae 2015). Body architect, science fiction artist, filmmaker, inventor and fourth-generation sewer, McRae aims to find fantastical solutions to potential problems such as the 'crisis of touch', or lack of it, which demands inventive interventions that can soothe society's physical and emotional needs. 'Curious about the human consequences of bypassing the womb and that first hug of a "mother" [and] envisioning a new generation of children having radically different formative years, developing new types of sensitivities and neurobiological quirks' in a future where children could be grown in a scientific laboratory, McRae investigates how these future sensitive humans could find new ways for intimacy and togetherness.

Designed to compensate for the lack of human touch in early life by virtue of their origins having bypassed the womb, *Heavy Duty Love*, *Compression Carpet* (Figure 3.2) and *Compression Cradle* are mental health machines that sandwich the body between layers of soft, padded materials and simulate the protective and comforting embrace of a parent or womb. Touch and comfort are also themes in McRae's *Solitary Survival Raft* (Figure 3.3), built as 'a buffer between the occupant and the world … a machine that comforts a single body as they drift into the unknown … her body a sort of seed vault and storage facility preserving the very sense that's under threat – touch' (McRae 2023). Although *Compression Carpet* and *Solitary Survival Raft* are not 'costume' in the traditional sense, they are worn and attached to the body, a fundamental aspect of the artworks. Both part of McRae's *Future Survival Kit*, *Compression Carpet* rolls up and is carried on the back like a snail's shell while the performer in the *Solitary Survival Raft* wears a second body on their back to embrace and comfort their solitude.

3.2
Lucy McRae, *Compression Carpet*, 2019. Photograph by Ariel Fisher. © Lucy McRae.

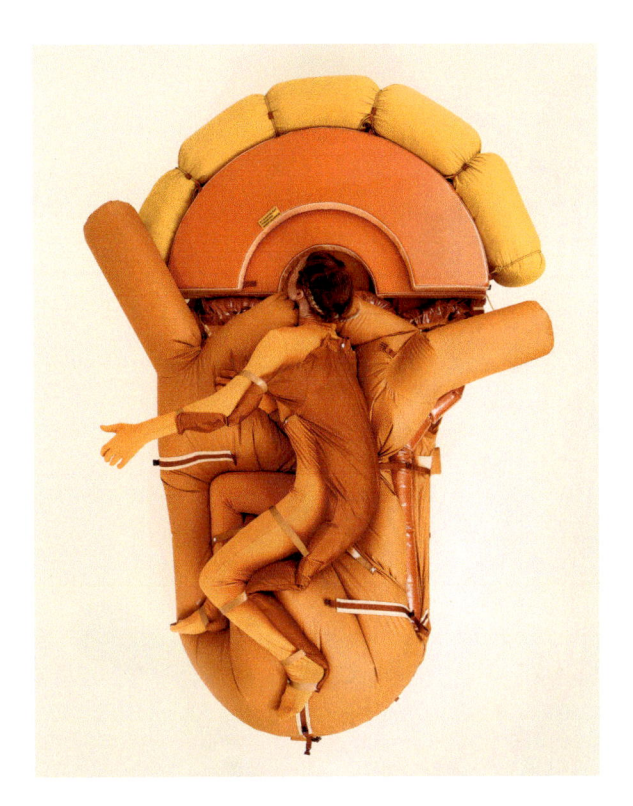

3.3
Lucy McRae,
Solitary Survival Raft, 2020.
Photograph by Ariel Fisher. © Lucy McRae.

NICK CAVE

Nick Cave's *Soundsuits* (Figures 3.4 and 3.5) bridge the worlds of art, fashion and dance. Recalling some of Leigh Bowery's 'Looks' or Maurice Sendak's *Wild Things*, the costumes are sewn, knitted, crocheted and adorned with recycled materials, sequins, children's toys and human hair. 'Some are durable; others more fragile. But all, based on the human body, look as if they could easily spring into motion. The potential for dance is implicit in all of them' (Finkel 2009), their size and shape dictate the movements of the performers.

The *Soundsuits* appear joyful and playful but they have an underlying seriousness. In an interview in the *New York Times*, Cave described how he plays with ideas of identity, masquerade and anonymity in his costumes:

> 'When I was inside a suit, you couldn't tell if I was a woman or man; if I was black, red, green or orange; from Haiti or South Africa', he said. 'I was no longer Nick. I was a shaman of sorts'.
>
> (Finkel 2009)

Cave's first *Soundsuit* was created as a reaction to police brutality and the beating of Rodney King in 1991. Feeling a sense of extreme vulnerability as a black man he built a protective garment from twigs which made a sound as he moved.

■ **Insubordinate Costume**

3.4
Nick Cave, *Soundsuit*, 2010. Photograph: James Prinz © Nick Cave.

Blurring the Boundaries

3.5
Nick Cave, *Soundsuit*, 2015. Photograph: James Prinz. © Nick Cave.

> The sound was a way of alarming others to my presence. The suit became a suit of armor where I hid my identity. It was something 'other'. It was an answer to all of these things I had been thinking about: What do I do to protect my spirit in spite of all that's happening around me?
>
> (O'Grady 2019)

Since 1991, he has created more than five hundred *Soundsuits* which are used in productions of dance and performance as well as displayed in exhibitions. His work addresses racism, homophobia, oppression, loss and remembrance through the celebration of beauty, which he sees as a sign of optimism and the future (O'Grady 2019). In this he is inspired by 'carnival tradition, and the use of costumes and mask to extend the body as a way to think about a jubilation and joy, and a casting off the prior year's crap and moving into renewal, into the next year' (Guggenheim Museum 2022) with hope.

PERFORMING CHARACTER

As noted by Monks, Barthes and Lublin, a character on stage can be understood through the costume the actor or performer is wearing (Monks 2010; Barthes 1972; and Lublin 2011). Likewise, individual and collective identities can be understood through the clothing we choose to wear. In her book *Seeing Through Clothes*, historian, Anne Hollander discusses the performative nature of clothing, stating that 'dress is a form of visual art, a creation of images with the visible self as its medium' (Hollander 1993: 311). This idea of dress as a form of visual art has been expanded by some who have chosen to live their lives as a work of art such as Marchesa Luisa Casati in the early twentieth century, Leigh Bowery in the 1980s and early 1990s and contemporary artist Daniel Lismore, who have envisaged their dressed bodies as an artistic canvas or living sculpture. According to fashion theorist José Teunissen this creation of images particularly

> characterises contemporary (avant-garde) fashion and performance art in its research into the body, its relationship to 'the individual', to the world around it, and the experiments with which it is attempting to reinterpret and redefine this relationship.
> (Teunissen 2011: 15)

The phenomenon of character creation, both human and online, has grown exponentially in the twenty-first century, as the many photos in the book *Not A Toy, Fashioning Radical Characters*, illustrate. In their essay, 'Characters on Parade: Contemporary Character Design Invades the Catwalk', Gregg Duggan and Hoos Fox note that

> Second Life, gaming, and virtual reality have established an alternative arena for multiple activities or personalities, providing an outlet for anonymous expression. Avatars stand in for our physical bodies, and we are no longer tied to our genetic make-up but can choose our Character traits and how we want to look, and we can act in ways we would never dare to in reality.
> (Gregg Duggan and Hoos Fox 2011: 9)

Gregg Duggan and Hoos Fox believe that, through this combination of fashion and 'contemporary character design', which could be defined as a form of Insubordinate Costume, a new art form has emerged which although frequently 'devoid of traditional narrative elements – most notably a plot – [is] firmly rooted in the world of performance and theatre' (Gregg Duggan and Hoos Fox 2011: 9).

LEIGH BOWERY

Leigh Bowery, like the Marchesa Casati, lived his life as a work of art and used experimental costume as a form of visual communication, both in the costumes he designed for Michael Clark and in the outfits he created for himself for his appearances on the London club scene. The maxim for his own club, *Taboo*, which ran on Thursday nights between 1985 and 1986, was 'dress as though your life depends on it, or don't bother' (Tilley 1997: 53) and Bowery would create a different outfit every week where, as fashion designer Rifat Ozbek said 'he always outdid himself' (Swindells and Burston 2016). His designs evolved throughout the 1980s and early 1990s and became more and more surreal as:

> Bowery evolved from a fashion designer into an aesthetic revolutionary ... Bowery was not simply dressing up; it was his lifestyle and commentary on the mundane,

3.6
Leigh Bowery, Session II, Look 9, 1989, from the book *Leigh Bowery Looks* by Fergus Greer. Courtesy of Fergus Greer.

■ Insubordinate Costume

3.7
Leigh Bowery, *Session VII, Look 34*, 1994, from the book *Leigh Bowery Looks* by Fergus Greer. Courtesy of Fergus Greer.

a joke about appearance. His collections or 'looks' were based on himself manipulating his body with clothing and make-up. Working outside the comfort zone, he developed a clothing aesthetic that few would dare follow. Original, provocative, evolutionary; Bowery manipulated clothing to totally change one's appearance, like a form of cosmetic surgery ... His dress style hailed from club culture, and the concepts of dressing up and masquerade.

(Healy 2002)

A series of photos by Fergus Greer (Figures 3.6 and 3.7) illustrate the larger-than-life characters Bowery created by modulating and exaggerating parts of his body through costume. Bowery wrote in his diary which is quoted in Sue Tilley's book *The Life and Times of an Icon*:

I think that firstly individuality is important, and that there should be no main rules for appearance and behaviour. Therefore I want to look as best I can, through my means of individuality and expressiveness.

(Tilley 1997: 97)

The Insubordinate Costumes of fashion designers Alexander McQueen, Gareth Pugh and Craig Green, performance artists Nick Cave and Pyuupiru and performer Lady Gaga all reflect playful, and apparently frivolous, characteristics inherited from Bowery's work and his continuing influence on the fashion world and in contemporary performance art should not be underestimated (Marshall 2021: 77). Insubordinate misbehaviour in costume creation also continues in the work of contemporary drag artists, such as David Faulk/Mrs Vera of Verasphere, whose mixture of recycled materials, kitsch and the spectacular often displays an underlying playfulness and rebellion.

DANIEL LISMORE

Labelled by Aimee Farrell in *Vogue* as England's most eccentric and flamboyant dresser (Farrell 2016), artist and sustainable fashion advocate Daniel Lismore has been compared to Leigh Bowery, although he states that his way of dressing is a way of life not a performance, and that he is not out to shock (Cochrane 2022). In his TED talk Lismore describes how he uses his body as a canvas to create masterpieces, curating his collection of over 6000 eclectic pieces of clothing, vintage fabric, jewellery, armour and various objects into heavily embellished, three-dimensional tapestries. His 'costumes' are collages, assemblages of extraordinary items that he that he reuses and recycles *ad infinitum*. He is constantly changing, reinventing and recreating himself, noting 'these artworks are me. I am art. I have lived as art my entire adult life. Living as art is how I became myself' (Lismore 2019).

ANDREY BARTENEV

Russian multidisciplinary artist, Andrey Bartenev has also created his own colourful and extravagant persona, immediately recognisable for his flamboyant and humoristic dress style. 'His work can be described as a hybrid practice between conceptual fashion and costume for performance' (Vainshtein 2019). In his costumed performances he merges theatre with visual arts and believes that in order 'to be able to express yourself through images … your soul has to be overloaded either with philosophical contemplation of some sort, or with poetic rhythms' (Timofejev 2017) Bartenev sees his performances 'as an ironic take on fashion shows …parodying the catwalk' although he notes 'that the poetics of the catwalk are becoming more complex, and that the fashion shows he is competing with are evolving too' (Bartenev 2006–07: 90–1). Bartenev's inspiration is eclectic, both in his personal style of dress and for the productions he designs such as *The Botanic Ballet*, 1992, staged, for the *Untamed Fashion Assembly* in Jurmala, Latvia (Figure 3.8) and *The First Snowflake Fallen on the Ground* from the 1993 performance of the *Snow Queen* (Figure 3.9). *The Botanic Ballet* was inspired by childhood play modelling the fruit out of snow, fruit that he 'hardly ever got to see in real life, because it was practically impossible to transport them to Norilsk' (Timofejev 2017) and by St Basil's Cathedral in Red Square in Moscow, whereas the costume for *The First Snowflake Fallen on the Ground* was created using hundreds of postcards by Gilbert and George. Bartenev describes the entangled connections that inspire his creativity:

■ Insubordinate Costume

3.8
Andrey Bartenev, *Botanic Ballet*, 1992 Moscow. Photo by Hans-Jurgen Burkart. © Andrey Bartenev.

3.9
Andrey Bartenev, *The Snow Queen*, 1994, Yurmala Beach, Latvia. Photograph by Vladimir Fridkes © Andrey Bartenev.

Once you start creating, you produce a result that is a tangle, a knot of this inexplicable neural interaction. And you cannot discern whether it is a kind of response to the early 20th century culture or to Bauhaus, or a distillate of constructivism, or an expression of yourself. It is impossible to tell precisely. Because such is the peculiarity of our brain – soaking everything up and then re juxtaposing and re-projecting it.

(Timofejev 2017)

SASHA FROLOVA

Bartenev's work has had a notable influence on contemporary Russian artists including Sasha Frolova and Roman Ermakov. Bartenev mentored the Russian sculptor, costume designer and performance artist Sasha Frolova who has a large social media following. She defines herself as a visionary artist trying to 'foresee the future by creating its innovative aesthetics today ... characterised by flexibility, mobility, fluidity – properties that will determine the life and modus operandi of future generations' (Sharma 2022). Frolova creates, and performs as a 'live sculpture', in elaborate inflatable costumes and sculptures in latex which blur the boundaries between fashion and art. Dressed from head to toe in latex, she appears as a variety of characters with voluminous inflatable hair, including pseudo-popstar *Aquaaerobika* and *Marie Antoinette* (Figure 3.10).

Frolova frequently uses bright colours in her costumes, such as *Fontes Amoris Pink* (Figure 3.11), believing that 'color can influence human consciousness bypassing our control, and its intensity compensates for the invisibility of emotions and feelings' (De Vos 2020). She is inspired by nature and biomorphic shapes and maintains that the latex is the co-author in her design process: 'The material itself creates the shape and I am carried away by this co-creation – you never know how the pattern will swell, you try to calculate and this is a very interesting and intriguing process' (Sharma 2022).

ROMAN ERMAKOV

Roman Ermakov also creates live sculptures, a combination of architecture, art, fashion and performance. His work is inspired by geometric forms, repetitive shapes and colourful elements and recalls the creations of the Bauhaus costume parties. The human body moving in space is fundamental to his ethos although the body is not always visible in his costume constructions. In the series *Black Light* 2009–18, for example, the costumes are made to be seen in the dark with an ultraviolet light. The bright fluorescent structures glow in the dark while the black-clad body disappears completely. Ermakov describes his live sculptures as 'architecture of the body ... a reflection of the world of my emotions and impressions' where 'the relationship between music and the light, form and movement are called to unite all the images and help to enter a new reality' (Ermakov 2018).

POLINA OSIPOVA

Contemporary performative characters often use social media channels such as Instagram and TikTok to disseminate their art. Aesthetics and eye-catching imagery have become fundamental in the age of smartphones and internet scrolling. Multimedia designer Polina Osipova has a strong online presence through the photos and videos she posts on Instagram of herself wearing and performing in the surreal objects, wearable sculptures and masks she creates. Frequently encrusted with jewels or pearls, they are inspired by her Chuvash culture and traditions. In one photo she has long branches springing from her fingers, in another

■ **Insubordinate Costume**

3.10
Sasha Frolova Performance in the Catherine Hall of the Grand Tsaritsyno Palace, 2018. Photographer: Irina Voiteleva. Photoshoot for TUSH Magazine 44. Models: Sasha Frolova, Ivan Matyushin, Daria Nikiforova. Assistant: Yana Khromova © Sasha Frolova.

3.11
Sasha Frolova, *Fontes Amoris. Pink*, 2020, latex costume. Photograph: Gleb L.adygin. Director of photography: Kate Bugrova © Sasha Frolova.

she is wearing protective armour made from framed family photos. Some of her work is interactive using mechanical wire contraptions to paint her face, pour liquid into a glass or rotate different photos of eyes in front of her own.[5]

GENA MARVIN

Characters like Bartenev, Frolova, Ermakov and Osipova's creations can be considered aesthetic works of art but other manifestations have deeper and darker connotations, as in the work of Gena Marvin and Pyuupiru. Guerrilla performance artist Gena Marvin plays with the concepts of 'beauty' and 'creature drag', using fear, violence and trauma from her past experiences to fuel her creativity and bring childhood nightmares to life. The tall, spindly, monstrous alien creatures she creates from recycling discarded items, have surreal bulbous growths, appendages and long dangling fingers and they totter or run around on preposterously high heels.[6] The documentary *Queendom*, filmed by Agniia Galdanova's between 2019 and 2023, follows Marvin's development as a queer trans in Russia where anti-LGBTQ+ legislation is becoming ever stricter. She defines her performances as political drag, protesting in full costume about the detainment of Alexey Navalny, LGBTQ+ rights and the invasion of Ukraine, wrapping her body in tape to evoke 'a country where there is no freedom and where the freedom of my body was not permitted' (RFI 2022). In 2022 she became a refugee in Paris after being arrested at an anti-war demonstration in Moscow.

PYUUPIRU

Pyuupiru's extreme costume explorations were also born from trauma. Footage for the documentary *Pyuupiru 2001–2008* was filmed over a period of seven years by Daishi Matsunaga and follows the life and thoughts of contemporary Japanese artist Pyuupiru. In a recent interview with Takashi Haga, she describes the years during the making of the film as a period of intense darkness as she underwent gender affirming surgery and explored questions of gender dysphoria, loneliness, life and death, love and hate, anxiety and desire through the *Planetaria* series of character creations (Haga, 2023). The nine wearable bodies simultaneously represent the planets in the solar system and nine re-interpretations of herself as a person struggling with their own identity. The costumes with bulbous growths and extra appendages were knitted over a period of three and a half years, all but one in bold stripes. The *Goddess* photographic series, which Pyuupiru began in 2010, again explores identity and portrays the artist in different guises such as *Iris Dancing in the Air* and *Hecate Crushed by Grief*.

BJÖRK AND LADY GAGA

The performers Björk and Lady Gaga utilise character creation as part of their public appearances. Björk's iconic style is conceptual. She creates alternative personae by wearing thrift shop clothing or choosing the most avant-garde fashions by designers such as Rei Kawakubo for Comme des Garçons, Junya Watanabe,

Martin Margiela, Hussein Chalayan, Iris van Herpen and Noir Kei Kagami and ethereal headwear by Maiko Takeda. Lady Gaga can be seen as parodying the use of costume as a protest to dismantle the traditional ideas of glamour that are usually associated with pop and film stars. In a 2021 video for *British Vogue*, she describes some of her iconic performative looks such as the *Meat Dress* designed by Franc Fernandez, the *Fire Bra* designed by Tom Talmon Studio, *The Egg* designed by Hussein Chalayan, the inflatable spike dress by Jack and the inflatable tentacle dress by Irving Dayne Henderson and Vex Clothing. She has always used fashion and costume as an artistic statement, noting:

> I do believe in art for art's sake. I also believe in intentional art. And I believe that you can, if you choose, choose to live an artistic life where art is every moment of your being in every second of every day. People say all the time that they think I hid in fashion but I was never hiding. I was screaming.
>
> (Lady Gaga 2021)

FASHION AND PERFORMANCE

> As performance and fashion practice both increasingly move into new and site-specific contexts and as focus is extended around conceptual and experimental approaches, the divisions between clothing designed as conceptual fashion and clothing designed as costume for performance have arguably become less clear.
>
> (Bugg 2013: 1)

Throughout history, clothing has been used to enclothe, protect, adorn and express personality, but it has also been used to alter, constrict, manipulate, emphasise, or exaggerate parts of the body (Marshall 2021: 23) 'to achieve fashion's goal through subtle visual adjustments of proportion, less subtle prostheses, and, often, deliberate physical changes' (Koda 2001: flyleaf). In recent years runway shows have become ever more theatrical, with concept pieces often shown alongside the general collection. Extreme fashions on the runway, with their exaggerated forms and materials not usually associated with wearable clothing, are very effective in 'promoting the brand, generating editorial attention and press, and ultimately driving sales' (Gregg Duggan and Hoos Fox 2011: 9) as they are photographed and reproduced worldwide in newspapers, magazines and across the internet. In an interview with the BBC, avant-garde designer, Craig Green, whose past collections have included wooden structures (Autumn/Winter, 2013) and inflatables (Autumn/Winter, 2022), acknowledges the importance of creating strong, attention-grabbing visual images:

> We don't sell the pieces with wooden elements, for example, but a lot of those more extreme kind of sculpture pieces end up as part of museum collections. We make those pieces because it's about creating a world or a strong visual, but then we also sell jackets and shirts and things that are more accessible for people.
>
> (McIntosh 2018)

Like other artistic media, fashion has become increasingly more conceptual with several designers explicitly uprooting traditional ideals of beauty and bodily norms (Marshall 2021: 33) on the runway. José Teunissen, writing in *Not a Toy: Fashioning Radical Characters*, notes that

> Instead of beautifying the body and clothing it with identity and personality, [fashion designers] are searching for the ominous, unsettling fantasies and meanings that the clothed human figure can also communicate.
>
> (Teunissen 2011: 15)

The use of performative Insubordinate Costume, which often conceals body and face, means that the focus is placed firmly on the garment rather than on the beauty of the model (Marshall 2021: 33). Francesca Granata likens 'the constant play with garments' traditional function, and its attendant disruptions of expectations … to carnival humour and its temporary disruption of hierarchies' (Granata 2017: 101).

The relationship between fashion, theatre and performance further consolidated during the 1980s and 1990s as fashion designers collaborated on dance pieces which gave them the opportunity to experiment with a different medium.

MICHAEL CLARK, BODYMAP AND LEIGH BOWERY

In an interview for the *Financial Times* in 2013, dancer and choreographer, Michael Clark, explained why, at the beginning of his career in the 1980s, he preferred to work with friends who were fashion designers and artists rather than trained theatre designers who he believed might be too accommodating:

> I wanted to collaborate with people who had ideas on the same level as me, who weren't just going to be told what to do … I wanted people who were going to challenge me as well.
>
> (Jobey 2013)

Clark's choreography was inspired by strong visual images: platform shoes, prosthetics, backside-baring costumes with exaggeratedly long sleeves by BodyMap (Figure 3.12), polka-dot costumes by Leigh Bowery. Playful, fun and often consciously outrageous, the costumes inspired Clark's choreography and frequently influenced the dancers' movements. The visual impact of the costumes for Clark's productions such as *New Puritans* (Figure 3.13), 1984, *not H.AIR*, 1985, *our caca phoney H. our caca phony H.*, 1985 and *No Fire Escape in Hell*, 1986, contravened the expectations of the audience and critics and provoked the subsequent interest in the flamboyant and provocative design choices (Marshall 2021: 45–6).

■ **Insubordinate Costume**

3.12
Michael Clark and Ellen van Schuylenburch in a publicity shot for *Do You Me? I Did*, 1984. Costumes by BodyMap. Photograph by Richard Haughton. Courtesy of Richard Haughton.

3.13
Michael Clark in a publicity photograph for *New Puritans*, 1984. Photograph by Richard Haughton. Courtesy of Richard Haughton.

Clark has since acknowledged that the visual elements of his early performances frequently upstaged his choreography (45):

> To be honest, it annoyed me that people would talk about the costumes and the props and not about the actual dance. I was trying to help people see what was underneath all that.
>
> (Jinman 2018)

Although the idea of using challenging costume designs was extremely appealing to Clark, it appears that the actual result was irritation at the fact that the costumes received more press coverage than the choreography (Marshall 2021: 46). Since Clark's early comments in the 1980s, the agency of costume has been more fully acknowledged and contemporary costume designers are as experimental as fashion designers or artists, as the final section of this book demonstrates.

RÉGINE CHOPINOT AND JEAN PAUL GAULTIER

Famous for the ruched orange cone bra corset dress from his Autumn/Winter 1984–85 collection, *Barbès*, and the cone bra Madonna wore for her *Blond Ambition* tour in 1990, Jean Paul Gaultier designed the costumes for sixteen of French choreographer Régine Chopinot's ballets between 1983 and 1993. The most famous of these was the 1985 *Le Défilé* (*The Fashion Show*), part fashion parade part ballet where

> the costumes are not just the subject of the work, they are also genuine partners. As a result of their weight, their texture 'the fabrics appear to be animated through their own kinetic potential, and the dance, that awakens it, has to adapt and integrate its reactions'.
>
> (Numeridanse 2012; Suquet 2010: 33)

The costumes 'intensify morphological particularities and sometimes invent them, with prostheses and accessories' (Suquet 2010: 31), combining humour with historical references, like the heavy eighteenth-century pannier crinolines in white cable-knit wool.

MERCE CUNNINGHAM AND REI KAWAKUBA

In 1997 Rei Kawakuba's designs for the Merce Cunningham dance *Scenario* (Figure 3.14) and her Spring/Summer *Comme des Garçons* collection *Body Meets Dress, Dress Meets Body* are the first examples of her playing with padding and body modulation in order to

> explore and question assumptions about female beauty and notions of what is sexually alluring and what is grotesque within the Western vocabulary.
>
> (Granata 2017: 40)

As the Metropolitan Museum of Art's Costume Institute *Rei Kawakubo/Comme des Garçons: Art of the In-Between* retrospective exhibition of 2017 showed, it

◾ **Insubordinate Costume**

is a theme which has continued to intrigue her as her work continues to move away from wearability towards the surreal. With her sculptural fashions Kawakubo blurs the boundaries between art and fashion challenging 'our ideas about fashion's role in contemporary culture' (The Met 2016). Speaking about her work, Rei Kawakubo said:

> I have always pursued a new way of thinking about design by denying established values, conventions, and what is generally accepted as the norm. And the modes of expression that have always been most important to me are fusion imbalance … unfinished … elimination … and absence of intent.
>
> (The Met 2016)

In 1919, twenty-two years after her costume designs for Cunningham's *Scenario*, Rei Kawakuba was asked by Olga Neuwirth, the first female composer to be commissioned by the Vienna State Opera, to design the costumes for a new opera based on Virginia Woolf's novel, *Orlando*. Neuwirth specifically wanted Kawakubo to design the production as she felt that her 'abstraction of body, enlargement of body, deconstruction of body [and] androgynous way of thinking about fashion, art and life' (Menkes 2019) complimented the musical score. The costumes draw inspiration from Kawakubo's fashion designs as well as historical references, technological materials and a touch of pantomime. The costumes included flat dresses similar to her Autumn/Winter 2012 *2 Dimensions* collection, tailored jackets with extra sleeves like her *The Infinity of Tailoring* collection of Autumn/Winter 2013 and abstract armour like her *18th-Century Punk* collection of Autumn/Winter 2016. Just as the link between *Scenario* and the *Body Meets Dress, Dress Meets Body* collection was apparent, the *Orlando* costumes are closely related to the Comme des Garçons Spring/Summer 2020 menswear and womenswear collections.

3.14
Rei Kawakubo's costumes for Merce Cunningham's *Scenario*, 1997. Photograph by Timothy Greenfield-Sanders. Courtesy of Timothy Greenfield-Sanders.

THE NETHERLANDS DANCE THEATER AND VIKTOR & ROLF

Viktor & Rolf collaborated with experimental theatre director Robert Wilson on both the surreal dance piece *2 Lips and Dancers and Space* for the Netherlands Dance Theater in 2004, where one of the dancers wore a long flowing purple wig, and on the opera *Der Freischütz* (*The Freeshooter*) in 2009. The costumes for *Der Freischütz*, which was based on a German folk tale in which a huntsman enters a pact with the devil, are extravagant and playful with a child-like fairytale ambience. While the choir was dressed in black neoprene with matching wigs, the lead singer wore 'the most exaggerated costume ... a huge singing bouquet of flowers ... vaguely reminiscent of something like a Meissen figurine' (Browne 2009). Others are dressed as trees or in white dresses captured under voluminous white hunting nets. Viktor & Rolf note that they 'feel very much at home in Bob's world. It's a very original and specific world he created, where time seems to have a different logic and people are abstractions Somehow we understand each other's universe' (Browne 2009).

Viktor & Rolf's runway shows also blur the borders between fashion and performance art. From their 1999 *Russian Doll* collection, which saw the Dutch designers dress one model on stage with successive garments one on top of the other, to the giant doll heads of the *Action Dolls* Autumn/Winter 2017 couture collection, from the tulle ball gowns with perfect holes cut into the skirts from the Spring/Summer 2010 *Cutting Edge Couture* collection or worn upside-down in their haute couture Spring/Summer 2023 collection to their 2015 *Wearable Art* series, where the models parade wearing broken Renaissance paintings complete with gold picture frames and *Performance of Sculptures*, haute couture collection, Spring/Summer 2016, Viktor & Rolf's designs are theatrical and their shows highly performative.

MARIE-AGNÈS GILLOT AND WALTER VAN BEIRENDONCK

Unconventional Belgian fashion designer Walter Van Beirendonck designed the playful costumes for Marie-Agnès Gillot's *Sous Apparence* at the Paris Opera Ballet in 2012. The style of the costumes, in pleated and folded tulle, the traditional tutu material used in an unexpected way, is recognisably linked to his fashion designs with bold shapes and colours. Bright green fir trees, a peach-coloured topiary bush and a giant blackberry covered the dancers' heads and torsos completely. In an interview with the Opéra National de Paris he describes the collaborative and experimental working process and the ideas behind the costumes, noting that Marie-Agnès Gillot wanted to introduce the idea of restriction of movement into the choreography and was inspired by the 'walking sculptures' that Van Beirendonck had designed in the past. The result was 'a kind of surreal garden' with 'the dancers almost like creatures' in 'very bright colours on the one hand but also with pastel shades and a lot of flesh colour' (Van Beirendonck 2012).

In the 1980s, Walter Van Beirendonck was one of the Antwerp Six, Belgium's influential avant-garde fashion collective. His conceptual art-meets-fashion designs use humoristic elements that often border on the absurd, in much the same way as the artwork of the Dada and Surrealist movements. He sets out to shock and jolt the fashion world into having a social conscience with themes that cover issues such as ecology, war, and AIDS:

> Inflatable balloon masks printed with the words 'Blow Job'. Horn prostheses on models' foreheads. Hairy T-shirts. Vests with wings. Tulle sculptures shaped like clipped trees. Blow-up doll bodysuits with long, snaky phalluses. Those are just some of the wearable oddities that have sprung from the fertile mind of Walter Van Beirendonck, who's ... bridged the gap between art and fashion, proving that garments could also express extreme concepts ... with ample humor.
>
> (Saad 2011)

DAMIEN JALET AND HUSSEIN CHALAYAN

In 2015, Hussein Chalayan devised, designed and directed the production of *Gravity Fatigue* together with choreographer Damien Jalet. Chalayan and Jalet worked closely on the collaborative process, with Chalyan insisting that the costumes should be 'dictating the grammar of the choreography not simply dressing it' (Mackrell 2015a). The performance was divided into eighteen tableaux which explored the theme of migration and the sense of displacement that it can entail, by 'exploring the body in states of disorientation and strangeness' (Mackrell 2015b). Many of the over one hundred costumes constricted the movement of the dancers and inspired the choreography, like the much-photographed *Elastic Bodies*, a long loop of fabric which stretched between two dancers linking and defining their movements.

Likewise, Chalayan incorporates performance into his fashion shows. The Autumn/Winter 2000 *After Words* collection was conceptual and played with the idea of transformation with pieces of furniture morphing into clothing:

> This show bordered on a 1970s 'happening': four models wearing grey shift-dresses approached these chairs, removed the covers and then put them onto their bodies. The last model wearing a similar dress delicately stepped into the middle of the table, lifted it up and transformed it into a skirt ... This wasn't, however, an exercise in theatricality for the sake of theatricality ... The show was inspired by refugees of war, people forced to flee their homes, carrying their worldly possessions on their backs.
>
> (Stansfield 2016)

DAMIEN JALET AND IRIS VAN HERPEN

Dutch experimental fashion designer, Iris van Herpen's couture collections are also performative. She works with technology, avant-garde textiles, three-dimensional printing and innovative engineering techniques to create unique, metamorphic and scenographic fashion pieces, whose sculptural forms are often inspired by the geometrical patterns of the natural world. Van Herpen's work bridges, not only the boundaries between fashion, theatre and performance, but also those of science, architecture and engineering (Marshall 2021: 109). In an interview with *Vogue*, she describes how her working methods 'create garments that combine experimental technology with traditional craftsmanship. This interdisciplinary research creates a constant dialogue and new knowledge and challenge for the atelier' (Borrelli-Persson 2017).

Van Herpen, who trained in classical ballet as a child, believes fashion is an artform that is closely related to dance and describes her designs as being 'about exploring movement in all its complexity' (Finney 2022). In 2018, she collaborated with choreographer Damien Jalet, on Opera Vlaanderen's production of *Pelléas et Mélisande* in Antwerp, Belgium, stating in conversation with Jalet:

> I think of the body as a sculpture … I have the human anatomy as my muse, so it's a bit more abstract … In my work, in every piece I make, I'm looking for the movement and the aliveness that dance can express … I put the material on and I start testing it myself, and I start interacting with it and seeing the way it moves. And then often that influences my next motion in the draping process.
>
> (van Herpen 2020)

SASHA WALTZ AND IRIS VAN HERPEN

Perhaps the most spectacular of van Herpen's dance designs can be seen in Sasha Waltz & Guests 2017 production of *Kreatur* which explores the 'phenomena of existence against the background of a disrupted society: power and a lack of power, dominance and weakness, freedom and control, community and isolation' (Waltz 2017). The dancers appear in different costumes and include diaphanous clouds that cocoon and protect the body and faceless creatures whose long spikes protrude outwards like a sea urchin.

ALEXANDER MCQUEEN

Rebellious, provocative and transgressive, Alexander McQueen's runway shows were always theatrical, bordering on performance art. According to Andrew Bolton, curator of the *Alexander McQueen: Savage Beauty* exhibition 'The runway was where McQueen's fantasies and creative impulses were given free reign. He used the runway to express the purity of his creative vision, imbuing his collections with strong conceptual narratives' (Bolton 2011: 18). McQueen stated that he 'was quite happy just doing the performance, happy working as a performance artist … It was all about making a statement and the communication of that statement' (Frankel 2011: 26).

With eclectic historical references and exaggerated shapes, McQueen questioned the traditional ideals of beauty and often hid the models' faces behind masks, cages, headwear and distorted make-up. The runway show for McQueen's Spring/Summer 1999 collection was held in a disused warehouse. Ex-ballet dancer and model Shalom Harlow describes wearing dress No. 13 for the finale, which was inspired by Rebecca Horn's installation of two shotguns firing red paint at each other:

As soon as I gained my footing, the circular platform started a slow, steady rotation. And it was almost like the mechanical robots were stretching and moving their parts after an extended period of slumber [then] they began to spray and paint and create this futuristic design on this very simple dress. And when they were finished, they sort of receded and I walked, almost staggered, up to the audience and splayed myself in front of them with complete abandon and surrender.

(The Met 1999)

PAULA ULARGUI ESCALONA

Like the new generation of performance artists, young contemporary fashion designers are using the internet and social media as a means to communicate and disseminate their fashions and voice their ideas, concerns and solutions. Highly attuned to current ecological and sustainable issues, Spanish eco-fashion designer Paula Ulargui Escalona has developed a way to work with nature in order to create performative garments that sprout grass, seeds, moss and mushrooms in an aesthetic alliance which becomes part clothing part living sculpture. Collaborating with Jonathan Anderson to grow pieces for Loewe's Menswear 2023 runway show, these pieces are not for everyday wear but were chosen to grab the attention of the press and public and to advocate sustainability and a back to nature mentality.

TERRENCE ZHOU

New York-based Chinese fashion designer Terrence Zhou creates sculptural clothing with bold abstract body-morphing silhouettes inspired by modernism, spheres and globes, or by underwater creatures. 'In the workshop, my dress took up so much room you couldn't unsee it. There was an element of performance to it, and at that point, I knew this was what I wanted to explore with my clothes' (Smith 2021). His extreme designs went viral on social media and have since been worn by singers Lizzo, Christina Aguilera and Rina Sawayama. He believes in immersive storytelling and that, even though many of his designs may appear unwearable, 'the concept of wearability changes over time, corresponding to contingent norms and expectations of space. We all now have an identity through the virtual world … where new generations are not shying away from showing their personalities and pursuing uniqueness' (Barbakadze 2023). In 2022 Zhou and his fashion brand Bad Binch TongTong entered the metaverse with a series of NFTs (non-fungible tokens) where 'the designs, considered impossible to wear and function in real life, are now able to be collected as digital artworks, empowering the owners to share on social media as part of their online identities' (Law 2022).

Just as in the early twentieth century, when avant-garde artists experimented with Insubordinate Costume as a response to the advent of the mechanised age, industrialisation and war, many contemporary designers and practitioners are exploring the potential of costume to open up a discussion of cultural and societal issues. Although Insubordinate Costume in performance may be considered a niche artform, it has become more widespread in recent years: seen on the runway, at the Met Gala, on opera and ballet stages and in drag performances. The boundaries between the artistic and performative disciplines of theatre, dance, performance art and fashion are dissipating and many examples of Insubordinate Costume transcend formal classification. As Monks observes: there are 'multiple ways in which costume works' (Maclaurin and Monks 2015: 2).

A strong emphasis on experimentation remains, with designers focusing on shape, materiality and the body in movement. Technical advances such as three-dimensional printing, laser-cutting and innovative textiles have made a notable impact on design and opened up new creative potentials for the future. The digital age allows for the widespread distribution of information and the online sharing of images and films through websites and social media, which gives the opportunity for contemporary designers and artists to bring their work into contact with a wider audience. As such, the audience for costume-led performances may be live or online, knowledgeable about the subject or approaching it for the first time, they may have actively searched for the performance or happened upon it by chance by browsing the internet or because certain algorithms mean it is shared on their social media pages.

NOTES

1. Centre of Theatre Research (www.ctrteatro.it)
2. From a private conversation with Sonia Biacchi at the exhibition 'Architetture per i corpi. I costumi-sculture di Sonia Biacchi' (Architecture for bodies. The costume-sculptures of Sonia Biacchi) at the Centro culturale Candiani in Mestre.
3. https://www.daisycollingridge.com/WORK
4. https://www.lucymcrae.net/lucyandbart https://www.barthess.com/lucyandbart
5. https://www.instagram.com/polinatammi/?hl=en
6. https://www.instagram.com/genamarvin/reels/).

REFERENCES

Barbakadze, Nini. 2023. 'Terrence Zhou Unwearables.' *Metal Magazine*. https://metalmagazine.eu/en/post/interview/terrence-zhou accessed [11/10/23].

Barbieri, Donatella, and Sofia Pantouvaki. 2016. 'Towards a Philosophy of Costume', *Studies in Costume & Performance* 1 (1): 3–7. https://doi.org/10.1386/scp.1.1.3_2.

Bartenev, Andrey. 2006–07. 'Veselaya Nauka Perfomansa' ('The merry science of performance'). Interview with Olga Vainshtein quoted in Vainshtein, Olga. 2019. 'Fashioning the 'Performance Man': Costumes and Contexts of Andrey Bartenev', *Critical Studies in Men's Fashion* 6 (1 & 2): 22. Intellect. https://doi.org/10.1386/csmf_00003_1.

Barthes, Roland. 1972. 'The Diseases of Costume', in *Critical Essays*, 41–50. Translated by Richard Howard. Evanston, Illinois: Northwestern University Press.

Biacchi, Sonia. 2015. *Architecture per i Corpi*. Venezia: Marsilio Editori.

Bolton, Andrew. 2011. 'In Search of the Sublime.' in *Alexander McQueen,* edited by Claire Wilcox. London: V&A.

Borrelli-Persson, Laird. 2017. 'An Interview With Iris van Herpen on the Eve of Her 10th Anniversary Show in Paris.' *Vogue*. 2017. https://www.vogue.com/article/iris-van-herpen-haute-couture-anniversary-interview accessed [13/10/20].

Brecht, Bertolt, and John Willett. 1964. *Brecht on Theatre: The Development of an Aesthetic*. Edited and translated by John Willett. New York: Hill and Wang.

Browne, Alix. 2009. 'High Note | Viktor & Rolf at the Opera.' *New York Times*. https://archive.nytimes.com/tmagazine.blogs.nytimes.com/2009/04/28/high-note-viktor-and-rolf-at-the-opera/ accessed [07/11/20].

Bugg, Jessica. 2013. 'Fashion & Performance: Materiality, Meaning, Media.' https://www.academia.edu/14810304/Fashion_and_Performance_Materiality_Meaning_Media.Academia.edu accessed [13/09/20].

Bul, Lee. n.d. 'Lee Bul.' Thaddaeus Ropac. https://ropac.net/artists/31-lee-bul/ accessed [13/06/23].

Campion, Chris. 2017. 'Interview: Punk Prosthetics: The Mesmerising Art of Living Sculpture Mari Katayama.' *The Guardian*. https://www.theguardian.com/artanddesign/2017/mar/06/mari-katayama-japanese-artist-disabilities-interview accessed [02/05/23].

Cochrane, Lauren. 2022. '"I just want to be left alone": Artist Daniel Lismore on Life as a Living Sculpture.' *The Guardian*. https://www.theguardian.com/artanddesign/2022/feb/14/i-just-want-to-be-left-alone-artist-daniel-lismore-on-life-as-a-living-sculpture accessed [15/06/23].

C.T.R. 2023. https://www.ctrteatro.it/sonia-biacchi/ accessed [04/06/23].

D'Agostino, Ivana. 2015. 'Sonia Biacchi and the Abstraction of the Form. Analysis of Her Costume Making as an Absolute Creative Act', in *Architetture per i Corpi*. Venezia: Marsilio Editori.

De Vos, Joanna. 2020. *Sasha Frolova. Fontes Amoris*. Moscow Museum of Modern Art. https://mmoma.ru/en/exhibitions/gogolevsky/sasha_frolova_fontes_amoris/ accessed [04/05/23].

Ermakov, Roman. 2018. 'Roman Ermakov.' Al-Tiba9 Contemporary Art. https://www.altiba9.com/roman-ermakov accessed [08/04/23].

Farrell, Aimee. 2016. 'England's Most Eccentric Dresser Shows His 3,000-Piece Wardrobe in an Exhibition.' *Vogue*. https://www.vogue.com/article/daniel-lismore-be-yourself-fashion-exhibit-scad-atlanta accessed [11/05/23].

Finkel, Jori. 2009. 'Nick Cave, Dreaming the Clothing Electric, at the Yerba Buena Center.' *The New York Times*. https://www.nytimes.com/2009/04/05/arts/design/05fink.html accessed [01/05/21].

Finney, Alice. 2022. '"Fashion is a form of art and it's so closely related to dance" says Iris van Herpen.' *Dezeen*. https://www.dezeen.com/2022/07/19/iris-van-herpen-fashion-art-dance-interviews/ accessed [08/04/21].

Frankel, Susannah. 2011. 'Introduction', in *Alexander McQueen: Savage Beauty* by Andrew Bolton. New York: Metropolitan Museum of Art.

Fritsch, Lena. 2013. 'Lee Bul Untitled (Cravings White) 1988, Reconstructed 2011.' Tate. https://www.tate.org.uk/art/artworks/lee-untitled-cravings-white-t13992 accessed [08/08/23].

Giussani, Bruno, and Lucy McRae. 2015. 'The Human of the Future | Intel and WIRED Present: Upstarts | WIRED.' https://www.youtube.com/watch?v=HgfTIrlh4to&ab_channel=WIREDUK accessed [22/04/23].

Granata, Francesca. 2017. *Experimental Fashion Performance Art, Carnival and the Grotesque Body*. London, New York: I.B. Tauris & Co. Ltd.

Gregg Duggan, Ginger, and Judith Hoos Fox. 2011. 'Characters on Parade: Contemporary Character Design Invades the Catwalk', in *Not A Toy: Fashioning Radical Characters*, edited by Valerie Steele, Jose Teunissen, and Vassili Zidianakis, 352. Berlin: Pictoplasma.

Guggenheim Museum. 2022. *Nick Cave: Forothermore*. Guggenheim Museum. https://www.youtube.com/watch?v=EAw4bemr0NQ&ab_channel=GuggenheimMuseum accessed [08/09/23].

Haga, Takashi. 2023. '12 Years have Passed since the Release of the Movie 'Pyuupiru'. World-famous Artist Pyuupiru's Current Location.' *New Tokyo*. https://the-new-tokyo.com/pyuupiru/ accessed [18/09/23].

Healy, Robyn. 2002. 'Taboo or Not Taboo, the Fashions of Leigh Bowery.' *NGV*. 2002. https://www.ngv.vic.gov.au/essay/taboo-or-not-taboo-the-fashions-of-leigh-bowery/ accessed [26/04/20].

van Herpen, Iris. 2020. 'The Big Ideas: Why does Art Matter? Where Dance and Fashion Collide. A conversation between the designer Iris van Herpen and the choreographer Damien Jalet on the creative process.' https://www.nytimes.com/2020/05/30/opinion/dance-fashion-herpen-jalet.html accessed [08/04/21].

Hollander, Anne. 1993. *Seeing through Clothes*. Oakland, CA: University of California Press.

Jinman, Richard. 2018. 'Why the Wild Boy of Dance, Michael Clark, Has Toned down His Act.' *The Sydney Morning Herald*. https://www.smh.com.au/entertainment/why-the-wild-boy-of-dance-michael-clark-has-toned-down-his-act-20180115-h0i9jf.html accessed [27/04/20].

Jobey, Liz. 2013. 'Michael Clark: "Extreme Is Good for Me."' *Financial Times*. https://www.ft.com/content/59836b32-4cc2-11e3-958f-00144feabdc0 accessed [27/04/20].

Koda, Harold. 2001. *Extreme Beauty The Body Transformed*. New York: The Metropolitan Museum of Art.

Lady Gaga. 2021. 'Lady Gaga On The Meat Dress and 19 Other Iconic Looks | Life In Looks', *British Vogue*. https://www.vogue.co.uk/video/watch/life-in-looks-lady-gaga accessed [03/05/21].

Law, Julienna. 2022. 'Bad Binch TONGTONG Brings Eccentric Silhouettes to the Metaverse', *Jing Daily*. https://jingdaily.com/bad-binch-tongtong-nft-xtended-identity/ accessed [30/09/23].

Lehmann, Hans-Thies. 2006. *Postdramatic Theatre*. Translated and with an introduction by Karen Jürs-Munby. London and New York: Routledge.

Lismore, Daniel. 2019 'My Life as a Work of Art.' *Ted Talk*. https://www.youtube.com/watch?v=8q7D4EmbSCw&ab_channel=TED accessed [11/05/23].

Lublin, Robert I. 2011. *Costuming the Shakespearean Stage: Visual Codes of Representation in Early Modern Theatre and Culture*. Abingdon: Routledge. https://doi.org/10.4324/9781315574448.

LucyandBart. 2010. https://www.barthess.com/lucyandbart accessed [21/01/20].

Mackrell, Judith. 2015a. 'Gravity Fatigue Review – Catwalk-like Rhythm Diminishes Chalayan's Dazzle.' *The Guardian*. https://www.theguardian.com/stage/2015/oct/30/gravity-fatigue-review-hussein-chalayan-sadlers-wells-damien-jalet accessed [02/06/21].

Mackrell, Judith. 2015b. 'How Hussein Chalayan Fashioned a Dance Where Costumes Rule.' *The Guardian*. https://www.theguardian.com/stage/2015/sep/10/hussein-chalayan-gravity-fatigue-dance-choreography-fashion-interview accessed [02/06/21].

Maclaurin, Ali, and Aoife Monks. 2015. *Costume Readings in Theatre Practice*. London: Palgrave Macmillan.

Marshall, Susan. 2021. *Insubordinate Costume*. Doctoral thesis, Goldsmiths, University of London. https://doi.org/10.25602/GOLD.00031204.

McIntosh, Steven. 2018. 'Men's Fashion Week: How Craig Green Caught the Stars' Attention - BBC News.' *BBC Website*. http://www.bbc.co.uk/news/entertainment-arts-42430335 accessed [03/05/21].

McRae, Lucy. 2023. *Solitary Survival Raft*. https://www.lucymcrae.net/solitary-survival-raft accessed [09/06/23].

Menkes, Susy. 2019. 'At The Vienna Opera, A Female Composer, Transgender Story, and Costumes by Comme.' *British Vogue*. https://www.vogue.co.uk/fashion/article/at-the-vienna-opera-a-female-composer-transgender-story-and-costumes-by-comme accessed [02/06/21].

Monks, Aoife. 2010. *The Actor in Costume*. London: Palgrave Macmillan.

Numeridanse. 2012. 'Le Défilé.' *Numeridanse*. https://www.numeridanse.tv/en/dance-videotheque/le-defiley accessed [02/06/21].

O'Grady, Megan. 2019. 'Nick Cave.' *New York Times*. https://www.nytimes.com/interactive/2019/10/15/t-magazine/nick-cave-artist.html accessed [02/06/21].

RFI. 2022. 'Russian LGBT Artists Find Sanctuary in Paris.' *RFI*. https://www.rfi.fr/en/health-and-lifestyle/20220630-russian-lgbt-artists-find-sanctuary-in-paris accessed [11/07/23].

Saad, Shirine. 2011. 'If Anyone Can Dream the World Awake, It's Walter Van Beirendonck.' *Hint Fashion Magazine*. http://www.hintmag.com/post/august-27-2011-1500 accessed [10/03/21].

Sharma, Manu. 2022. 'Sasha Frolova Discusses Latex, Artistic Synthesis and her Performance Practice.' *Stir World*. https://www.stirworld.com/see-features-sasha-frolova-discusses-latex-artistic-synthesis-and-her-performance-practice accessed [04/05/23].

Smith, Michael. 2021. 'Terrence Zhou is the Internet's Favourite Designer.' *1 Granary*. https://1granary.com/designers-3/terrence-zhou-is-the-internets-favourite-designer/ accessed [11/10/23].

Stansfield, Ted. 2016. 'When Hussein Chalayan Turned Furnishings Into Fashion.' *AnOther Magazine*. www.anothermag.com/fashion-beauty/8248/when-hussein-chalayan-turned-furnishings-into-fashion accessed [02/06/21].

Suquet, Annie. 2010. *Chopinot*. Le Mans: Ed. Cénomane.

Swindells, Dave, and Paul Burston. 2016. 'What Made Leigh Bowery So Legendary?' *Timeout*. 2016. https://www.timeout.com/london/nightlife/what-made-leigh-bowery-so-legendary accessed [17/11/20].

Teunissen, Jose. 2011. 'Beyond the Individual: Fashion and Identity Research.' In *Not A Toy: Fashioning Radical Characters*, edited by Valerie Steele, Jose Teunissen, and Vassili Zidianakis, 352. Berlin: Pictoplasma.

The Met. 2016. 'Rei Kawakubo/Comme Des Garçons: Art of the In-Between.' The Metropolitan Museum of Art. 2016. https://www.metmuseum.org/press/exhibitions/2016/rei-kawakubo accessed [17/06/21].

The Met. 1999. 'Dress, No. 13, spring/summer 1999.' https://blog.metmuseum.org/alexandermcqueen/dress-no-13/ accessed [09/07/20].

Tilley, Sue. 1997. *The Life and Times of an Icon*. London: Hodder & Stoughton Ltd.

Timofejev, Sergej. 2017. 'Andrey Bartenev: "Artist Is Like a Giant Jellyfish".' *Arterritory*. https://arterritory.com/en/visual_arts/interviews/20569-andrey_bartenev_artist_is_like_a_giant_jellyfish/ accessed [06/05/23].

Vainshtein, Olga. 2019. 'Fashioning the "Performance Man": Costumes and Contexts of Andrey Bartenev.' *Critical Studies in Men's Fashion* 6 (1 & 2). Intellect. https://doi.org/10.1386/csmf_00003_1.

Van Beirendonck, Walter. 2012. 'Sous Apparence: Interview with Walter Van Beirendonck.' Opéra national de Paris. https://www.youtube.com/watch?v=3C6z4nP55Yo&ab_channel=Op%C3%A9ranationaldeParis accessed [10/01/23].

Waltz, Sasha. 2017. 'Kreatur. Sasha Waltz & Guests.' https://www.sashawaltz.de/en/creation-by-sasha-waltz-world-premiere-in-june-in-berlin/ accessed [10/05/23].

Warner, Marigold. 2023 'Why I Make Art.' *LensCulture*. https://www.lensculture.com/articles/mari-katayama-why-i-make-art

Weber, Hugh. 2022. 'Lucy McRae Interview.' https://thegreatdiscontent.com/interview/lucy-mcrae/ accessed [09/06/23].

4 Contemporary Runway, Contemporary Costume

Felix Choong

Conceptual showpieces have long provided designers with an opportunity to experiment with their medium. Although destined to never truly be worn, once seen on the runway they go on to exist as museum pieces, as images in fashion spreads or in paparazzi shots. In each case, they are brought out for a fleeting moment before being returned to the garment bags, acid-free tissue paper and temperature-controlled cabinets of the archives. These creations embrace fashion's symbiotic relationship to capitalism, acting as a unique form of brand publicity while presenting audiences with garments that have significant conceptual and artistic value.

The interactions between the spheres of art and fashion are dynamic; however, it is still rare for clothes to be considered on the same critical level as works of art. They resemble each other as aesthetic categories but are ultimately defined by different systems – in particular, systems of labour and production – that keep these notions clearly distinct (Ugelvig 2020: 7). Art and performance, both of which predate capitalist modernity, have managed to sustain a connection to values we hold in high regard, despite the commercial underpinnings of their contemporary iterations. In contrast, fashion is inextricably linked to capitalism and frequently regarded as superficial in comparison to other artforms (Evans 2013: 1). While the history of Western fashion dates back at least 700 years, the emergence of the French haute couture system in the mid-nineteenth century was instrumental in establishing how the current fashion system operates. The technological parameters of the runway have developed since the first fashion shows in France, Britain and the USA in the late nineteenth and early twentieth century; its underlying performativity remains intact. Artistic strategies that were used by trailblazing designers, such as Charles Frederick Worth, Lucile and Lucien Lelong, continue to be employed today. They understood that couture houses could function like theatres, marketing to diverse audiences through staging, musical arrangement, lighting and other dramatic devices that, in Lucile's case, included erotically named dresses such as *Come to Me*, *The Sighing Sound of Lips* and *Unsatisfied* (Evans 2013: 35). The runway flips the relationship between culture and commerce, where culture is treated as a commodity, economic value grafted onto a model's body (Evans 2013: 115). These early strategies of spectacle blurred the lines between the performance of fashion and bodies in movement

DOI: 10.4324/9781003341000-6

and the performance of designers and their brand identities (Kollnitz and Pecorari 2022: 14).

While fashion may look to art for new stylistic trends, it cannot assume the same levity and criticality that art can. There is less opportunity to challenge the fundamental hierarchies, prejudices and exploitations that exist within its industry because it is a business in much more overt ways than art, and it is therefore expected to produce quantifiable results (McKenzie and Lipscombe 2020: n.p.). Fashion constantly contends with complex modalities of looking. Blunting the fashion buyer's calculations of a garment's saleability, titillating the individual's materialistic desires, and satiating the press's need for endless novelty are all demands that fashion needs to satisfy in its cyclical debuts. French literary theorist and philosopher Roland Barthes notes that fashion transforms the body from an organism into an abstraction, making it a site of intense imagining (Barthes 2010: xi). As such, garment construction, runway presentation and styling can all be viewed as artistic strategies that exemplify fashion's conceptual and artistic value. In treating these garments as discursive sites that challenge and reconfigure the border between art, performance and fashion, I look to the 'insubordinate' creations of Jonathan Anderson at Loewe, and Matty Bovan and Craig Green at their namesake labels, to open up a wider discourse on contemporary, ready-to-wear fashion. Each ensemble was chosen for its ability to exist in between the fictional and spectacular act of performance that happens in the here-and-now, and the real worldliness of performativity that constructs identity (Kollnitz and Pecorari 2022: 3). If performance can be seen as operating in the realm of fiction, performativity is a concept used to address the effects of shaping the real. Fashion continuously moulds our identities and bodies, in both material and immaterial ways, which can be seen to employ the *modus operandi* of both performance and performativity (Kollnitz and Pecorari 2022: 4). Jonathan Anderson's duo of car dresses for Loewe in Fall/Winter 2022 illustrates society's obsession with and relationship to modernisation, even as concerns mount around our ability to integrate with these advancements. Matty Bovan's dramatic ball gown for Spring/Summer 2019 dissolves time by creating an intricate layering of transgressive garments and historical styles that embody a spirit of defiance in the face of current British politics. Craig Green's rubber cocoon for Fall/Winter 2022 is a monument in motion, ruminating on ideas of control and preservation. In each example, the body and garment are activated by one another. Through alteration and adornment, the ensembles offer a theatricalisation of life that performs and interrogates wider themes related to the body, society and culture.

For Loewe's Fall/Winter 2022 womenswear collection, the brand's creative director Jonathan Anderson devised a collection which references the transition from the industrial age into the twenty-first century. Anderson referred to the season's offerings as *primal*, reducing garments down to their essential forms, inserting Surrealist motifs and utilising new advancements in textile fabrication to reflect a fascination with mechanisation and automation (Mower 2022a: n.p.). The collection traced a subtle historical progression from a pre-industrial to a consumer society. This could be seen through the car dress and its allusion to the mass production of automobiles, through the emancipated female embodied in prints and pursed-lip bodices, and in the advent of leisure time seen through tubular, slouched and stacked knits.

Looks 4 and 5 were a pair of mini trapeze dresses, each with a three-dimensional printed skeleton of a car suspended in stretch satin: one black, one silver (Figures 4.1 and 4.2). A child-sized car immured under an adult-sized dress, an intervention on the garment's body-conscious silhouette distorts the body's natural lines, replacing it with something rigid, angular and cumbersome. A Vivienne Westwood *mini-crini* updated for the twenty-first century. In perverting the boundaries between organic and inorganic and human and mechanical, the human figure becomes a literal and metaphorical vehicle. The dress was paired with trainers that look freshly pulled from a plastic mould, residual tendrils still intact, still waiting to be sent to quality control. It is as if the model has stepped straight off the assembly line and onto the runway. She is the essence of capital in motion, decades in the making.

The advent of Fordist ideas that linked mass production to mass consumption in the early twentieth century led to a new aesthetic that saw culture and commerce collide. As fashion shows moved further into the realms of spectacle and indirect advertising, the industrial aesthetics of the production line began to permeate shows. Models marched out at speed in quick succession, producing a more modernist, streamlined and rationalised body. Models became increasingly regulated and uniform in appearance offering a blank canvas that contrasted

4.1
Loewe Fall/Winter 2022, Look 4. © Violette Meima @ Viva Model Management Paris.

4.2
Loewe Fall/Winter 2022, Look 5. © Estrella Gomez @ IMG Models.

with each season's exploration of novelty. In 1924, the French couturier Lucien Lelong introduced his kinetic line, practical clothing for the modern woman that highlighted a newfound freedom of movement, with the imperative that they be shown in motion and not in static pose (Evans 2013: 116). The imperative to show fashion in motion found another analogue in the development of the *Concours d'Élegance et Automobiles*, high society events originally dating back to seventeenth-century France. To enhance their prowess, cars were presented alongside female models, mostly recruited from fashionable society and dressed in the latest fashions by the leading Parisian couturiers. This created a compelling symbiosis that suggested that both woman and car were a singular entity and produced an erotic exchange between mass production and elite fashion styling.

German scholar Siegfried Kracauer coined the term *mass ornament* to describe the aesthetic expression of capitalism through the geometric arrangements of human bodies for the purposes of entertainment and attraction. This was embodied, for example, in the chorus lines of the Tiller Girls, whose formation in the 1890s coincided with the first fashion shows. Identically dressed and matched in weight and height, they linked arms around one another's waist as they tapped, kicked and gestured in unison. Modelled on the humming and whirring of industrial machinery, the Tiller Girls choreography organised the performers in a way which obliterated the individual, presenting the audience with an indissoluble cluster whose staged movements mimicked a mechanised loom or the threshing drum of a combine harvester. As such, the Tiller Girls became reduced to a linear system for the purpose of entertainment. In constructions of this sort, the individual performer has no grasp on the totality of the act, but consciously takes part in its assembly. This level of engagement represents a significant component of modernity; the demand for calculability can render us invisible and sacrifice individual personality. Machines were built to be subservient to the craftsman, mimicking the natural movements of the human. The Tiller Girls choreography reverses this relationship. The chorus line represents an aesthetic reflection of the prevailing economic system, where workers no longer operate the machine but are themselves its tools and prosthetics (Kracauer 1995: 78).

Mass ornamentation and the runway both privilege the optical allure of movement disengaged from any narrative or psychological identification with the human form. Alienating the image of the body from the idea of individual personality and sentiment works to privilege motion over emotion (Evans 2013: 245). The hands in the factory, the legs of the Tiller Girls and the model on the catwalk are all aligned. As each embarks on its preordained set of movements, the figure of the woman becomes not just a commodity but also a mass-produced article (Benjamin 2008). The mechanical intervention required to construct the Loewe dress, to create an effect that would be difficult to achieve by hand, conveys a sense of flatness and coldness, which adds to its impersonality and potential for dehumanisation. Understanding its construction and establishing where the human hand stops and the computer starts is difficult to pinpoint. The three-dimensional printed fabrication of the car represents a shift from the deskilled device of the readymade to the skilled manufacture of the facsimile or duplicate (Foster 2020: 48). The Loewe dress enacts the impact of industrialisation on the body and captures our obsession with technology, modernity and novelty by making the speed at which things change its own fertile subject matter. It exists both as a showpiece that will never be widely produced and as a replica of a commodity, an original and a simulacrum at once.

As a performative act, the car gestures to a children's toy or game of dressing up and gives off the sheen and sleek quality of a brand-new ride. It articulates both the promise and the threat of the future – the potential for progress, novelty, technological mastery and harmony and the danger of automation, the dissolution of human individuality and agency are distilled in one. The car dress forges an uneasy relationship between biology, technology and commerce. Historically, we have seen depictions of the female form selling products; now she is literally depicted as a vehicle selling the product. There is an erotic frisson that makes the dress both alluring and chilling, simultaneously provoking and complicating our desires. Is it the feminine body that we desire? Or the dress? Maybe the car? Perhaps the amalgamation of all three? Anderson's vision for the twenty-first century is one colonised by desires and illusions. The ubiquity of the commodity is epitomised by the model being dressed as one. By using a car as an intervention on the silhouette, the dress is 'push[ed] … towards something that can be nonsensical … that can be irrational', as Anderson remarked (Mower 2022a: n.p.). The postmodern, post-production body is presented as wholly irrational, liberated from the realm of commerce and allowed to gestate as a conceptual piece. The prevailing view of modernism is that our bodies become dissociated and fetishised, ultimately empty and machinable elements (Evans 2003: 165). Industrialisation and the advancements of technology that were created to liberate us have instead come to subjugate us. The latest advances in AI technology has meant that cars can drive themselves, written documents can be fabricated from mere prompts, and faces and bodies can be rendered in proxy of real people. We are slowly outsourcing ourselves to digital coding and are unable to stop. At its crux, the dress can be seen to embody how we have become victims to our own inventiveness, where technological advancements meant to enrich our lives have outpaced our ability to integrate with them, rendering workforces obsolete as automation offers greater efficiency, lower risk and costs (Foster 2020: 62). The performativity of the car dress re-engineers everyday consumerism and the 'white heat' of technology to reveal sinister truths about our excessive consumption (Wilson 1963: n.p.).

For the opening look of Matty Bovan Spring/Summer 2019 a ball gown woven in pink, yellow and metallic thread, spews a mass of tulle, caught in the commotion of a messy network of cable ties and ribbon (Figure 4.3). Castaways and found items reworked by the deft hands of milliner Stephen Jones create structural marvels. A rose trellis protrudes skywards from the model's head with creeping vines, fake flowers and a gardening glove pinching a single rose, gardener's net cascades over the model's face. Haphazard in appearance, artisanal in construction. The opening ensemble is a sensory overload taking whimsical detours through history – the grandeur of Marie Antoinette's eighteenth-century dresses, whispers of a Chanel tweed, the decadence of a Christian Dior evening gown, coupled with an ostentatiousness and penchant for embellishment to

■ Insubordinate Costume

4.3
Matty Bovan
Spring/Summer
2019, Look 1. ©
Shaun James Cox.

match that of Christian Lacroix. The tension between past, present and future are performed with gleeful application. Inauthentic recreations, authentically Matty Bovan. The collection explored the concept of *sempiternity*, used to describe the property of existing within time but infinitely into the future (as opposed to eternity, understood as existing outside time). By nature, fashion is both temporal and sempiternal, it constantly eschews the old for the new, but its demand for change, novelty and renewal is ceaseless. Through intricate construction and collage, Matty Bovan reconfigures time as labyrinthian and mediated, allowing the juxtaposition of the historical alongside the contemporary. Fashion history is then, less a chronological succession of events, objects and people and more a force that scrambles time and challenges linearity (Pecorari 2014: 67). The dress becomes a *heterotopia*, a concept which French philosopher Michel Foucault theorised to describe sites and objects, such as mirrors, cemeteries and prisons, that simultaneously represent, contest and invert reality. Fashion is reticent, it panders as much as it challenges, it takes into account every occurrence, every judgement, every shift before it makes its own statement. Like its predecessors, the dress and its accompaniments were made in response to its environment. The theatricality of Christian Dior's designs provided a serene mask to the anxieties of the postwar period after the Second World War, Coco Chanel's calculated austerity in response to the *Belle Époque* fashions, was agile and full of movement, modern and futurist in spirit, Christian Lacroix's decadence in the 1980s, a salve to the decade's economic strife. For Matty Bovan, designing against the backdrop of British austerity, exacerbated by social inequality and the United Kingdom's decision to leave the European Union, the dress is a visual embodiment of the turbulence of contemporary British society. It is the descendant of a long lineage of garments that have embodied a spirit of change and defiance in their time.

A surreal historicism colonises the terrain of the 'new'. A layering of historical periods woven into a single dress approximates the past through established representations of the period. The American literary critic Fredric Jameson argues that the plundering of history by contemporary visual culture creates a postmodern carnival, the incessant return to the past a kind of deathly recycling that empties history of its meaning, rendering it bankrupt and only good for costume drama and fantasy (Evans 2003: 24). While modern society has indeed rendered everything into images and everyone into image junkies, Bovan's excavation of the past is not history repeating itself, but a study of history and identity asserted through repetition (Stagg 2019: 93). Camp is a rediscovery of history's waste. By asserting that there is good taste in bad taste and vice versa, camp retrieves not only what has been excluded from serious high-cultural 'tradition' but picks up more unsalvageable and discarded material discovered anew (Granata 2017: 96). It is the mode of enjoyment and witty hedonism found in camp that Bovan utilises with its many gestures of irony, parody, pastiche, naïveté, theatricality, extravagance, artificiality, exaggeration and aestheticism. The outfit demonstrates luxury while, at the same time, mocking it, adopting camp's philosophy of transformation and incongruity and allowing aesthetic absurdities to exist in the realm of high culture and desire. Fixed notions of time, taste, and sensibility collapse in on themselves rendering established norms obsolete and envisioning new ones in their stead.

Through a complex programme of reference and amendment, the ensemble is a physical incarnation of time unfurling. Rather than constructing the artifice of transcendent beauty, a deconstructivist approach highlights the mechanics of production, of permanent and accelerating change that governs much of contemporary global life and culture. Fashion's inherent contradictions are instead laid bare, the traces of construction visible, as a way of examining upheaval and strife. When the structure of the design appears under attack, silhouette distorted, seams displaced, hemlines skewed, inflicting the underskirt with a tangle of plastic and ribbon that dangles and clumps together, it all suggests a vision of elegant chaos, of being in the eye of the storm. While the fantasy of probing the body's interiority is common in contemporary art, it is habitually disavowed in fashion due to its emphasis on surface, perfection and polish (Evans 2003: 144–5). The use of deconstruction sensibilities, explored by Martin Margiela, Rei Kawakubo and Yohji Yamamoto in the 1980s and 1990s, was a critique of established norms of beauty and convention. Matty Bovan's designs share a renewed interest in these techniques utilising displacement, inversion and unconventional materials to suggest that we are in a stage of turbulence akin to the close of the last century. Not dissimilar from how a painting is painstakingly created, the opening ensemble is an exercise in layering through a gradual, meticulous build-up of materials and colour. Bovan's exuberant bricolage reflects the frenzied and insecure age in which we live. The limits of taste and respectability are tested, the parameters of each being constantly broken down and rehashed. Beneath this veneer of theatricality and extravagance in all its frippery beats the decisive heart of a modernist, a

■ Insubordinate Costume

gleeful dystopian creativity bred from an Orwellian moment in time. As a performance, Bovan repositions fashion as politically subversive and revolutionary in spirit, where history is made histrionic, virtue is born out of duplicity, and legitimacy is conferred on what it pretends to ridicule.

Look 10 of Craig Green's Fall/Winter 2022 menswear collection was comprised of a white medical-grade latex cloak with undulating folds, that sheathed the upper torso and obscured the face, white utility trousers and beige trainers (Figure 4.4). Green noted that the collection was about 'being able to experience things in reality and touch things … kind of for comfort, but also for suffocation' (Mower 2022b: n.p.). Throughout, mohair and satin were turned inside out, felt more than they were seen, while mould castings of Adidas Stan Smiths became footwear in themselves. These items explored an introspective experience of a garment's materiality in lieu of an outward presentation of comfort and luxury. Expansive and restrictive explorations of form, silhouette and construction probed the body's spatial relationship to its environment. The rubber sheath is a mobile monument that ruminates on ideas of control, whether that be for pleasure, preservation, or care.

Look 10 provokes the viewer's *sight-knowledge* or *tactile epistemology*, both terms Laura Marks, a philosopher and scholar of new media and film, coins to describe an intimate knowledge of the tactile experience of fabric (Evans 2013: 177). Marks suggests that particular objects can create a mimetic experience, triggering specific material and textured areas of corporeal knowledge that twist emotions back and forth between titillation and repulsion. The performativity of

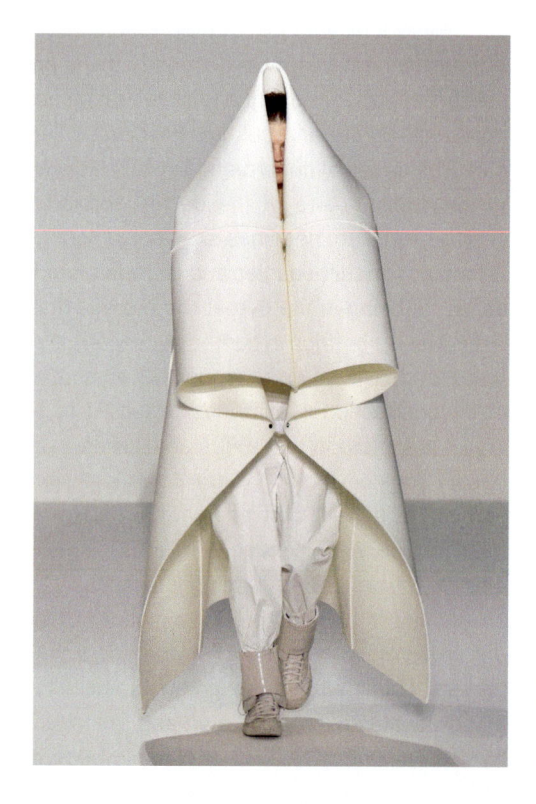

4.4
Craig Green Fall/Winter 2022, Look 10. © Filippo Fior/Imaxtree.com.

the ensemble prioritises the wearer's experience, but it does not diminish the viewer's. One can understand the sensation that is provoked through sight-knowledge alone. In utilising a material produced by a factory that specialises in manufacturing medical pieces, the use of rubber references the body as an entity that is porous and leaking, in need of containment. Hands that are hidden for fear of contagion, trousers that are evocative of hospital scrubs, recall an ecclesiastical image of a saint-like chaplain visiting a sickly patient. The ensemble plays out our fears of contagion and the obsessive moral policing of bodily borders that characterised the politics of blame and responsibility of the HIV/AIDS crisis in the 1980s and 1990s that re-emerged with COVID-19 (Granata 2017: 2). Illness here is not rendered through unsightly growths, protuberances or ailments but through a clinical and sanitised cloaked figure.

Convexities are smoothed out, the body's waste omitted, all kept veiled and secret. The grotesque realism of the sick body does not need to be physicalised and would appear gratuitous when a recent mass event like the COVID-19 pandemic reels in the minds of the masses. Instead, Green employs a visual medical lexicon conceptually. The monochromatic hues of white convey purity, cleanliness and peace, but are also symbolically linked to death, mourning and rebirth. The performativity of this gesture situates illness, in its physical and psychosomatic manifestations, as a state that offers a transgressive and alternate perception of the body in the wake of trauma. By offering readings of both mourning and rebirth, the performance here acts as a spatial metaphor for excavating loss in the present, which encourages the viewer to look frankly at these forms and resist a certain temptation to deny reality and reflect nostalgically on a time when things were allegedly simpler, better (Steyerl 2012: 5).

Dissociation and self-preservation from the troubles of the world is an understandable response. In times of strife, people often turn inwards, reclaiming the body as the only thing that can be controlled. Enveloped in rubber, the body is encased in a protective cocoon. Inspired by iron maidens and iron lungs, the first a medieval torture instrument resembling a coffin, the second an antiquated, life-prolonging medical apparatus, both functioning through encasement. A tension is created where the performative gesture of the cloak complicates the perception of the garment as remedial or harmful. Not only is the viewer's gaze denied by the wearer, the wearer's ability to see is negated in its scanning capabilities (Ross 2006: 111). Sheltered from this voyeurism, the wearer's extreme proximity to the rubber cloak intensifies the realm of interiority. The price for such protection is claustrophobic; it creates the idea of isolation rather than preservation where there is friction between the outward aesthetic appearance of the garment and the inward sensation of wearing it.

Hal Foster refers to containment as a particular kind of bondage that nourishes simultaneous desires for absolute submission and total freedom (Foster 2020: 42). While rubber was initially used to make raincoats, hats and domestic items such as gloves, it became associated with S&M fetishists before gradually being integrated into mainstream fashion, where it offers designers a shorthand for sexuality and deviancy. In the past, the single most popular rubber fetish was the mackintosh, a rubberised raincoat, invented in 1823 by Charles Macintosh.

The Mackintosh Society, one of the oldest fetishist organisations in the world, was founded in England taking its name from the coat while, as early as 1926, enthusiastic letters about the garment appeared in the fetish magazine *London Life* (Steele 1996: 148). Abstracted by Green into a sheath, the shroud defies easy categorisation; organic and artificial, space-age and medieval, perverse yet unthreatening, it resists our tendency to naturalise clothing. The magic of the fetish is that it neutralises fear turning something otherwise threatening and repulsive into something titillating and rewarding. In cultural historian Valerie Steele's book *Fetish*, rubber enthusiasts remarked that rubber 'feels' nice, which is important for people living in an insecure world (Steele 1996: 151). Asphyxiating rubber, confined limbs, loss of vision, Craig Green's bondage plays between submission and release. The fissure at the centre of the cocoon offers respite creating a visual oscillation between public and private that collapses the synthetic separation of performance and real life. Fashion sits at the crossroads of theatricality and reality, wholeheartedly revelling in both. Performing in this liminality, the boundaries of commercial and experimental fashion, sexuality, wellness, interiority and exteriority, visibility and invisibility, life and death are trespassed. What Craig optimistically gestures is that strife can be revised as a lucrative opportunity for restoration where bondage, control and deficiency offer the conditions for release and renewal.

Showpieces have become a mainstay in a collection, offering designers the opportunity to test the possibilities of their medium while undertaking a successful marketing strategy that defines a brand's vision through the circulation of vivid images. While these creations reflect how design and fashion are anchored in specific moments of capitalist production and consumption, they also reflect the social and cultural upheaval of the time. What is impressive is that these concepts can be engineered to work within the restrictions of a commercial business and become machine washable at 30 degrees (McKenzie and Lipscombe 2020: n.p.). The ensembles by Jonathan Anderson for Loewe, Craig Green and Matty Bovan bypass definitions of art, design, and ready-to-wear fashion through rigorous, conceptual underpinnings that cannot be ignored. These designers are subverting the powers at play in our consumerist society where garments, such as these, are imbued with a distinct visual language whose constructed representations of life may offer an astute understanding of the conditions we find ourselves living through.

REFERENCES

Barthes, Roland. 2010. *The Fashion System.* London: Vintage Classics.
Benjamin, Walter. 2008. *The Work of Art in the Age of Mechanical Reproduction.* London: Penguin Great Ideas.
Evans, Caroline. 2003. *Fashion at the Edge.* London, New Haven: Yale University Press.
Evans, Caroline. 2013. *The Mechanical Smile.* London, New Haven: Yale University Press.
Foster, Hal. 2020. *What Comes After Farce?: Art and Criticism at a Time of Debacle.* New York: Verso Books.

Granata, Francesca. 2017. *Experimental Fashion Performance Art, Carnival and the Grotesque Body.* London, New York: I.B. Tauris & Co. Ltd. https://doi.org/10.5040/9781350986312.

Kollnitz, Andrea, and Marco Pecorari. 2022. *Fashion, Performance and Performativity.* London: Bloomsbury. https://doi.org/10.5040/9781350106215.

Kracauer, Sigmund. 1995. *The Mass Ornament: Weimar Essays.* Cambridge, MA: Harvard University Press.

McKenzie, Lucy with Beca Lipscombe. 2020. 'Atelier E.B Back-to-Back.' In *Atelier E.B Passer-By.* France: Lafayette Anticipations - Fondation d'entreprise Galeries Lafayette.

Mower, Sarah. 2022a. 'Loewe Fall 2022 Ready-to-Wear Collection.' *Vogue.* Available at: https://www.vogue.com/fashion-shows/fall-2022-ready-to-wear/loewe [Accessed 10/04/2023].

Mower, Sarah. 2022b. 'Craig Green Fall 2022 Ready-to-Wear Collection.' *Vogue.* Available at: https://www.vogue.com/fashion-shows/fall-2022-menswear/craig-green [Accessed 08/06/2023].

Pecorari, Marco. 2014. 'Contemporary Fashion History in Museums', in *Fashion and Museums: Theory and Practice,* by Marie Riegels Melchior and Birgitta Svensson. London, New York: Bloomsbury. https://doi.org/10.5040/9781350050914.ch-003.

Ross, Christine 2006. *The Aesthetics of Disengagement.* Minneapolis, MN: University of Minnesota Press.

Stagg, Natasha. 2019. *Sleeveless.* Pasadena, CA: Semiotext(e).

Steele, Valerie. 1996. *Fetish: Fashion, Sex and Power.* New York: Oxford University Press.

Steyerl, Hito. 2012. *The Wretched of the Screen.* Berlin: Sternberg Press.

Ugelvig, Jeppe. 2020. *Fashion Work 1993-2019: 25 Years of Art in Fashion.* Bologna: Damiani.

Wilson, Harold. 1963. *'Labour and the Scientific Revolution' a Policy Statement Made to the Annual Conference of the Labour Party, Scarborough, 1963 by the Leader, Mr Harold Wilson.* L'Université de Pau et des Pays de l'Adour. Available at https://web-archives.univ-pau.fr/english/TD2doc2.pdf [Accessed 15/07/2023].

PART 3

THE INSUBORDINATE HERE AND NOW

5 The Insubordinate Here and Now
Susan Marshall

THE INSUBORDINATE HERE AND NOW: INSUBORDINATE COSTUME IN CONTEMPORARY RESEARCH

As noted in the introduction, the study of performance costume has become an established area of research in recent years, proving that costume is not 'far too trivial or playful for serious scholarship' (Monks 2010: 10). A theoretical framework is evolving with current research interests looking at different aspects of costume and the relationship between theory and practice. This is being furthered by many practitioners who are consolidating their work by undertaking doctoral research. Costume is under the lens and is being investigated as, among other things, a protagonist of theatre-making and dramaturgy, and a tool to experiment with identity and embodiment. The areas of research that are particularly relevant to the study of historical and contemporary examples of Insubordinate Costume are those surrounding costume and the body, New Materialism, the agency of costume and theories about play and playfulness.

THE BODY

The body is central to extensive research in the field of costume as costumes remain static and lifeless without the performer's body to animate it. Questions surrounding the body are particularly pertinent to the phenomenon of costume as performance where the symbiotic link is especially evident. In the introduction to *The Cambridge Introduction to Scenography*, McKinney and Butterworth note that 'it is sometimes hard to distinguish clearly between what is achieved through the performer's body and movement of the performer's costume' (McKinney and Butterworth 2009: 6). Jessica Bugg highlights this in her article 'Emotion and Memory; Clothing the Body as Performance', stating that by 'placing the emphasis on the costume and the body as a text or narrative ... the performance is the costume and the body's responses to it' (Bugg 2013: 97). When costumes are the inspiration behind a performance,

> the notion of costume as an extension of the performer's body and mind suggests a correlation between how the costume is used to create the performance and the identity of the performer themselves. A dancer will interact in a different way

to an actor, but two dancers may also interact differently as individual experience and memory colour the perception and embodied experience of the performers.

(Marshall 2021b: 42).

In the mid-twentieth century, influenced by philosophers Edmund Husserl and Martin Heidegger, the phenomenological philosopher Merleau-Ponty challenged Cartesian theories of mind–body dualism and identified the body as fundamental to our perception of the world, as understanding consists of both mental and bodily experience:

> we are our body … we are in the world through our body … we perceive the world with our body. [P]erceiving as we do with our body, the body is a natural self and, as it were, the subject of perception.
>
> (Merleau-Ponty 2013: 206)

In his essay 'Eye and Mind', Merleau-Ponty describes the body as 'a thing among things … caught in the fabric of the world' (Merleau-Ponty 1964) which Italian linguist Patrizia Violi also notes in her article 'How our Bodies Become Us: Embodiment, Semiosis and Intersubjectivity' suggesting that, although perception is uniquely personal, 'the body is not an isolated entity, but the result of a complex set of interactions with the environment and with others, where intersubjectivity plays a crucial role' (Violi 2009: 57). Somatics, like phenomenology, emphasises bodily perception. The term derives from the Greek word *sōma*, the body. Somatic practices, which include Body–Mind Centring, the Alexander technique, the Feldenkrais method and Laban movement analysis, aim to increase bodily awareness and wellness. Practitioners such as Sally E. Dean work with movement techniques using costume and objects to provoke internal sensations in the body.

THE POLITICS OF THE BODY

Kathleen Lennon and Susan Bordo note that the body is never neutral: 'The body as lived is always a body in a situation, a body always subjected to culture' (Lennon 2010) and 'a site of struggle' (Jaggar and Bordo 1989: 28). With the rise of second-wave feminism in the 1960s

> feminism inverted and converted the old metaphor of the 'body politic', found in Plato, Aristotle, Cicero, Seneca, Machiavelli, Hobbes and many others, to a new metaphor: 'the politics of the body'. In the old metaphor of the body politic, the state or society was imagined as a human body … Now, feminism imagined the human body as itself a politically inscribed entity.
>
> (Bordo 1993)

Since the avant-garde experiments of the early twentieth century, Insubordinate Costume has often been used as a platform for social, cultural and political comment and as a way to subvert norms and conventions. In her article 'Fashion and the Fleshy Body: Dress as Embodied Practice', Joanne Entwistle writes about the subversive nature of clothes when they flout convention:

> Bodies that do not conform, bodies that flout the conventions of their culture and go without the appropriate clothes are subversive of the most basic social codes.
> (Entwistle 2000: 323)

Many examples of Insubordinate Costume can be seen to alter, constrict or exaggerate certain aspects in order to investigate themes surrounding the body. Oscar Schlemmer's *Triadic Ballet*, conceived while he was teaching at the Bauhaus, for example, reflects his interest in the subject of the body in space as do Alwin Nikolais's dance costumes and Rebecca Horn's prosthetics. The fascination with mechanisation at the beginning of the twentieth century led to experiments in trying to improve or overcome the limitations of the human body, or even to remove it completely from the equation as suggested by Edward Gordon Craig in *The Mask* in 1908. Craig proposed using Über-marionettes instead of actors so that '[n]o longer would there be a living figure to confuse us into connecting actuality and art; no longer a living figure in which the weakness and tremors of the flesh were perceptible' (Craig 1908: 11). Throughout history the natural shape of the body has been modified and altered for aesthetic reasons in the name of fashion, but artists and designers manipulate the body through their use of Insubordinate Costume*s* in order to play with and subvert notions of normality and diversity, questioning and subverting gender and bodily norms as well as aesthetics. Leigh Bowery's self-created alternative personae and radical characterisations in the 1980s, for example, have exerted an enormous influence on both performance and fashion (Marshall 2021b: 32) and can be seen in Lady Gaga's experimental costumes, Pyuupiru's performance art and Gareth Pugh's fashions, to name but a few. Cultural scenographer Rachel Hann associates the subversive quality of costume with body politics and conscious performativity in her article 'Debating Critical Costume: Negotiating Ideologies of Appearance, Performance and Disciplinarity':

> Approached as an interventional practice, costume represents a potential strategy for subverting the ongoing repetitions of body politics. The theatrical charge of costume is innately related to its conscious 'othering' of the act of appearance.
> (Hann 2017: 5)

In *Experimental Fashion, Performance Art, Carnival and the Grotesque Body* Francesca Granata discusses the growth of interest in aestheticism, anti-aestheticism and the grotesque since the 1980s noting that 'undisciplined' bodies 'can be read as provocations and attempts to escape what Michel Foucault referred to as the "anatomo-politics" of the human body'[1](Granata 2017: 2). If 'the unexpected, surprise and astonishment, are an essential part and characteristic of beauty' (Baudelaire 2006: 41), Baudelaire's phrase 'Le beau est toujours bizarre' (Baudelaire 1868: 217) could be a *leitmotif* for many Insubordinate Costumes whose aesthetic is often deliberately 'bizarre', questioning the traditional ideals of beauty (Marshall 2021b: 39).

NEW MATERIALISM, THE AGENCY OF COSTUME AND THING-POWER

In a costume-based performance the costume as object becomes the costume as subject. The costume is given poetic space which, as Bachelard wrote, transforms it into something more than an object: 'To give an object poetic space is to give it more space than it has objectivity; or, better still, it is following the expansion of its intimate space' (Bachelard 1994: 202). Current interest in the agency of costume has led to the analysis of costume within the context of New Materialism theories which consider the agency and discursive possibilities of materials (Barad 2006; Bennett 2010; McKinney 2015). Unlike previous materialism theories that share 'a conception of matter as essentially passive, non-performatively constituted, and discretely self-contained' (Gamble, Hanan, and Nail 2019: 113) without 'creative agency' (Gamble, Hanan, and Nail 2019), Jane Bennett, in her book *Vibrant Matter: A Political Ecology of Things*, refers to 'thing-power' and aims to 'theorize a materiality that is as much force as entity, as much energy as matter, as much intensity as extension' (Bennett 2010: 20). In acknowledging the interdependency of human and non-human elements, Bennett writes that the mind has a greater capacity for thought and that 'bodies enhance their power in or as a heterogeneous assemblage'[2] (23). Insubordinate Costume can be considered to be an assemblage of human and non-human elements with the 'ability to make something happen' (24) 'in a reciprocal exchange between bodies and materials' (McKinney 2015: 127). In her chapter 'Vibrant materials: the agency of things in the context of scenography' Joslin McKinney discusses Tim Ingold's theory of animate life where materials have the 'capacity to become active participants, incomplete potentialities' (126) that fulfil their potential through human interaction. Insubordinate Costumes are active participants in the dramaturgical process as performers interact with them to bring forth, as Ingold suggests, the 'potentials immanent in a world of becoming' (Ingold 2013: 31). 'Thing-power', in this case, 'costume-power', affects and is affected by the body, together they have greater power, together they increase the mind's capacity for thought, together they generate a performance … [The] costumes are activated by the performers but, simultaneously, the performers are activated by the costumes, which act like prosthetics, changing the body through extension and altering their physical perception (Marshall 2021a: 295, 166–7).

PLAY

Insubordinate Costume can be considered within the context of both play and playfulness. The element of play, visible in Schlemmer's *Triadic Ballet* or Michael Clark's early work, is a recurrent theme which can be observed throughout most instances. Where costume is the instigator of performance the performers need to play with the costume to discover its hidden potentialities and to find a creative approach to movement and the costume in space. 'The costume, and its obstructions, leads, or rather, demands, a heuristic process: improvisation, exploration, play' (Marshall 2021b: 49). In *Psychological Types*, Jung wrote that

> if the play expires in itself without creating anything durable and living, it is only play; but in the alternative event it is called creative work … The creation of something new is not accomplished by the intellect, but by the play instinct acting from inner necessity. The creative mind plays with the objects it loves.
> (Jung 1976: 123)

Many theorists, such as Friedrich Froebel, John Dewey, Abraham Maslow and Jean Piaget[3] (Froebel 1887; Dewey 1910; Maslow 1943; Piaget [1951] 2013) agree that the concept of play is fundamental to creativity and intrinsically linked to experiment, exploration, research, discovery and learning. Creative solutions are found through play, for children and adults alike. In analysing the characteristics and significance of adult play in his seminal work of 1938, *Homo Ludens: A Study of the Play Element in Culture*, Johan Huizinga claims that 'pure play is one of the main bases of civilization' (Huizinga 2016: 5). In her article 'Playful Invention, Inventive Play' in the *International Journal of Play*, Monica M. Smith writes about the *Invention at Play* exhibition at the Smithsonian Institute in Washington which 'provided visitors with opportunities to learn how play fosters creativity and invention' (Smith 2016: 246). With reference to Fergus Hughes book *Children, Play, and Development* and Robert Weisberg's book *Creativity: Beyond the Myth of Genius*, Smith describes the characteristics of creativity:

> Creativity can be described in three dimensions: (a) a personality characteristic – attitudes toward oneself and the world characterised by mental flexibility, spontaneity, curiosity, and persistence; (b) an intellectual process – a way of thinking, an approach to problem-solving that includes making unusual connections or associations; relying not only on conscious linear thought, but also on intuition and imagination … generating rich visual images; asking original questions; and (c) a resulting creative product and original contribution to the appreciation understanding or improvement of the human condition.
> (Hughes 2010; Weisberg 1993; Smith 2016: 246)

Smith continues by asking: 'Why do humans play? What are the practical functions of play? How is play linked to child development?' and notes that 'some consensus has emerged: play, in all its forms, shapes habits, knowledge, and skills that form a basis for lifelong talents' (Bekoff 1998; Pellegrini and Smith 1998; Smith 1982; Smith 2016: 247). Importantly she states that humans 'retain many childlike characteristics during adulthood [and that] this retention of juvenile attributes has been linked to brain plasticity (Bjorklund 1997), species adaptability (Wilson 1998) and creativity' (Smith and Ward 1999; Smith 2016: 247).

Play theorist Gunilla Lindqvist writes about a 'playworld' (Lindqvist 1996). Lindqvist is talking about child's play but the concept is not dissimilar to the concept of *oikos*,[4] discussed by Bonnie Marranca in her book *Ecologies of Theater*

(Marranca 1996), where she likens the theatre environment to an ecosystem, a fine balance of different organisms that create a whole world. The idea of entering a different reality is described by John Berger in his essay 'Ev'ry Time We Say Goodbye' where he writes about how a narrative can engulf us completely in its own world:

> When we read a story, we inhabit it. The covers of the book are like a roof and four walls. What is to happen next will take place within the four walls of the story. And this is possible because the story's voice makes everything its own.
>
> (Berger 1992: 15)

As in a book, a 'playworld' or 'new reality' is created in the theatre. Insubordinate Costume can be considered a 'playworld' in itself, 'a kind of travelling scenography' (Pavis 2003: 177) a 'three-dimensional world for the body in movement that tells a story' (Barbieri 2012). Each costume creates its own world, 'an environment for the performer' (Pavis 2003: 178) which appropriates space and acts as a catalyst for creative ideas.

It could be argued that an element of play and/or playfulness is discernible in all historical and contemporary instances of Insubordinate Costume which, positioned as the primary creative motivator, can be used as a research tool. The varied and innovative examples can be seen to have pushed boundaries and explored new meanings of creativity but they can also be examined in a cultural context as they frequently reveal contemporary social, political and aesthetic influences. Costume is now being employed to explore and research the pertinent questions of the twenty-first century in much the same way as the artistic movements of the early twentieth century investigated the possibilities of the costumed body as a scenic element in examining questions of embodiment, modernity and power (Marshall 2020). Current costume research is also looking at the pertinent questions of climate change, ecology and sustainability both as subject matter and as methodology, with numerous designers incorporating recycling and upcycling into their creative practice. Play can be frivolous but, as artist David Hockney wrote in his book *That's The Way I See It*, 'People tend to forget that play is serious' (Hockney 1993: 133).

NOTES

1. Michel Foucault refers to the 'anatomo-politics of the human body', in *The History of Sexuality, Vol. 1. An Introduction* (New York: Random House, 1978), 139.
2. Gilles Deleuze and Félix Guattari wrote about the concept of assemblage in 1980 in their book *A Thousand Plateaus*. The idea that an assemblage of human and non-human elements has the ability to make something happen is crucial to the idea of Insubordinate Costume as the costume and performer collaborate in symbiosis to generate a performance.
3. Educationalist Friedrich Fröbel introduced the first kindergarten in 1837 as a garden of children where each child could be nurtured and encouraged to grow. As an aid to learning through creative play, Fröbel identified and created twenty 'play gifts' and 'occupations' that help develop skills and become progressively more complex as the child grows and develops. John Dewey, American philosopher, psychologist, and educational reformer, wrote How We Think (1910); Abraham Maslow, American psychologist,

wrote *A Theory of Human Motivation* ([1943] 2013) and Jean Piaget, French psychologist who wrote *Play, Dreams and Imitation in Childhood* ([1951] 2013)

4 *Oikos* in Greek can be translated as home or place to live.

REFERENCES

Bachelard, Gaston. 1994. *The Poetics of Space*. Boston: Beacon Press.

Barad, K. 2006. *Meeting the Universe Halfway: Quantum Physics and the Entanglement of Matter and Meaning*. Durham, NC: Duke University Press. https://doi.org/10.2307/j.ctv12101zq.

Barbieri, Donatella. 2012, 'Costume re-considered: From the scenographic model box, to the scenographic body, devising a practice based design methodology that re-focuses performance onto costume' in *Endymatologika 4: Endyesthai (to Dress): Historical, Sociological and Methodological Approaches: Conference Proceedings*, Athens, 9–11 April 2010, Nafplion: Peloponnesian Folklore Foundation, pp. 147–52.

Baudelaire, Charles. 2006. *Intimate Journals*. Mineola, New York: Dover Publications.

Bekoff, Marc. 1998. 'Playing with Play: What Can We Learn about Cognition, Negotiation, and Evolution?', In Denise Dellarosa Cummins and Colin Allen, eds., *The Evolution of Mind*, 162–82. New York: Oxford University Press.

Bennett, Jane. 2010. *Vibrant Matter: A Political Ecology of Things*. A John Hope Franklin Center Book. Durham, NC: Duke University Press. https://doi.org/10.1215/9780822391623.

Berger, John. 1992. *Keeping a Rendezvous*. New York: Vintage.

Bjorklund, David. 1997. 'The Role of Immaturity in Human Development.' *Psychological Bulletin* 122 (October): 153–169. https://doi.org/10.1037/0033-2909.122.2.153.

Bordo, Susan. 1993. 'Feminism, Foucault and the Politics of the Body', in *Up Against Foucault: Explorations of Some Tensions Between Foucault and Feminism*, edited by Caroline Ramazanoglu. London: Routledge. https://doi.org/10.4324/9780203408681-14.

Bugg, Jessica. 2013. 'Emotion and Memory; Clothing the Body as Performance.' in *Activating the Inanimate: Visual Vocabularies of Performance Practice*. Critical Issues, 97–108. Oxford: Inter-disciplinary Press. https://doi.org/10.1163/9781848881211_01.

Craig, Edward Gordon. 1908. 'The Actor and the Über-Marionette', in *The Mask*, Vol. 1, No. 2, edited by Edward Gordon Craig. Florence: Arena Goldoni.

Dewey, John. 1910. *How We Think*. Lexington, MA: D.C. Heath & Company. https://doi.org/10.1037/10903-000.

Entwistle, Joanne. 2000. 'Fashion and the Fleshy Body: Dress as Embodied Practice.' *Fashion Theory* 4 (3): 323–347. https://doi.org/10.2752/136270400778995471.

Froebel, Friedrich. 1887. *The Education of Man* (W. N. Hailmann, Trans.). International Education Series. New York: D. Appleton. https://archive.org/stream/educationofman00fruoft/educationofman00fruoft_djvu.txt. https://doi.org/10.1037/12739-000 accessed [10/09/20].

Gamble, Christopher N., Joshua S. Hanan, and Thomas Nail. 2019. 'What is New Materialism?' *Angelaki* 24 (6): 111–134. https://doi.org/10.1080/0969725X.2019.1684704.

Granata, Francesca. 2017. *Experimental Fashion Performance Art, Carnival and the Grotesque Body*. London; New York: I.B. Tauris & Co. Ltd. https://doi.org/10.5040/9781350986312.

Hann, Rachel. 2017. 'Debating Critical Costume: Negotiating Ideologies of Appearance, Performance and Disciplinarity', in *Studies in Theatre and Performance* 39 (4): 1–17. https://doi.org/10.1080/14682761.2017.1333831.

Hockney, David. 1993. *That's the Way I See It*. San Francisco: Chronicle Books Llc.

Hughes, Fergus P. 2010. *Children, Play, and Development*. Thousand Oaks, CA: SAGE Publications.
Huizinga, Johan. 2016. *Homo Ludens A Study of the Play Element in Culture*. Kettering, OH: Angelico Press.
Ingold, T. 2013. *Making: Anthropology, Archaeology, Art and Architecture*. Abbingdon: Routledge. https://doi.org/10.4324/9780203559055.
Jaggar, Alison M., and Susan Bordo. 1989. *Gender/Body/Knowledge: Feminist Reconstructions of Being and Knowing*. PMLA. https://doi.org/10.2307/462776.
Jung, Carl. G. 1976. *Collected Works of C.G. Jung, Volume 6: Psychological Types*. Translated and edited by Gerhard Adler. Princeton, NJ: Princeton University Press.
Lennon, Kathleen. 2010. 'Feminist Perspectives on the Body.' *Stanford Encyclopedia of Philosophy*. Stanford University. Center for the Study of Language and Information. https://plato.stanford.edu/entries/feminist-body/ accessed [10/07/20].
Lindqvist, Gunilla. 1996. 'The Aesthetics of Play. A Didactic Study of Play and Culture in Preschools', *Early Years* 17 (1): 6–11. https://doi.org/10.1080/0957514960170102.
Marranca, Bonnie. 1996. *Ecologies of Theater: Essays at the Century Turning*. PAJ Books: Art + Performance. Johns Hopkins University Press.
Marshall, Susan. 2020. 'Following the Threads of Scenographic Costume at PQ19', *Theatre and Performance Design* 6 (1–2): 165–181. https://doi.org/10.1080/23322551.2020.1785229.
Marshall, Susan. 2021a. 'Insubordinate Costume', *Studies in Costume & Performance* 6 (2): 283–304. https://doi.org/10.1386/scp_00052_3.
Marshall, Susan. 2021b. *Insubordinate Costume*. Doctoral thesis, Goldsmiths, University of London. https://doi.org/10.25602/GOLD.00031204.
Maslow, Abraham H. 1943. 'A Theory of Human Motivation', *Psychological Review* 50 (4): 370–396. https://doi.org/10.1037/h0054346.
McKinney, Joslin. 2015. 'Vibrant Materials: The Agency of Things in the Context of Scenography.' in *Performance and Phenomenology: Traditions and Transformations*, edited by Maaike Bleeker, Jon Foley Sherman, and Eirini Nedelkopoulou, 121–137. Abingdon: Routledge.
McKinney, Joslin, and Philip Butterworth. 2009. *The Cambridge Introduction to Scenography*. Cambridge: Cambridge University Press. https://doi.org/10.1017/cbo9780511816963.
Merleau-Ponty, Maurice. 1964. 'Eye and Mind', in *The Primacy of Perception*, 159–190. Evanston: Northwestern University Press.
Merleau-Ponty, Maurice. 2013. *Phenomenology of Perception*. Abingdon: Routledge. https://doi.org/10.4324/9780203720714.
Monks, Aoife. 2010. *The Actor in Costume*. London: Palgrave Macmillan.
Pavis, Patrice. 2003. *Analyzing Performance: Theater, Dance, and Film*. Michigan: University of Michigan Press. https://doi.org/10.3998/mpub.10924.
Pellegrini, Anthony D., and Peter K. Smith. 1998. 'The Development of Play During Childhood: Forms and Possible Functions', *Child Psychology and Psychiatry Review* 3 (2): 51–57. https://doi.org/https://doi.org/10.1111/1475-3588.00212.
Piaget, Jean. [1951] 2013. *Play, Dreams and Imitation in Childhood*. London: Routledge. https://doi.org/10.4324/9781315009698.
Smith, Monica M. 2016. 'Playful Invention, Inventive Play', *International Journal of Play* 5 (3): 244–261. https://doi.org/10.1080/21594937.2016.1203549.
Smith, Peter K. 1982. 'Does Play Matter? Functional and Evolutionary Aspects of Animal and Human Play', *Behavioral and Brain Sciences* 5 (1): 139–184. https://doi.org/10.1017/S0140525X0001092X.
Smith, Steven M., and Thomas B. Ward. 1999. 'The Evolution of Creativity', in *Evolution of the Psyche: Human Evolution, Behavior, and Intelligence*, edited by David H. Rosen and Michael C. Luebbert, 95–105. Westport, CA: Greenwood Publishing Group/Praeger.

Violi, Patrizia. 2009. 'How Our Bodies Become Us: Embodiment, Semiosis and Intersubjectivity', *Journal of Cognitive Semiotics* 4 (1). https://doi.org/10.1515/cogsem.2012.4.1.57.

Weisberg, Robert W. 1993. *Creativity: Beyond the Myth of Genius*. Books in Psychology. New York: W.H. Freeman.

Wilson, F. R. 1998. *The Hand: How Its Use Shapes the Brain, Language, and Human Culture*. New York: Pantheon Books.

6 On Creating Costume Generated Performances

Christina Lindgren

The *Costume Agency* Artistic Research Project[1] was supported by the Norwegian Artistic Research Program and affiliated with the Oslo National Academy of the Arts (KHIO). The project was led by Christina Lindgren, professor in Costume Design at KHIO, in collaboration with Sodja Zupanc Lotker, dramaturg and course leader of the MA in Directing of Devised and Object Theatre at the Theatre Faculty of the Academy of Performing Arts in Prague (DAMU). Lotker teaches, and develops methods for devising theatre, where things, place and matter play a central role. Lotker was artistic director of the Prague Quadrennial of Performance Design and Space (2008–15), where she curated *The Tribes* project, a 'walking exhibition' of costume.

At KHIO, the education in Costume Design is based within the Design department and is offered as a joint bachelor course with fashion design. Here, costume has traditionally been understood as an object independent of its performative context, where the quality of the costumes hinges on the originality, craft, and aesthetic qualities of the garments. As a response, I advocated for a collaboration with the performing arts departments, and an understanding of costume as a dynamic entity, consisting of four components: the garments, the performer's body, the action (for example, the choreography or direction) and the contexts (for example, the scenography, venue and cultural-socio-political contexts).

With our research experience, a postdramatic backdrop and a New Materialist approach, along with the openness of the Norwegian artistic research programme, there was an opportunity, and an urgency as well, to explore what costume can 'do', and how it can form a starting point for performance. Postdramatic theatre is a term introduced by theatre scientist Hans-Thies Lehmann in 1999[2] used to describe the de-hierarchisation of theatrical means and a theatre no longer based on representation in a mimetic-fictional way. According to Lehmann, 'The "style", or rather the palette of stylistic traits of Postdramatic Theatre, demonstrates the following characteristic traits: parataxis, simultaneity, play with the density of signs, musicalisation, visual dramaturgy, physicality, irruption of the real and the characterisation of theatre as situation/event' (Lehmann 2006: 86). The *Costume Agency* research project emerged in a performing arts landscape with diverse forms and genres, where text was no longer the main premise.

New Materialism is a interdisciplinary field of inquiry, that emerged at the millennium and paved the way for an understanding of the natural and social world which exists in a constant interaction. Some key concepts are described by thinkers, such as actor-network theory (Bruno Latour and others), agency (Karen Barad and others), vibrant materiality (Jane Bennett), performativity (Judith Butler and others) and situated knowledges (Donna Haraway), to mention a few. New Materialism proposes an understanding of humans and non-humans as connected, on an equal footing, where things and humans interact and perform in processes of cause and effect. This aligns with our understanding of costume as important to performance, and stimulated our curiosity on *how* costume performs.

With the theme of *Costume Agency*, the project hosted the Critical Costume 2020 Conference and Exhibition, a platform for both artistic and academic research. The *Costume Agency* workshops offered costume designers, dancers, lighting designers and dramaturgs, an opportunity to experiment with, and to unpack the potential of, a performance embedded in costume. A major output of the research was the publication of *Costume Agency Artistic Research* (Lindgren and Lotker 2023).

Costume Agency workshops were organised in order to explore whether it was possible to generate a performance from costume. With minor variations, the format was planned as follows: each workshop would include four designers, four performers, four sets of costume, two black box spaces, two weeks of rehearsals and consultations with the main researchers, as well as video and photo documentation on the final day. The process started with an open call for designers to apply to participate in the project with photos or drawings of their costumes and a description of their vision for a performance embedded in the costumes or of ideas they wanted to experiment with. The twenty-one co-researchers, who were mostly costume designers, had ideas about what they wanted to experiment with but several of them had no previous experience of leading a rehearsal process. After the selection, the designers were given the opportunity to choose which kind of performer they wanted to work with, for example, dancers or actors. Each workshop took place from Monday to Friday for two weeks. On the first day the costume designers brought their costumes, garments or materials and shared their visions and ideas. Each designer led their own explorations and had daily rehearsals with two performers, seven sessions of three hours each. In addition, there was an introduction meeting on the first day where basic information about the research project was laid out. The groups worked in theatre spaces with basic stage equipment, sound and lighting and discussed their ideas with a lighting designer. The designers met for consultations with Lotker and Lindgren, in addition to invited guests. All participants met in sharing sessions on Fridays, where they presented their work and helped each other to think and create. On the final day, the presentations were video recorded and photographed. After the workshop, the designers each wrote a reflective text on the process which were published in the *Costume Agency Artistic Research* book.

Some of the main findings from this research demonstrate that costume garments are in fact highly relevant as the starting point for a performance. When working from alternative starting points for a performance, new tools and methods are required, and these were found in the process. With their costume as the starting point, the designers searched for a method to unpack the latent potential.

The creative collaboration with performers who had a willingness to experiment, was crucial for the level of advancement that was achieved. Each of the designers and their teams developed a distinct and original performance of approximately twenty-five minutes, expressing the belief that it had the potential to be developed into a full-length performance. The costumes that were brought on the first day showed a wide span of diversities and, likewise, so were the performances these generated. Many of the performances challenged traditional categories of forms and genres, and thus can be seen to contribute to the expansion of the range of expressions in the performing arts.

A CONVERSATION BETWEEN ZOFIA JAKUBIEC, SIGNE BECKER AND CHRISTINA LINDGREN OSLO, AUGUST 2023

The following is an edited conversation between costume designers Zofia Jakubiec,[3] Signe Becker[4] and myself following the end of the *Costume Agency* project in which we discussed their work and some pertinent questions that arose from the workshops, as well as experiences outside Costume Agency. We spoke about how to create a performance with costume as the nontraditional starting point, how to lead the process, how to work with dramaturgy and how to compose with all the elements that form the entity of a performance such as light, sound, space and the performers. All three of us work in mainly non-commercial independent theatres or dance venues in Norway and receive support from governmental funds which promote original, experimental art forms and expression. The rehearsal period with professional performers and the creative team is normally six to eight weeks in Norway. As well as designing costumes, we have experience in all creative aspects of a performance both as initiator of a project and as director or choreographer.

COSTUME AS A STARTING POINT

Zofia: In my project for *Costume Agency*, I wanted to sew as much choreographic knowledge and scores for the dancers into the costume as possible. So, I designed a costume where the dancers were connected (Figure 6.1). The design decided the placement, range of movement and a lot of other things, rules that couldn't be broken. I believe that a garment has the choreography within it, and that's what I'm interested in. I sew the choreographic score into the garment so I don't have to say it, it's just there.

Christina: What happens at first when you are designing costumes and the choreography, when and where do you get the ideas?

Zofia: I get a lot of experimental costumes ideas from my own dance practice. I am inspired by Ohad Naharin's Gaga movement language and the way he works with imagination. I use images that can generate the movement both when I work alone and with others. Images such as imagining that your skin gets tighter on the whole body like wearing gloves that are too tight or perhaps your skin gets too loose and you are swimming inside a gigantic skinsuit. Having these kinds of images in my mind, while

On Creating Costume Generated Performances

6.1
Zofia Jakubiec, *Experimental costume designed for Costume Agency Workshop*, KHiO, 2021. Photograph by Espen Tollefsen.

moving, brings different movement qualities to the process and triggers my imagination towards creating 'weird' costumes. Three people sharing, and sometimes trapped inside, one skin is an outcome of that. A more private inspiration was also my pregnancy, as when I joined the workshop my daughter was five months old and I had newly experienced sharing my skin, and body, with another person. The imagination I am talking about is very physical. I like to work with dancers that share my passion to move and research that kind of imagery. The choreography is an act of composition for me, and the same goes for the design, I put those two processes together and work very intuitively.

Signe: This sounds clear to me. I especially understand this intuitive part. I have worked in the same way, but I very seldom have this very clear idea. I never investigate a specific thing with a specific costume. Performance is so many art forms in one, and everything influences everything else. I understand this complexity.

UNPACKING THE POTENTIAL OF THE COSTUME

Signe: I very often start from an idea or a feeling, or a theme, something that I want to explore. For example, in *Skeleton Woman* (Figure 6.2), for Costume Agency Workshop #3, I wanted to investigate the theme of feminine power or gender hierarchies with the costumes. In contrast to the image of femininity portrayed throughout history, I wanted to make it raw and grotesque and to communicate that through the costumed figure. That's why *Skeleton Woman* played with the traditional proportions of the human body by having super high platform shoes, oversized pants made

■ Insubordinate Costume

6.2
Signe Becker, *Skeleton Woman*, 2020. Performance by Becker/Langgård, Black Box Teater/Kunstnernes Hus, Oslo. Photograph by Alette Schei Rørvik.

of a super thick textile and an upper part, which is not a normal upper part, but rather a bomber jacket that is held up by one hand. On top of that, the hand holds a skeleton head. It's a kind of shifting person, which is uncanny, because it does something with the human proportions and can collapse and move in a very non-human way. The costume was the starting point, but not the only one. Maybe that's because I don't work that strictly as an artist, I kind of look for emotions too.

Zofia: I think this is almost an opposite way of working to my project, because I started with this idea of movement that I wanted to explore. In the rehearsals, the dramaturg Sodja Lotker asked me what my performance was about but I had not decided yet. I had raw movements but I still need to create a story because it can be many things. I hope I will be able to develop the project further in the future and find the narratives.

Signe: I often make something just because I'm interested in the visual qualities or the material. And then the answers to the question of context and content come by doing.

Christina: My designs for Babyopera's *Dragon Zoo*,[5] a performance for children, were inspired by dragons in Chinese mythology, where dragons are connectors between the earth and the sky, between the human and the gods. The idea was to make a zoological garden, where there was no narrative, more a place to visit and experience the creatures. The costumes were present from the very start and we searched for the sounds, shapes and movements of each individual dragon during the rehearsals, trying to find their characters and temper. We explored movement based on the possibilities and limitations of the costumes and developed sequences.

DRAMATURGY EMERGING FROM COSTUME

Signe: I think even if you're a costume designer or a scenographer, if you make performances, you work in the same way as a director or a choreographer, because you search for the dramaturgy, develop a timeline and investigate how the elements communicate with each other. In *Skeleton Woman*, we had nine dancers wearing the same type of costume. We explored how they worked individually, as a group and even as a lump, as one object. To me, it was important that the form of the performance was one whole, and that the overall dramaturgy shouldn't be too easy and predictable. The nine performers gather as a lump in the beginning. before emerging from the lump as individuals. They then take off their jackets and their heads are revealed, but their faces are still covered by a thin skin-like silicone mask. Finally, they leave, and never come back, not even for the applause, the incident is over. You never see the real faces of the performers. You might be waiting for them to remove their masks; ask where is the human? Where are all these beautiful women inside the costumes? But they never appear: They are still grotesque and intangible as they sing their way out of their costumes and away from the performance space. To me it was important to keep this kind of uncanniness. Not the easy way. I wanted to keep it a bit rough, hard, and not delightful. You get a glimpse of this character, a glimpse into a life, but you are not given any concrete answers. Like a passing wind. The whole history of the female and of femininity is in this wind. I tried to put 2000s years of repression into thirty minutes.

Zofia: I also work in the same way as directors and choreographers when it comes to dramaturgy. I am very intuitive, it's about finding the right dynamics. What I'm looking for is a balance between very structured and free moments with improvisation, because I see the value in both movement-wise.

Christina: The Babyopera performance of *Dragon Zoo* (Figure 6.63) has a nonlinear dramaturgy; the dragons are present as if it was in a zoological garden, children visit them and get to know them by watching them. Rather than telling a story, it's about getting to know the creatures through their presence, by how they look and what they do. As part of a tour to Russia, the performer Katja Henriksen Schia and I held open one-hour workshops after the performances for both children and adults. The twenty-five participants were guided to animate the stiff, thin, white paper as if it was a dragon skin, then to dress in the 'skin' and be transformed into dragons. The adults were instructed to talk as little as possible, but rather to support and communicate non-verbally with their children. It was extraordinary and beautiful to see the ongoing transformation, and how the adults enjoyed being part of the illusion of the presence of fifteen dragons in the room. The whole event was dedicated to experiencing the creatures magically

■ Insubordinate Costume

6.3
Christina Lindgren, *Dragon Zoo*, 2017. Performance by Dieserud, Lindgren and Skar. Det Norske Teater, Oslo (2017). Photograph by Siren Høyland Sæther.

come alive and perform merely by being present. A nonlinear, circular or spiral dramaturgy can be a useful structure for performances for small children, as it can for costume-generated performances.

COMPOSING WITH ALL THE ELEMENTS

Signe: I think of light, sound, movement, costume and scenography at the same time. It's very connected. It's not that I make the light, and the sound and everything, but I think of all elements because it's all about the wholeness of the image, such as how a particular costume works with the lighting.

Christina: For me performance is like a world coming alive and I'm interested in that. I like to express myself by creating a universe and show what is happening there and then I need all the elements as these are creative tools. I like to have all the tools.

Signe: It's hard to avoid all the elements because, even if you have a performance without any electricity, there is a light and, even if you're standing still, things look different after ten minutes because something happened in your head during those ten minutes. You can't avoid thinking about all the elements as one entity.

Christina: So, you work in parallel with all the elements?

Signe: Yes, but this has been a struggle ever since I was educated twenty years ago which is why I have chosen to mainly work in the freelance field. In the traditional theatre institutions, you only work with light and costume in the last weeks and I prefer to have everything from the very beginning. To me the process and investigation of the material has always been extremely important. I need to test it: How does this talk, how does this work, how does this perform?

Christina: When we worked on *Dragon Zoo* I wanted to explore whether we could include text in performances for children 0–3 years. I invited a dramatist, Maria Tryti Vennerød, to join but when she saw the costumes, she said we didn't need any text, as the dragons were packed with information and sensation in their physicality, presence, movement, and sound. We decided that we still wanted to try with text and that she should join the rehearsals at a later point in the process after the performers had worked on characterising the dragons. The dramatist observed the performers improvisation and responded by writing words she imagined these dragons could think, dream or say. She created beautiful poems and rhymes which we then selected and tested different ways to say them. We found that the words added something to the dragons, something emotional, sweet, funny, absurd. The text enriched the performance but it was crucial to find the character of the dragons and the atmosphere of the zoo first so the text could emerge. The order of things made a huge difference.

COLLABORATING AND COMMUNICATING WITH PERFORMERS

Signe: It has been super important to me that the dancers in *Skeleton Woman* are skilled dancers. Almost every one of them was also a choreographer, so that they were very used to searching for material and meaning and to be part of the whole thing. Since I'm not a choreographer, I'm not able to choreograph in that way. It's been very much a collective work. *Skeleton Woman* wouldn't have become what it is if not, I think.

Christina: Were you and the composer part of the improvisations, or were you standing, observing, and feeding back to the dancers?

Signe: Yes, we were leading the rehearsals, investigating what the costume could do, and what the dancers' bodies could do in such a costume. We had all the dancers dressed in the costumes at the same time, and then we gave them tasks like, for example: try to be a lump where only the pants are visible and your upper parts are hidden, then slowly find your way out of the lump and spread out. We found all the choreographic material by testing out different things. The composer and I were the directors, looking from the outside and feeding back to the dancers and deciding what to try out next.

Zofia: I like to work with dynamic movement. Contrasting movements with both super slow motions, then crazy fast movements. For *Costume Agency* I started my research from the movement/choreographic score that I placed in the costume. I prepared a short choreographic sequence that I taught the dancers and instigated some improvisation tasks. I like to work with improvisation, but it is important to me that this narrowed down during the process to what is allowed and not, what is right and what is wrong, what works and what doesn't work. In this way the improvisation is more and more specific and composed. Each production is a playground first and then specific rules develop during the process. I like to work with movement dynamics and body visibility is often important. Choreography

	is an act of composition; design is an act of composition as well. I see the potential in merging those two processes together. It is important how we communicate. As I am a former dancer, I know how dancers work, the language they speak, the terminology they use and what rehearsals look like so that's what I use when I choreograph.
Christina:	Do you, Zofia, sometimes enter the rehearsal floor, move and say, I want this or that? Do you dance together with them?
Zofia:	Yes.
Signe:	Me too. I was one of the performers in the original cast of *Skeleton Woman*, and sometimes I still am if we haven't got enough dancers I step in. You don't need complex dance skills to be part of this performance but you do need to like to crawl around hidden in a non-breathable costume, and to sing.
Christina:	I carefully select collaborative partners and performers based on the type of performance that is to be created. In the last two operas for toddlers, I wanted to create a baroque universe with the scenography and costume, with performers appearing as strange time-travellers. I wanted movement, sound, scenography and costumes to be tightly connected. It was clear that we needed an expert in baroque dance and performers that could simultaneously dance, play baroque instruments and sing in the baroque opera tradition. I searched for performers that are good at simultaneously moving and singing and have had the privilege to work with some that are really good at both! Craftmanship is so important!

THE ROLE OF THE ARTISTIC LEADER

Christina:	You both mentioned that you work in the same way as a director or choreographer when deciding the dramaturgy of a production. Is that right?
Zofia:	I think we work the same way as choreographers and directors when we get the chance to lead the performance. I am inspired by Sharon Eyal and her company L-E-V. She's based in Paris, and studied the Batsheva Dance Company and Gaga movement language. She has this very nice balance of constructed, mechanical movement and wild improvisation in her works. She is concerned with physicality. She collaborates with Dior designer Maria Grazia Chiuri, who designed the costumes for her latest productions while L-E-V took part in the Dior fashion shows. I really like this recent connection between fashion and dance. The wild movements of the dancers and their tight costumes are in contrast to the measured walking of the models with their voluminous dresses. The costumes for the performances of L-E-V company are very complex and very minimalistic at the same time and often consist of leotards that appear tight on the body like a second skin.
Signe:	I don't know if I ever have called myself a director. When we did *Skeleton Woman*, I suddenly had to say: Oh yeah, I'm a scenographer, but sometimes I relate to my role as a scenographer in quite an expanded way. Maybe this could be called visual choreography. I don't know.

Christina: So, you mean that it's difficult to say that we are directors but that we are actually many things, like directors, scenographers, and performers at the same time?

Signe: Yes. Often, I feel that I must define myself: Who am I now? But the fact is, that it is just me there and I work with different elements ... as an artist.

Christina: Does this mean that there is a kind of freedom, to put aside the categories and the roles?

Signe: In a way but it is important for me to say that I would never be able to choreograph the way a real choreographer would. The premises are different when I choreograph from a visual point of view.

Zofia: I think the situation is still hierarchical in the traditional theatres and opera houses but that the distinction between roles is more and more fluid on the independent scene. Working with smaller projects and independent groups, like I do, there are less and less strictly defined roles.

Christina: The limits seem to have been dissolved; in a way they have disappeared. The tasks are being done by everyone and therefore the roles are not so clear anymore. Is this the way you see it?

Signe: Yes, that applies for the way we work on smaller projects and in smaller groups.

Zofia: In my experience, a task is given by the director, the choreographer or someone else during the creative process. The task can be very open but the task is not instructive and does not, for example, ask the dancers to perform specific movements. It is more open, for example, asking the dancers to move like growing grass. And then the dancers may perform something unexpected. The choreography is created like this, the task comes from whoever is leading.

Christina: Do you mean that although there is a leader, they are not necessarily the director or choreographer?

Zofia: Yes. And the leader doesn't have all the answers, it's not like a traditional ballet company.

ROLES, HIERARCHIES AND POWER STRUCTURES

Christina: In those cases, when the creation of costume generated performances are led by a costume designer, does this have consequences on the traditional hierarchies and power structures in the creative process?

Signe: In a way I would say it's just the same, it's just that you are the one that has got the power, there is still a hierarchy. *Skeleton Woman* is made together with the nine dancers, but it is signed by me and Ingvild Langgård, the composer. So, there is still a power structure there, just that now it has shifted, and the power is transferred to me.

Christina: So, there is still an aspect of power?

Signe: As long as you have a leader and one that makes the final decisions, there is a power structure. But maybe the power of the materials has shifted. Normally they have less power but by letting the costume and the objects play the main role, you give them power and that breaks with tradition.

	Breaking with tradition shifts the hierarchy and is powerful. That's good, isn't it?
Zofia:	I feel that on the independent scene, it is shifting anyway and everybody works together.
Christina:	From my experience, in a production where the costumes and scenography are the starting point, all involved are aware of the power of the things, and they respect and somehow listen to them. The whole team listens to them because they are the key to the development of the whole idea of the performance.

COSTUME GENERATED PERFORMANCES AS GENRE, STYLE AND ARTFORM

Christina:	I find that costume generated performances have their roots in the history of the performing arts. Loïe Füller, Oscar Schlemmer/Bauhaus, Tadeuz Kantor, Romeo Castellucci, Kirsten Delholm/Hotel Pro Forma and Verdensteatret, to mention but a few, have all paved the way for costume generated performances. At the core of these performances I see the appearance, presence, and action of the costumed performer as human, animal-like beings, creatures or abstract beings. The appearance, presence and action are what create sensations, emotion and meaning for the audience which could be defined as the central and primary objective of the performance.
Signe:	A performance generated from costume could be anything or everything. It's hard to say. It could go in any direction. Maybe one obvious thing to say is that it has more of a visual focus. It is perhaps more object oriented, but, at the same time, costume is also very connected to the moving body.
Zofia:	Costume research is quite a new phenomenon so maybe it doesn't have to be categorised yet. I think it's nice that experimental costume can be found in many different places both in academic research and on stage. When dancers and choreographers are open to experimental costume, costume can be an important part of a lot of different styles and performances in different genres.

COSTUME AND THE PERFORMANCE SPACE: THE NEED FOR DRAMATURGY, CHOREOGRAPHY AND STRUCTURE VERSUS LETTING THE COSTUME REMAIN IN AN EXPERIMENTAL COSTUME CONTEXT

Signe:	When you are in a performance setting, you are there because you want to make a performance, so you need some structure and you work with all the elements as light, sound and space. You can't avoid working with all the elements.
Zofia:	Choreography doesn't limit the experimental costume context; it depends on what you want.

Christina: I agree, I need all the elements because they are creative tools. What can performative costume be outside of a traditional performance setting?

Signe: It's hard to tell because it depends on so many things but I guess that if performative costume is presented outside a performance context, then you would call it something else.

Zofia: It would be an installation or a sculpture or something else.

The conversation shows that the three designers found much in common. For all of them it is crucial to start the creative rehearsal process by exploring the costumes. The dramaturgical structure often emerges from intuitive work in rehearsals, based on how scenes of different qualities, dynamics, visual compositions and mood are generated by the costume, as well as how different scenes communicated with each other. All three expressed the importance of working with performers as creative collaborators.

Creating a performance from costume is difficult to preplan, as it is difficult to predict how the costume will behave and interact with the other elements. It is necessary to experiment and improvise during rehearsals. It was agreed that working with all the elements simultaneously is important to all as everything is connected and the wholeness of the image is fundamental. Although mostly they would not call themselves a director or choreographer, all three designers identify with the work of the director or choreographer. First, as they are leading the process, giving tasks, and feeding back to the performers; second, by working with the entity of all elements; and third, by composing with time and deciding on the dramaturgy. The process of costume generated performances, however, is not the traditional process of a director or choreographer. A choreographer traditionally starts with ideas for movement while a director traditionally begins with a text or ideas for dramatic action. In performances that start from costume, the process begins with 'things', non-human parts that are physical and non-verbal. There is a continuous need to put aside the will of the creators and find the right tools to understand what the costume wants to 'do'. This way the interplay between human and non-human can unfold in a subtle and complex way.

The processes, tools and methods described by these three designers, aligns well with what the twenty designers of Costume Agency described, which is interesting as the visual results demonstrate a great span of variety. For the designers, the costumes led the way in the creational process. Linnea Bågander expressed that 'The dancers experienced that being in the costumes evoked emotions as well as motions and these became the foundation and led the dramaturgical explorations'. Maria Vidal said: 'We realized the interesting findings were … about the shapeless creatures and the infinite possibilities this particular design was giving'. And Snezana Pesic noted that 'Each garment's fragility, materiality, and restrictiveness was regarded as relevant to shaping performers' behaviour on stage' (Lindgren and Lotker 2023: 151).

In Costume Agency, the designers leading the process, the performers, the team and the audience, were in a collective process of listening to the sensorial, poetic and complex language of the costume. They attentively observed the changes and explored how costume can create meaning and emotion. To grasp what happens in a costume generated performance, is a time-consuming, complex and thrilling task. which is one of the reasons why the three designers find it so inspiring to work this way.

NOTES

1. Costume Agency Artistic Research Project: www.costumeagency.khio.no and www.costumeagency.com
2. Hans-Thies Lehmanns book, *Postdramatisches Theater*, was first published in German in 1999.
3. Zofia Jakubiec: www.zofia.jakubiec.com
4. Signe Becker: www.signebecker.com
5. Christina Lindgren: www.babyopera.no

REFERENCES

Lehmann, Hans-Thies. 2006. *Postdramatic Theatre*. Abingdon/New York: Routledge. https://doi.org/10.4324/9780203088104.

Lindgren, Christina. 2023. 'Conversation with Zofia Jakubiec and Signe Becker about Leading Processes of Generating a Performance from Costume.' Transcription from zoom video conference meeting August 17th, 2023.

Lindgren, Christina and Sodja Lotker (eds). 2023. *Costume Agency Artistic Research Project*. Oslo: Oslo National Academy of the Arts.

7 Listening with Costume – A Material-Discursive Listening Practice

Charlotte Østergaard

INTRODUCTION

This chapter is a dialogue between practice and theory and between human and non-human companions about what *listening with costume* might imply. Whereas hearing is the passive process of perceiving sound through our ears, listening requires attention, understanding and interpretation. It is an active skill that involves knowledge, memory and our imagination and it may call upon our other senses. Moreover, listening is an action that we can cultivate in particular ways when we collaborate with both humans and inanimate objects. Listening with costume can change the concept of just wearing or using a costume if we listen to its 'inner voice'. Careful listening fosters a deeper involvement with the material or costume which thereby takes on a greater role in the design and performance process. My quest is to speculate on how we, as costume designers in collaboration with our colleagues in costume and performance-making situations, can cultivate our listening cultures in ways that make us aware of how we listen. Listening with costume is a material-discursive practice, a term used describe how materiality and thought intertwine to produce meaning. Through the practice of careful listening we can cultivate our lydhørhed (responsiveness and attentiveness) towards both the material properties or qualities of the textile or costume and the embodied experience of wearing the costume, without one subordinating the other. In the TED talk 'The Difference Between Hearing and Listening', composer Pauline Oliveros says that 'listening is a mysterious process that is not the same for everyone' (Oliveros 2015). She emphasises the fact that listening is subjective and that we never listen in the same way. This chapter approaches aspects of what listening with costume might entail and puts forward the idea that how we listen, and to whom or what, can change or challenge the way we collaborate with both materials and performers.

SITUATING THE ARTISTIC RESEARCH(ER)

My artistic research is informed by Donna Haraway, scholar, professor emerita of the history of consciousness and eco-feminist, who, in *Situated Knowledge: The Science Question in Feminism and the Privilege of Partial Perspective*, writes that 'situated knowledges are about communities, not about isolated individuals'

(Haraway 1988: 590). Haraway suggests that knowledge is produced in communities of human and non-human elements that are present in, and part of, a specific research situation. In the context of costume research, this implies that I, as researcher, create communities by entangling with, and having dialogues with, both human (for example, performers) and non-human (for example, textile materialities or costume) participants. Haraway continues by writing that 'the moral is simple: only partial perspective promises objective vision' (Haraway 1988: 583). Haraway argues that there is no objective truth and that what seems like 'the truth' is always perceived from a subjective perspective. Partiality implies that, as research is always conducted from a particular perspective, it is important that the researcher should situate themselves for the research to be understood in context. Please note therefore that this chapter is written from my perspective as a costume designer and researcher and that the entanglement between human bodies and crafted materialities is essential to my practice. With this chapter I argue that it matters how we listen to the different human and non-human participants that we collaborate with in the creative processes of thinking-with and doing-with.

COSTUME THINKING

At the (online) Critical Costume conference in 2020, scenographer and scholar Sofia Pantouvaki introduced the term *costume thinking*. Pantouvaki argues that:

> costume thinking is not about costume or design, as much as about critical thinking through costume – a means to articulate how costume becomes a tool for analysis, negotiation, communication, experimentation, expression of ideas and behaviors. Beyond designing for the body, costume thinking addresses the philosophical dimensions of human existence and the ways in which costume creates space for critical thinking.
>
> (Pantouvaki 2020)

Pantouvaki's *costume thinking* provides a valuable argument which highlights the fact that costume is more than a product (the costume itself) and more than a service to a performance. Importantly, costume can be considered a critical and reflective practice which includes 'a way of *think[ing] through* as well as to *act* or *do*, and even to *be* as a researcher' (Barbieri and Pantouvaki 2020: 5).

The educational theorist Donal Schön introduced the concept of the reflective practitioner that refers to how practitioners think and reflect in specific situations and how they reflect on the complexities of their experiences. Building on Schön's notion of reflective practice, Victor J. Pitsoe writes that 'central to reflective practice is the assumption that the quality of our actions is not independent of the thinking we are able to do before and in the process of our actions' (Pitsoe 2013: 212). This implies that the practice of critical thinking and doing are interdependent. Moreover, critical costume practice, such as sketching, making or performing, aways involves human and non-human others. Thus, our doing and thinking as costume designers involves and/or evolves around other humans, such as collaborators, audiences or reviewers, and other non-humans, such as materials, light or sound. Whatever the costume and performance-making setting is, whether institutional or independent, costume designers 'think-with a host of companions' (Haraway 2016: 31) and form temporal relationships and/or communities. Just like thinking, listening is a critical practice. In doing-with and thinking-with it matters how we listen to our companions, both human and non-human. The companions that I refer to in this text are performers as human companions and textile materialities as non-human companions.

LISTENING VERSUS HEARING

In the TED talk 'The Difference Between Hearing and Listening', the composer and central figure in the development of post-war experimental and electronic music, Pauline Oliveros (1932–2016), says that

> to hear and to listen have a symbiotic relationship with a questionable common usage; we know more about hearing than listening. Scientists can measure what happens in the ear. Measuring listening is another matter that involves subjectivity … To hear is a physical means that enables perception. To listen is to give attention to what is perceived both acoustically and psychologically … When listening there is a constant interplay with perceptions of the moment compared with remembered experience.
>
> (Oliveros 2015)

Oliveros notes that, even though hearing and listening are interlinked, to hear and to listen are not the same. Hearing is the natural process of perceiving sound, whereas listening is a subjective action that we consciously choose to do. Oliveros suggests that listening is an interplay between the present and the past. For example, if I listen to a song that recalls a specific memory from my childhood, this memory will most likely affect how I experience the song in the present. In the context of listening to costume, this suggests that if I wear something that reminds me of an itchy sweater I wore as a child, the memory will most likely affect my wearing experience, in one way or another, in the present moment. Thus, consciously, or perhaps even subconsciously, I am listening to the sensorial and tactile sensation embedded and embodied in my memory.

Oliveros says that to listen is to give attention. Thus listening addresses situations where listeners actively and consciously choose to listen. The Danish word to be *lydhøre* translates to English as 'to be responsive'. However, *lydhørhed* (responsiveness) also includes the sense that a person is attentive (for example, observant, cordial and caring), flexible (for example, compromise-seeking and/or cooperative), benevolent (for example, considerate, helpful, tolerant, positive, kind, and/or straightforward), present and good at perceiving small nuances. Inherent in *lydhørhed* is a conscious attunement that enables relational exchanges with and between others, whether human or non-human. *Lydhørhed* (singular) addresses the personal and subjective ability to listen to others, including oneself. *Lydhørheder* (plural) is a reciprocal listening ability. *Lydhørhed* can, for example, illustrate how I, the costume designer, respond to the experience a performer has of a costume that I have designed/made. The performer might find that the costume is itchy or the materiality of the costume might awaken an unpleasant embodied memory. I can choose whether to listen to the performer's sensorial experience of the costume or not. But, if I choose not to pay attention, my lack of *lydhørhed* for the performer's experience might affect and even reinforce the performer's unpleasant sensation.

It is a conscious choice to listen to others, whether human or non-human, as well as a conscious choice when others listen to us. In this conscious choice we direct our *lydhørheder* towards each other. Oliveros argues that 'listening is what creates culture' (Oliveros 2005: 32). This suggests that listening is doing-with, where we can collectively cultivate and attune our *lydhørheder*. However, in our cultivation we might intentionally or unintentionally favour specific listening cultures and repeat specific listening patterns. Therefore we must ask ourselves, for example, whether our listening obeys, or is subordinate to, specific authorities, positions or hierarchies, or if our listening favours specific people, viewpoints or places, as well as being aware of how our backgrounds (for example, our families, the communities that we belong to, our education and the country that we live in) inform the way that we listen. Moreover, I suggest that listening always comes with expectations. The question is whether we are aware of the expectations that we have. For example, what do we mean when we say that someone is a 'good' listener? Is a 'good' listener someone that does not interrupt when we speak, that asks questions about what we say or that we think understands our viewpoints or experiences? In situations where we meet a 'good' listener does it mean that we must listen back? Is the act of listening an exchange where we indirectly calculate 'scores'? And how do we listen to what is not said and what we do not want to hear? What do we not listen to? How do we humans listen to non-humans, and can non-humans listen to us? I pose these questions to you the reader, as the listener.

KIN-MAKING WITH NON-HUMAN COMPANIONS

In my practice as a costume designer, I have often been hired to design as well as to produce costumes. For me, this double role has blurred the borders between the creative design process and the more concrete realisation phrase. Hence, I do not always know where the designing ends and the making starts, as sketching and making the design complement one another and are a part of my conceptual thinking process. The textile materialities that I choose during the design-making process, are chosen to serve the aesthetic expression of my designs. At the same time, my designs, and the way that I use textile materialities, are also highly influenced by, for example, a director's or choreographer's overall aesthetic vision for a performance. My experience has shown me that my design-making process is also informed by how we collaborate as a team, how we think-with and listen to each other,

Besides my work as a freelance costume designer, my practice also includes more independent artistic projects that allow me to explore costume in other ways. These artistic projects allow me to dig deeper into the strong relationship I have with textile materialities. To use Haraway's words, when I craft, I am 'sowing worlds' that are 'opening up the story of companion species' (Haraway 2016: 118). Instead of aiming to accomplish a predefined aesthetic vision in these projects, I remain open to different possibilities as I listen to the materiality of the textiles during the crafting process and craft the relationship I build with the materials into the costumes. If during the design/making process I listen to the material and try to understand how it wants to behave, I am less in control, the material becomes more insubordinate, a protagonist. By 'sowing worlds' the costume appears to take on a new life of its own, growing and developing in surprising ways.

Crafting, for me, suggests an action that includes the use of some kind of material that is often non-human. For example, I use specific textiles when I craft a costume. At the same time, craft also describes the techniques that often include handling specific tools, we craft our bodies to become skilful in particular ways. For example, we use specific techniques and tools to become skilled at sewing, drawing, dancing, and many other actions. Actions and/or skills that might seem simple but that are often complex to learn and master. Donna Haraway combines academia and science fiction in her research that, for me, opens up the idea of speculative worlds where humans must cultivate crafting and caring skills in order to include non-human species and/or companions. She suggests that 'kin making is making persons, not necessarily as individuals or as humans' (Haraway 2016: 103). As such, crafting could be considered a kin-making process where the non-human textiles become more than just inanimate companions. Kinship is thus a way of listening to and with the textiles when I craft, and it is only when I listen carefully that I 'hear' the particularities that each type of textile contains and understand the qualities of the materials.

If I consider crafting as making kin with textile materialities, then it has consequences on how I enter the process. For example, it matters what type of costume I am crafting and how specific a vision I have of the costume that I want to craft, whether I already know in detail how I envision the costume to be or whether I only have an outline of an idea. If I envision a specific costume idea, I need to focus, for example, on how the technical methods I use inform and form the textiles in specific ways. If, however, I only have an outline of a costume that I want to craft, I may explore different techniques and textiles. The latter implies that I have an idea but at the same time I am not fully sure where I am heading, which can be challenging, but it also implies that I am open-minded to how the techniques and the textiles inform each other. In this kind of kin-making process the costume emerges as a metaphorical and non-verbal dialogue with, and between, the techniques and the textiles, where I act as 'interpreter'. I may find that I need to change or alter a technique in relation to, as an effect of, or as a response to, the type of textile I am using, or vice versa, and this may potentially change my relationship to both. Experience has taught me that the results that emerge are often quite different than I had imagined prior to the crafting process.

7.1 Charlotte Østergaard, the crafting image: screenshot from the video *Knotting Connections* (2022). In the video (made for the performance and activist collective Becoming Species) I share my knotting (crafting) practice. Videographer and editor: Charlotte Østergaard.

When I craft, I make kin with the textiles, I listen with my hands. The way that I use my hands shows how I listen to the materials. Often my entire body is activated. For example, soft and fragile textiles need to be handled carefully so they do not tear, whereas rough and heavy textiles are more stubborn and make me more forceful. The textiles that I use often have different properties that I might or might not be aware of: some are woven, others are knitted, some are organic others are synthetic fibres. In the kin-making process, these properties are part of what I am making kin with, whether I am fully aware of them or not. The properties of the textiles will affect me *as well as* affecting the way that I listen to them. I suggest that, if I am willing to attune my *lydhørhed* by listening to the properties of the textiles, they will craft my crafting of the costume and they will also craft my body.

Although I describe my crafting as a kin-making process, I am not able to predict how the specific costume that I have crafted will affect the humans that will wear it. I suggest that once a costume is crafted it becomes its 'own' non-humankind – a costume companion. Even though the costume companion might have traceable traces of my kin-making process, the traces are potentially only traceable to me. Moreover, the traceable traces will most likely transform when someone (myself, a performer or someone other) wears the costume. Thus, as soon as the costume is crafted, I must re-attune my *lydhørhed* and make kin with the costume companion that it has become.

7.2
Entanglements: screenshot from video that as a part of the textile artwork *Entanglements* exhibited at *Material Thinking* – 1st International Material Art Biennale in China (2022/23). Videographer and editor: Charlotte Østergaard.

INTERDEPENDENCY AND LISTENING

In my artistic costume projects, the costume companion becomes intrinsic to the performers in the performance-making process. The performers dress in, wear, explore, improvise and perform in the costume companion. The way that I host the situation has an impact on how the performer and I listen to the costume companion and to each other. As the costume designer, I may choose to direct the situation which implies that I decide, or even control, how we make kin with the costume. Alternatively, I can be more inviting in my attitude towards the performer, inviting the performer to listen to, and make kin with, the costume companion in a way that matters to the performer not to me. The consequence of this is that I, the costume designer, might potentially not be able to understand how the performer listens to, or makes-kin with, the costume companion. Oliveros says that 'listening is a mysterious process that is not the same for everyone' (Oliveros 2015). The performer and I are two different humankinds, that will never listen in the same way and thus, we will most likely make kin with the costume companion in quite different ways. Whichever way I choose to host and listen, I cannot escape my responsibility in the process.

Writing about K.E. Løgstrup's philosophy of the ethical demand, theologian Eva Skærbæk states that 'ethics is the responsibility of *I*, the demand is personal' (Skærbæk 2010: 45). This means that I am responsible or accountable for the way that I approach others (humans as well as non-humans). Skærbæk reminds me that, in situations with a performer, I have a responsibility, not only for how I have crafted a costume, but also for how the costume companion might potentially craft the situation. Skærbæk continues by noting that if, as Løgstrup suggests, an ethical life is fundamentally relational, we have a responsibility to care for and uphold the well-being of others as 'interdependence means that every one of us are I's as well as Others' (Skærbæk 2010: 45). Skærbæk's words resonate as an acknowledgement of the fact that the performer, the costume and I, are interdependent. This suggests that I must attune my *lydhørhed* towards the performer's experience and towards the kin-making process that occurs between the performer and the costume companion. Skærbæk writes that 'independence without any link to dependency leaves both parts ignored, invisible and unloved' (Skærbæk 2009: 51) which implies that if I, as costume designer, do not show that I am also dependent on the performer, the performer will become invisible in the situation. A performer's sense of invisibility can arise in situations where I do not welcome and listen to the performer's experience, viewpoints, creative ideas, or other inputs – however challenging I might find them.

Oliveros suggests that 'we need to be listening in all possible modes to meet the challenges of the unknown – the unexpected' (Oliveros 2010: 41). I suggest that if we, as costume designers in the kin-making process, listen to our human and non-human companions, we can attune our *lydhørhed* to include the unexpected. Oliveros argues that 'quantum listening is listening to our listening. The field expands to embrace all kind of listening, with openness to all possibilities' (Oliveros 2010: 51). Thus, as a costume designer and researcher, I must listen to how I listen, and I must learn from the way that I listen. If I listen to my human and non-human companions, if I listen to how we make kin, I might have to accept the unexpected but, by embracing this, I might also learn from the unexpected. The unexpected potentially opens up and expands my capacity to listen and my perspective on the costume companion that I have crafted. *Listening with costume* is a listening strategy that openly invites human and non-human others to connect in many different ways. Oliveros writes that 'listeners practicing cultural flexibility would be aware of the profound interdependence of all beings and all things' (Oliveros 2010: 58). *Listening with costume* is acknowledging that costume designers, performers and non-human materials are interdependent in the costume and performance-making process and it is through this interdependency that we can cultivate and attune the way that we listen to each other.

LISTENING WITH COSTUME IN CONTEXT OF INSUBORDINATE COSTUME

Writing about the concept of her modular Insubordinate Costumes, Susan Marshall notes that

> modular Insubordinate Costumes ... encourage open-ended play where the potential combination are seemingly endless. By playing with the modular costumes, exploring and investigating their mechanisms, performers discover the different creative possibilities that they offer. The performer, in a primary collaboration with the costume, discover its latent potential, without prejudgment or prescribed narrative context. The costume and its obstructions, leads, or rather, demands a heuristic process: improvisation, exploration, and play.
>
> (Marshall 2021: 48)

Rather having to be subordinate and embody the designer's (or someone else's) vision, Marshall's modular costumes give the costume modules agency and invite the performers to have agency and to be playful. The variations and combinations of Marshall's modular costumes are endless, and her invitation encourages performers to create and engage with their creations in ways that interest them. Marshall has no ambition or intention to direct or choreograph and thus the performers playful creativity can flourish in insubordinate ways.

Like Marshall's modular costumes, *listening with costume* invites humans to explore non-human matter and to discover how different people are affected by it. Sara Ahmed, scholar and writer working at the intersection of feminism, queer theory and postcolonialism, suggests that 'bodies are "directed" and they take the shape of this direction ... A direction is also something one gives ... orientations involve directions towards objects that affect what we do' (Ahmed 2006: 16, 18). This implies that the costume as a bodily companion will direct or orientate our bodies in one way or another, whether we are a performer, a designer or a witness. Just as Ahmed's object orientates the doing, I argue that we cannot *not* listen to how the material-specificity of a costume, as an intimate companion, will direct and affect our doing, whether we like it or not. I argue that, when we *listen with costume*, we enter an internal dialogue with, for example, the materiality, visuality and spatiality of the costume *as well as* an external dialogue with the other humans that we collaborate with.

Skærbæk writes that 'we are interdependent in the sense that we influence each other with what we do and say and by what we do not say and do; we are each other's authors' (Skærbæk 2010: 44). This suggests that, when we listen with costume, we are interdependent and our interdependency influences how we listen to and how we dialogue with each other in order to co-author or co-create the situation. Skærbæk argues that 'knowledge is to me an ongoing co-creational and situational process' (Skærbæk 2009: 63–4). *Listening with costume* challenges us to listen to other human and non-human companions in polyphonic ways in order to enable co-creation. The listening that I am advocating can potentially awaken the 'voice' that we 'normally' do not listen to. For me, listening has a consequence: how we listen, and to whom or what, can change or challenge the way we collaborate with materials and performers. As costume designers, we must never forget to listen and we must learn to listen in different directions.

In this chapter I have unfolded certain aspects of what listening with costume might imply and will end by sharing a few of the questions that I still linger on: Can I say that my listening is truly open-minded? What is it that I do not and will not hear? How can I lean to listen in a non-judgmental way? Is this possible?

REFERENCES

Ahmed, Sara. 2006. *Queer Phenomenology – Orientations, Objects, Others*: Durham, NC: Duke University Press. https://doi.org/10.1215/9780822388074.

Barbieri, Donatella and Sofia Pantouvaki. 2020. 'Costume and Ethics: Reflection on Part, Present and Future Entanglements', *Studies in Costume and Performance*, 5(1), 3–11. https://doi.org/10.1386/scp_00010_2.

Haraway, Donna. 1988. 'Situated Knowledge: The Science Question in Feminism and the Privilege if Partial Perspective", *Feminist Studies*, 14(3), 575–599. https://doi.org/10.2307/3178066.

Haraway, Donna. 2016. *Staying with the Trouble – Making Kin in the Chthulucene*. Durham, NC: Duke University Press. https://doi.org/10.2307/j.ctv11cw25q.

Marshall, Susan. 2021. *Insubordinate Costume*. Doctoral thesis, Goldsmiths, University of London. https://doi.org/10.25602/GOLD.00031204.

Oliveros, Pauline. 2005. Deep Listening: A Composer's Sound Practice, New York: iUniverse

Oliveros, Pauline. 2010. *Quantum Listening*. London: Ignnota.

Oliveros, Pauline. 2015. 'The Difference between Hearing and Listening.' *TED talks*, November 12, 2015. https://www.youtube.com/watch?v=_QHfOuRrJB8&t=4s accessed [02/09/23].

Pantouvaki, Sofia. 2020. '"Costume Thinking" as a Strategy for Critical Thinking.' Paper presentation at *Critical Costume 2020 Conference* (online). https://costumeagency.com/project/sofia-pantouvaki/ accessed [12/09/20].

Paulson, Steve. 2019. 'Making Kin: An Interview with Donna Haraway.' LARB Los Angeles review of books, published December 6, 2019. https://lareviewofbooks.org/article/making-kin-an-interview-with-donna-haraway/ accessed [12/12/22].

Pitsoe, Victor J. and Mago Maila. 2013. 'Re-thinking Teacher Professional Development through Schön's Reflective Practice and Situated Learning Lenses', *Mediterranean journal of Social Sciences*, 4(3), 211–218. Rome: MCSER Publishing. https://doi.org/10.5901/mjss.2013.v4n3p211.

Skærbæk, Eva. 2009. 'Leaving Home? The "worlds" of Knowledge, Love and Power', in *Teaching Subjectivity, Travelling Selves for Feminist Pedagogy*. Athena, 47–67.

Skærbæk, Eva. 2010. 'Navigating in the Landscape of Care: A Critical Reflection on Theory and Practice of Care and Ethics', *Journal of Health Care Analysis*, Online Oct. 2010, in journal June 2011, 41–50. https://doi.org/10.1007/s10728-010-0157-5.

8 Researching with and through Costume

Proposition for a Research Framework

Sofia Pantouvaki

What are the research possibilities that costume offers beyond its crucial role in co-creating characters and performances? This contribution focuses on performance costume as a means for new research and on processes of costume creation that enable new research methodologies to be established. When looking at costume not only as an artistic outcome integral to performance making – its most familiar and longstanding dimension – but also as a field for open-ended experimentation, costume's research potential emerges from its practice. The chapter examines contemporary methods and approaches for costume research through the costume itself as methodological research 'tool'. My interest is in providing a concise overview of the multiple dimensions and possibilities of performance costume as a means for systematic artistic research, specifically for carrying out practice-based or practice-led research. What differs between these and other ways of doing research *with* and *through* costume is that, in artistic research orientations, practice is not the object nor the outcome of the study, but the process that facilitates, implements, and completes the research.[1] The present chapter highlights approaches to costume practice as a platform for research, identifying current trends such as the connections between costume and sentient body and the relationship of costume with 'new' materials.

FROM RESEARCHING COSTUME TO RESEARCHING WITH AND THROUGH COSTUME

The more established methods for the study of performance costume, which could be labelled here as 'traditional' methods for costume research, are broadly known. They commonly regard researching costume as visual and material expression in relation to representation, design, body and performance. Methodologies for such costume-related research include archival research in theatrical archives and records, as well as in the creators' personal archives, into textual materials such as production books, wardrobe lists, notebooks, programmes or critics' reviews. The research of costume may also include the analysis of visual evidence, such as costume sketches or rehearsal and performance photographs. This type of research about costume covers a wide range of themes and periods, within historical performance (e.g. Isaac 2016; Dotlačilová 2020) as well as in recent or contemporary performance cultures (e.g. Nadoolman Landis 2012; Weckman 2021;

Hawkins 2022). The study of costume has also been well-established from the perspective of material culture analysis, examining costumes in museum archives and theatre collections, focusing on the material dimension of costume through which object biographies (and often, performer biographies, too) are formed (e.g. Barbieri 2012a and 2013; Lodwick 2021). Moreover, oral history analysis of the artists', technicians' and other collaborators' testimony has been increasingly used to reveal unseen aspects of costume practice historically and/or in the present (e.g. Wilkinson-Weber 2014; Taylor 2021). These methods frequently complement each other and converge through qualitative analysis – a well-established methodology in costume research.

Employing a diverse range of the above methods, for example, I focused on the costume collection of Yiannis Metsis from the Athens Experimental Ballet (1965–90). This involved implementing a multimodal research methodology tailored specifically for costume study (Pantouvaki 2019). In this particular case, the information derived from the costumes in the Athens Experimental Ballet collection as physical objects was examined in conjunction with evidence from other tangible materials like costume drawings, material samples, and stage photographs. Additionally, insights from intangible sources, such as the testimony of the costume designer, were integrated. This comprehensive approach offers a wealth of information for the study of costumes both on and off the stage. Adopting a multimodal costume research methodology brings together a diverse array of sources and analytical tools, as well as a system of various modes, including images, objects, and language/spoken discourse, which are systematically examined in combination and interaction. This approach transcends the confines of the visual and social semiotic tradition, where costume is primarily associated to visual messages, and instead fosters a more comprehensive study of costume as an embodied expression on both practical and theoretical levels.

Contemporary approaches to costume research encompass a thorough examination of the costume process, delving into its artistic dimensions and intellectual aspects from many angles. While traditional research methodologies persist, they undergo evolution shaped by the practical experiences and tacit knowledge of the researchers, many of whom now originate from the field of costume design, combining artistic insight with research expertise. The expert gaze of the costume practitioner-researcher, often relying on 'subjective, intuitive responses' (Barbieri 2013: 285), provides an informed interpretation rooted in deep knowledge and nuanced perception of the subject being studied. Moreover, 'when practitioners adopt the role of researchers their personal knowledge shapes the research process', as it 'brings a subjective input to the research because practitioner-researchers draw on their intuition as much as on the objective information they can access at the moment of practicing' (Vega et al. 2021: 6). This is evident, for instance, in the research collaboration between costume maker, historian and performers within the research project *Performing Premodernity*, which 'employs comparative research of material, visual and textual sources, and making and performing experiments', in which each member brought 'their expertise and way of doing that complement one another' (Dotlačilová and Kjellsdotter 2023: 155).

Simultaneously, mixed research methodologies in costume studies are renewed, frequently merging traditional approaches with contemporary methods that employ the costume as a 'methodological tool'. Additionally, artistic research methodologies, also defined as practice-based or practice-led research, have been introduced to the field of costume. To appreciate the distinction of these terms and their application onto costume research, it is useful to revisit the seminal paper by historian and educator Christopher Frayling at the Royal College of Art, titled 'Research in Art and Design' (1993).

Frayling had distinguished three ways of conducting research in the arts as follows:[2] Research *into* art and design, which includes historical research, aesthetic or perceptual research, and concerns a variety of theoretical perspectives on art and design with social, economic, political, ethical, cultural, iconographic, technical, material, etc., dimensions (Frayling 1993: 5). This type of research can be carried out by someone who does not practice in these fields, as the rules and research procedures are drawn from existing methodological models. Research *through* art and design is the next category and concerns art and design practices as a means of conducting research; it involves studio work, and the results are achieved and communicated through the activities of art, craft or design (ibid.). Today it is a largely recognisable and visible research method, of primary interest for the present study, and usually aims at formulating broader conclusions. Finally, research *for* art and design, in which the final product is an artefact and the thinking is 'embodied in the artefact, where the goal is not primarily communicable knowledge in the sense of verbal communication, but in the sense of visual or iconic or imagistic communication' (ibid.). As noted by Vega et al. (2021: 5), 'although these three categories have been contested, debated, and interrogated by many others, they have come to constitute one of the most authoritative points of departure in the literature of artistic and design research'.

Since Frayling's articulation of research methodologies for research in the arts, 'different interest groups' (academic and creative) 'have developed distinct terminologies to identify such orientations' that relate to the 'multiple and, at times, divergent directions' of the concept of research *through* art and design (Vega et al. 2021: 5). Hannula, Suoranta and Vadén (2005: 10) coined the term *artistic research* to indicate research that involves 'self-reflective and self-critical processes of a person taking part in the production of meaning within contemporary art'; the term has been widely used in the Nordic area in the past two decades (e.g. Arlander 2011; Varto 2018) in various fields of arts. However, as noted by Arlander (2011: 320), 'the terms practice-based research or performance as research are sometimes preferred in the performing arts, rather than art-based or artistic research … partly due to a different conception of art' in the context of performance making. Arlander (2011: 321) also writes that,

> artistic research can be practice-based, when artistic practice is more important than a specific artwork, or design oriented, when a specific object or artwork is produced. But this division is not strict, since many forms of design (stage design, costume design, light design, sound design etc.) are included in the performing arts.

In this definition, artistic practice relates to a process rather than a tangible artistic outcome; this explanation is problematic for the field of costume, where artistic practice may refer to either the artistic process of conceptualising and designing costume and/or to the creation of a (tangible) costume. In addition, the terms practice-based research (e.g. Candy and Edmonds 2018) and practice-led research (e.g. Mäkelä 2007) are often used interchangeably to refer to research driven by artistic practice. Yet, a refined look at the use of these terms reveals a diversity of approaches; for example, Mäkelä (2007: 157) focuses on the artefact as 'a method for collecting and preserving information and understanding' and examines how 'the final products (the artefacts) can be seen as revealing their stories, i.e. the knowledge they embody' as part of a practice-led approach.

One way to interpret these close connections would be to acknowledge that the research process is 'led' by the practice and the conceptual development of new ideas (new knowledge) is 'based' on the practice. On the other hand, the conceptual development of new ideas (new knowledge) is also 'led' by the practice, as the research process is 'based' on practice. Overall, these terms and approaches 'still suffer from a generalized lack of consensus even in their own academic circles' (Vega et al. 2021: 4) and, while they differ in terms of scope, objectives, stakeholder involvement and levels of artistic intention, 'what ties them together is a shared stance that advocates for the employment of practice as a platform of inquiry' (2021: 6). In that sense, research *through* art and design functions as a broader term encompassing these methodological approaches. As observed by Valle-Noronha (2019), 'utilizing personal knowledge, building on one's previous experiences, and accounting for the subjective nature of practice also constitute one of the common foundations that all of the above research orientations rely on'. This subjective quality is relevant to researching *through* costume as well.

PROPOSITION FOR A FRAMEWORK TO RESEARCH WITH AND THROUGH COSTUME: TERMS AND EXAMPLES

Costume research is currently interested in how concepts of research *through* art and design are shaped and delimited in relation to other research approaches that exist in the field of costume, and, therefore, how research can be further developed *through* costume practice. As previously mentioned, it's crucial to recognise that 'costume practice' encompasses multiple dimensions. This term not only pertains to the crafting of costumes as artefacts for adorning physical or virtual bodies but also involves the conceptualisation of ideas through a process of critical thinking (Pantouvaki 2020a). In this sense, it serves as 'a means of critically interrogating the body' (Hann and Bech 2014: 3), a process that may not necessarily culminate in a tangible design or material outcome.

So, how is research *with* or *through* costume shaped within the aforementioned orientations? Just as in diverse artistic disciplines, the field of performance costume presents a general lack of consensus and large variety in the terms and approaches it employs, even within the relatively small circle of costume research. This challenge stems from both the multitude of forms that costume research practices can assume and the influence of various academic institutions 'in defining and situating these practices as legitimate ways of producing knowledge that can academically qualify as such' (Vega et al. 2021: 5).

After several years of reflection and dialogue with peers,[3] I attempt a proposal for a formulation of these research orientations for costume, driven by and based on costume practice, as follows:

- Costume-based research (research *with* costume)
  where the means of carrying out the research is the creation of new costumes or the use of existing costumes (physical objects or digital/virtual designs) as a site for the production of new knowledge. In this case, creative costume work becomes a form of research, it complements the research and costume acts as a medium and a tool for researching. Through its qualities and possibilities as a creative artefact, costume forms the basis for the contribution to knowledge.

- Costume-led research (research *through* costume)
  where costume practice, its context and processes, forms a research condition that enables enquiry on issues that are not solely related to costume as an artefact. Here, costume and its processes of conceptualisation and realisation lead to the exploration of broader questions and themes, to the articulation of new perceptions (whether costume related or else), and to new research knowledge and theoretical or even philosophical thinking.

Some practical examples in which performance costume functions as a means for research serve to investigate this proposal.

In the solo performance *Electra* (2013), Stamatia Megla studied the dynamics of costume for the expression and materialisation of the character of Electra inspired by Sophocles' homonymous tragedy, while at the same time using the physical qualities of costume (shape, form, material) as a starting point for the creation of a new performance. Here, costume represents 'a "doing" of the character as well as its semiotic "describing"', holding within itself 'not only the body of the performer[s] but also the action of performing' (Barbieri 2017: 6). Through the costume, the designer has created a three-dimensional world in which the moving body can tell a story. The research here is costume-based and suggests new ways to use costume as a means and a space for experimentation beyond the text. This costume is a collaboration between designer, performer and material that 'embodies the text and becomes itself the text' (Barbieri 2012b: 149). The costume designer takes on an expanded role as the creator of an idea that is the starting point for the entire performance.

The specific project has emerged through the teaching practice of Donatella Barbieri, who, for over two decades, has been exploring movement-based and material-led approaches for the development of costume (2012b, 2021). Her costume-based research approach is inspired by the body-centred acting training ideas of Jacques Lecoq (Barbieri 2007) and Eugenio Barba, and is informed by the creative opportunities offered by Postdramatic Theatre 'which articulates performance in a way that does not prioritise text, performer or space' (Barbieri

2012b: 149). Her research has evolved as an ongoing practice of 'devising material-movement workshops as a radical departure from traditional designing' with the aim 'to re-define costume as agent and instigator in making performance' (Barbieri 2021: 197).

Following this work, the *Costume Agency* artistic research project (2018–23) led by Christina Lindgren and Sodja Lotker (2023), fully adopted a costume-based research approach, inviting designers to explore performance embedded in a garment and its materiality. This project developed in the context of Postdramatic Theatre as well, challenging and de-hierarchising the established structures in the performing arts by holistically exploring the full performative potential of garments. The research evolved around 'the complexity of the interactions of the four components (garment, body, action and context)' with the aim to 'investigate how costume affords dramaturgical change' (Costume Agency 2019: n.p.). This enabled an exploration of costume

> through, but also beyond, its traditional connections to the body to produce meaning relating to identity, ethnicity, age, gender, social status, etc., and inviting us to look at costume as a visual and spatial element that provokes dramaturgy that is not story-driven.
>
> (Pantouvaki and Příhodová 2021: 145)

The rich explorative individual research cases undertaken within this project with costume confirms that 'the approaches to costume as a performative element generating performance are abundant' (Lindgren and Lotker 2023: 13). While Lindgren (2021: 201) also notes that 'costume generated performances are about to be considered an established genre'.

A number of projects pertinent to costume-based research centre on the exploration of materiality regarding costume. Costume designer Dawn Summerlin experimented with an unconventional material when she used porcelain to create dance costumes in *Perceptive Fragility* (2015). Through a process of costume-based research, she investigated what knowledge stems from the body by observing 'how the body can be part of a material language … how it reacts, breathes, responds under the weight, and the physical restriction, temperature and kinaesthetic elements of the costume' (Summerlin 2019: 110). In this collaborative process, a choreography was created, eventually becoming a live performance, 'in which the costume was the guiding "text", the choreographic instigator and where dancing became the means of navigating a relationship with costume' (ibid.). The rehearsals gradually revealed further features of the costume based on the experience and sensory perception of the dancers and the intricate fragility of the porcelain material (Figure 8.1). The methodology followed stages with shifting control, 'between the material, the performer and the costume' (Summerlin 2019: 118).

In another example, director-designer Leo Fressato used real ice bars to make shoes and a bra for the costume of the performance *The Girl and the Autumn* (2007), creating movement in response to the pain the actor felt in their feet and on their skin from direct contact with the ice (Figure 8.2). Staged during wintertime

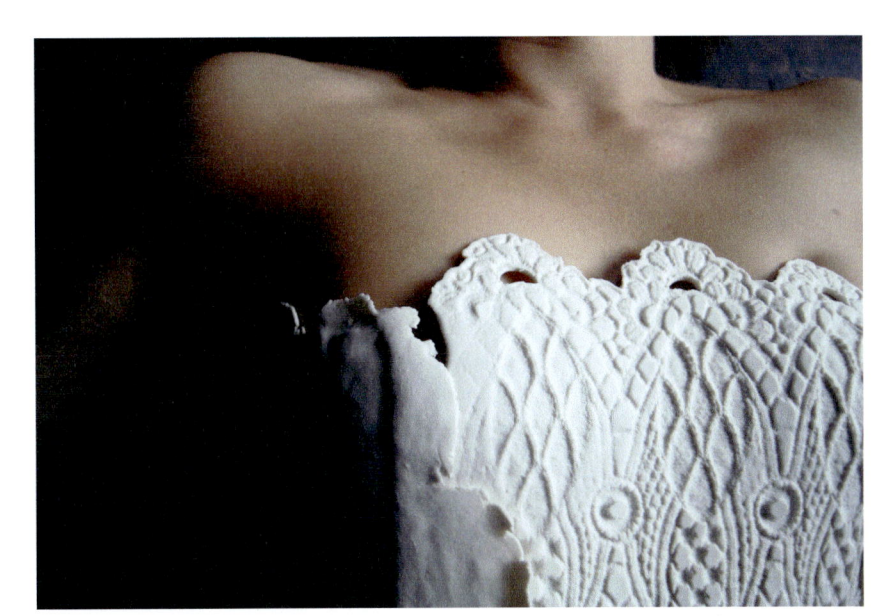

8.1
Perceptive Fragility, 2015. Costume designer Dawn Summerlin. First fitting in porcelain. Photograph by Dawn Summerlin, October 2014.

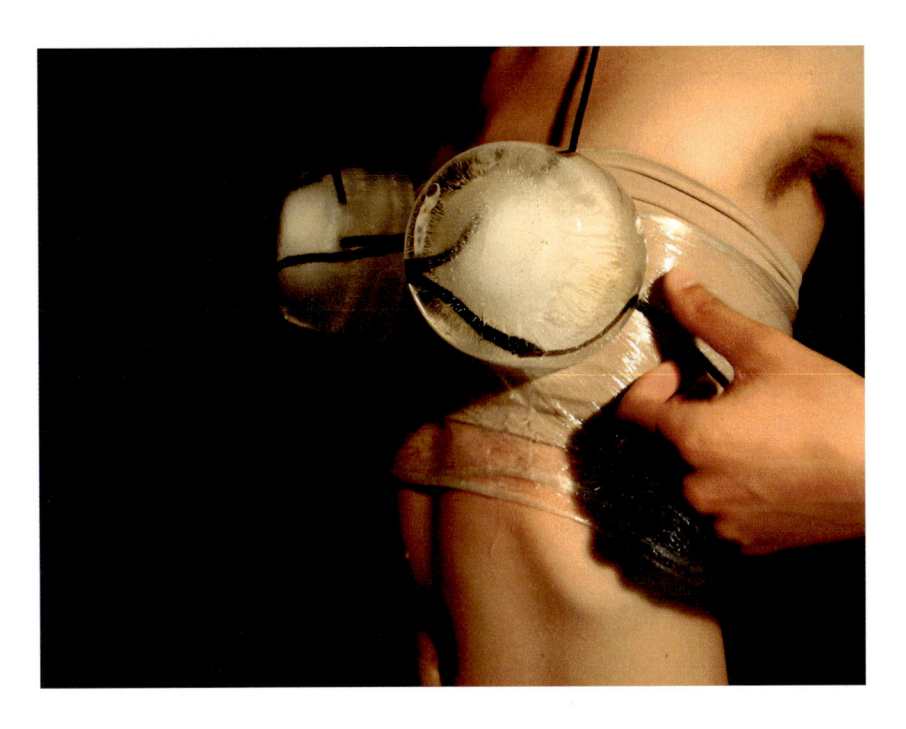

8.2
Penetrating Costume – The Girl and the Autumn, 2007. Director-costume designer Leo Fressato with Débora Vecchi and Elenize Dezgeninski. Tutor: Amabilis de Jesus. Teatro Novelas Curitibanas, Curitiba, Brazil. Photograph by Marcelo Deguchi.

in Curitiba, a cold and humid state capital in Southern Brazil, the costume evoked in the audience 'a feeling of inhospitality, of repulsion' (Silva 2010: 147). Here the costume served as a means of addressing the theme of the performance, namely sexual violence, by incorporating the metaphor of ice into its materiality (Pantouvaki 2020b). Under the supervision of Amabilis de Jesus da Silva, the costume-based research facilitated a material representation that conveyed the actor's physical and emotional experience of pain and penetration to the audience.

■ Insubordinate Costume

Costume designers Jeppe Worning and Charlotte Østergaard also experimented with materials in the project titled *MASK* (2017). The artistic conception of *MASK* arose from the restriction to only use materials and objects from everyday life (cutlery and paper tape) and from the requirement that the masks cover different, smaller or larger, parts of the body (Østergaard 2017). However, beyond researching the material, in this case, the costume designers-researchers studied the role reversal in their creative pair, provoking 'a critical dialogue between the sensorial feeling (inside) and the visual expression (outside) of the mask' (Østergaard 2018: 61). By adopting a three-dimensional sketching method on a 1:1 scale, they used each other as a three-dimensional bodily canvas, treating their bodies as an 'unformed surface' upon which variations of the 'mask' were created. Each of them had the possibility of experiencing the 'masks' from within through bodily and sensory perception (wearing it), while at the same time being able to maintain an external gaze as 'active observers' to their artistic expression. This method enabled the participants to shift between being wearer/carrier and maker/observer, alternating in these roles throughout the process. This specific experimentation serves as an example of costume-led research emphasising broader considerations beyond the costume itself, in this case, the mask. The focus extends to encompass various perspectives within costume practice, including the experiences from both the internal, as in wearing, and external, as in observing, viewpoints, and their interconnectedness. However, the project also yielded an artistic outcome, captured through photographs featuring a dancer whose movements were influenced by the weight and position of metal elements (cutlery), arranged in various 'mask' variations on his body (Figure 8.3).

In a final example, within my own costume-led research *through* costume under the overarching theme 'Designing through the Performer', I am dedicated to exploring the potential of personalised design beyond the constraints of specific character representation. Here, the focus shifts to the performer as an individual, acknowledging their private identity. The objective of this project is to cultivate an expanded and more intimate collaboration between the costume designer and the performers, aiming to forge stronger connections between performers and their costumes to elevate their onstage performance. In the production of *Don Giovanni Giocoso* (2014), characterised by historically informed costumes, my research delved into how the performers' personal memories and preferences could be visually integrated into their costumes. This costume-led research concentrated on infusing a more personal and familiar touch to the actor's costume by incorporating individually designed historical detailing. The embroidery patterns adorning the costumes were designed one-by-one for each specific actor, evolving through a collaborative sharing of personal experiences throughout the research process. As these costumes, rich in personal narratives in their design and materiality, were shown up close to the audience, they became a conduit for spectators to experience this intimate approach firsthand.

8.3
MASK #32, 2017. Costume designers Jeppe Worning and Charlotte Østergaard. Photograph by Thomas Cato.

APPROACHES TO RESEARCH WITH AND THROUGH COSTUME

The examples above illustrate that research *with* and *through* costume manifests through three primary trends. First, it centres on exploring novel approaches to the body, thereby redefining notions of physicality. Second, it delves into the investigation of diverse experiences and perceptions of costume, including through embodied and sensorial encounters. Lastly, research *with* and *through* costume frequently advances through experimentation with unconventional materials, reflecting a tendency to question and propose redefinitions of the materiality inherent in both body and costume.

In summary, in the various aspects and dimensions of performance costume as a research tool, we observe the following phenomena:

- New ways to create, and use, costume
- New design methods
- New creative collaboration processes
- New, often more horizontal, modes of collaboration
- New, often expanded, roles within creative teams
- Continuous experimentation with/through new materials
- New aesthetic expressions and meanings, consequence of all the above

In many cases, these perspectives overlap, therefore, these phenomena are combined.

■ Insubordinate Costume

This study emphasises the crucial role and contribution of practitioner-researchers to costume research, highlighting their deep understanding of the field and its expressions. Through this nuanced understanding, practitioner-researchers offer refined perspectives on costume creation, fostering expert discussions with social actors involved in the research. Research *with* and *through* costume introduces advanced analytical tools, facilitates communication opportunities, encourages critical discussions, and imparts robust skills to elevate the landscape of costume research. This engagement ensures a comprehensive exploration of the artistic, scholarly, and social contexts in which such practices unfold.

Consequently, this timely and robust contemporary evolution of research and research methodologies in the field of performance costume has given rise to various research programmes, academic networks, scholarly societies, and special interest groups that engage designers and designer-researchers. Additionally, it has facilitated the establishment of spaces and communities for the exchange of ideas (see, e.g. Barbieri and Pantouvaki 2016; Pantouvaki and Příhodová 2021). Collectively, these initiatives have carved out 'a space from which to reconsider the intersection of theory and practice through costume' (Barbieri 2023: 4).

Engaging in research *with* and *through* costume opens potential spaces and contexts to question, challenge, and overturn conventional notions ingrained in performance. Therefore, costume research holds the potential to shape our perspectives on broader issues, not only concerning the past and present of our societies and worlds but also in anticipation of the future.

NOTES

1 This phrasing is based on, and enriched from, Vega et al. (2021: 6).
2 Frayling's categories derive from the work of philosopher and literary critic Herbert Read, *Education through Art* (1944).
3 A preliminary articulation of the terms *costume-based* research and *costume-led* research as research lenses and distinct research approaches was undertaken in my paper 'Costume Thinking as a Strategy for Critical Thinking' at the Critical Costume 2020 conference (Pantouvaki 2020a).

REFERENCES

Arlander, Annette. 2011. 'Characteristics of visual and performing arts', in M. Biggs and H. Karlsson (eds.), *The Routledge Companion to Research in the Arts.* London: Routledge, pp. 315–332.

Barbieri, Donatella. 2007. 'The application of LEM to the teaching and practice of costume design for performance', in N. West (eds.), *Costume Symposium 2006. AIB.* The Arts Institute Bournemouth.

Barbieri, Donatella. 2012a. 'Encounters in the archive: Reflections on costume', *V&A Online Journal*, Issue No. 4 Summer 2012. Available: http://www.vam.ac.uk/content/journals/research-journal/issue-no.-4-summer-2012/encounters-in-the-archive-reflections-on-costume/. Accessed 10 January 2024.

Barbieri, Donatella. 2012b. 'Costume re-considered: From the scenographic model box to the scenographic body, devising a practice-based design methodology that re-focuses performance onto costume', in *Endyesthai (To Dress): Historical,*

Sociological and Methodological Approaches, Athens, 9–11 April 2010. Nafplion: Peloponnesian Folklore Foundation, pp. 147–152.

Barbieri, Donatella. 2013. 'Performativity and the historical body: Detecting performance through the archived costume', *Studies in Theatre and Performance*, 33(3), pp. 281–301.

Barbieri, Donatella. 2021. 'The Body as the Matter of Costume: a Phenomenological Practice', in Sofia Pantouvaki and Peter McNeil (eds.), *Performance Costume New Perspectives and Methods*. London/New York: Bloomsbury Academic, pp. 197–212.

Barbieri, Donatella. 2023. 'The agency of published research, a journal as the means to expand a nascent field', *Studies in Costume and Performance*, 8(1), pp. 3-9. https://doi.org/10.1386/scp_00082_2.

Barbieri, Donatella and Sofia Pantouvaki. 2016. 'Towards a Philosophy of Costume', *Studies in Costume and Performance*, 1(1), pp. 3-7. https://doi.org/10.1386/scp.1.1.3_2.

Candy, Linda and Edmonds, Ernest. 2018. 'Practice-based research in the creative arts. Foundations and futures from the front line', *Leonardo*, 51(1), pp. 63–69. https://doi.org/10.1162/LEON_a_01471.

Costume Agency. 2019. 'Workshops', *Costume Agency* website, 1 April. https://costumeagency.khio.no/?page_id=31. Accessed 10 January 2024.

Dotlačilová, Petra. 2020. 'Costume in the time of reforms: Louis-René Boquet designing eighteenth-century ballet and opera', Ph.D. dissertation. Stockholm: Stockholm University.

Dotlačilová, Petra and Kjellsdotter, Anna. 2023. 'Historically informed costume: Collaborative practice between maker, historian and performer', *Studies in Costume & Performance*, 8(2), pp. 155–174. https://doi.org/10.1386/ scp_00094_1.

Frayling, Christopher. 1993. 'Research in art and design', *Royal College of Art Research Papers*, 1(1), pp. 1–5.

Hann, Rachel and Bech, Sidsel. 2014. 'Editorial: Critical costume', *Scene*, 2(1+2), pp. 3–8. https://doi.org/10.1386/scene.2.1-2.3_2.

Hannula, Mika, Suoranta, Juha, and Vadén, Tere. 2005. *Artistic Research: Theories, Methods, Practices*. Helsinki: Gothenburg University and Art Monitor and University of Fine Arts.

Hawkins, Ella. 2022. *Shakespeare in Elizabethan Costume: 'Period Dress' in Twenty-First-Century Performance*. London: Bloomsbury.

Isaac, Veronica. 2016. '"Dressing the part": Ellen Terry (1847–1928): Towards a methodology for analysing historic theatre costume', unpublished Ph.D. dissertation. Brighton: University of Brighton.

Lindgren, Christina. 2021. 'Unfolding a vision embedded in a garment: Three tools from a toolbox for generating performance from costume design', *Studies in Costume and Performance*, 6(2), pp. 201–215. https://doi.org/10.1386/scp_00047_1.

Lindgren, Christina and Lotker, Sodja (eds.). 2023. *Costume Agency Artistic Research Project*. Oslo: Oslo National Academy of the Arts (KHiO).

Lodwick, Keith. 2021. 'Recording costume design in the theatre and performance collections at the V&A: Vivien Leigh and Oliver Messel', in S. Pantouvaki and P. McNeil (eds.), *Performance Costume: New Perspectives and Methods*. London/New York: Bloomsbury Academic, pp. 129–137.

Mäkelä, Maarit. 2007. 'Knowing through making: The role of the artifact in practice-led research', *Knowledge, Technology, and Policy*, 20(3), 157–163. https://doi.org/10.1007/s12130-007-9028-2.

Nadoolman Landis, Deborah. 2012. *Hollywood Sketchbook: A Century of Costume Illustration*. New York: Harper Design.

Østergaard, Charlotte. 2017. 'MASK project', *Charlotte Østergaard – Unfolding My World*. https://www.charlotteostergaardcopenhagen.dk/kunstnerisk-profil/mask. Accessed 12 January 2024.

Østergaard, Charlotte. 2018. '*MASK:* Dialogue between an inside and an outside perspective of costume', *Studies in Costume and Performance*, 3(1), pp. 61–80. https://doi.org/10.1386/scp.3.1.61_1.

Pantouvaki, Sofia. 2019. '"A touch of green with an Emerald Hue": A multimodal research methodology for the study of costume', in P. Dotlačilová and H. Walsdorf (eds.), *Dance Body Costume*. Leipzig: Leipziger Universitätsverlag, pp. 41–76.

Pantouvaki, Sofia. 2020a. 'Costume thinking as a strategy for critical thinking', *Critical Costume 2020* conference paper (online). https://costumeagency.com/project/sofia-pantouvaki/. Accessed 12 January 2024.

Pantouvaki, Sofia. 2020b. 'Novelty through performance costume: From material to immaterial dimensions', in Elise Breukers (ed.), *Innovation and Fashion: Proceedings of the ICOM Costume Committee Annual Meeting, Utrecht, The Netherlands, 10–15 June 2018*. Utrecht: Centraal Museum. http://costume.mini.icom.museum/wp-content/uploads/sites/10/2020/02/Sofia-Pantouvaki-Novelty-through-Performance-Costume.pdf. Accessed 12 January 2024.

Pantouvaki, Sofia and McNeil, Peter (eds). 2021. *Performance Costume: New Perspectives and Methods*. London and New York: Bloomsbury Academic.

Pantouvaki, Sofia and Příhodová, Barbora. 2021. '*Critical Costume 2020*: Investigating Costume Agency', *Studies in Costume and Performance*, 6(2), pp. 143–154. https://doi.org/10.1386/scp_00043_2.

Read, Herbert. 1944. *Education through Art*. London: Faber and Faber.

Silva, Amabilis de Jesus da. 2010. 'Figurino-Penetrante: Um Estudo sobre a Desestabilização das Hierarquias em Cena' [Penetrating Costume: A Study on the Destabilization of Hierarchies on Stage], unpublished Ph.D. dissertation. Universidade Federal de Bahia, Brazil.

Summerlin, Dawn. 2019. 'Perceptive Fragility: Movement and porcelain', *Studies in Costume & Performance*, 4(1), pp. 109–19. https://doi.org/10.1386/scp.4.1.109_1.

Taylor, Madeline. 2021. 'Technical skill, emotional intelligence, and creative labour: The collaborative work of costume realisation', unpublished Ph.D. dissertation. Melbourne: The University of Melbourne.

Valle-Noronha, Julia. 2019. 'Becoming with clothes: Activating wearer-worn engagements through design', Ph.D. dissertation. Espoo, Finland:Aalto ARTS Books.

Varto, Juha. 2018. *Artistic Research. What is it? Who does it? Why?* Espoo: Aalto ARTS Books.

Vega, Luis, Aktaş, Bilge, Latva-Somppi, Riikka, Falin, Priska, and Valle-Noronha, Julia. 2021. 'Shared authorship in research through art, design & craft', *Research in Arts and Education*, 1/2021, pp. 1–22. https://doi.org/10.54916/rae.119316.

Weckman, Joanna. 2021. 'The first premiere and other stories: Towards a history of the costume design profession in Finland', in S. Pantouvaki and P. McNeil (eds.), *Performance Costume: New Perspectives and Methods*. London/New York: Bloomsbury Academic, pp. 141–158.

Wilkinson-Weber, Clare M. 2014. *Fashioning Bollywood: The Making and Meaning of Hindi Film Costume*. New York: Bloomsbury Academic.

PART 4
THE PRACTITIONERS' VOICE

9 The Practitioners' Voice – Edited Interviews and Contributions

Susan Marshall et al.

INTRODUCTION

Contemporary practice in Insubordinate Costume is dynamic and varied, demonstrating a wide range of interests that range from social, cultural and political themes to artistic exploration and academic research. This section of the book gives voice to twenty-two contemporary artists, designers and key practitioners working in different parts of the world with costume as the instigator of performance. Some are colleagues and friends met at conferences or the Prague Quadrennial whilst others were discovered during my research. Their styles and techniques differ, they come from diverse artistic backgrounds and training and have different knowledge, some research within a university context, others are independent artists. Many practitioners who experiment with Insubordinate Costume try to find affordable and sustainable solutions because, although some have funding, others, like me, do not. Most design for traditional theatre productions alongside their experimental costume projects. Many of the costume performances take place outside of the traditional theatre setting in art galleries, museums and outdoor spaces, some invite audiences to actively participate. All but two of the practitioners in this chapter are women. Whilst one hypothesis for this could be that women are investigating the diverse possibilities of Insubordinate Costume as a reaction to centuries of sewing and needlework being considered 'women's work' and not a serious artform, many of the previous examples in this book are by men. Undoubtedly the growing awareness of the agency of costume, as well as the acknowledgement of costume as a serious artform, worthy of critical research, has had an impact on the increased number of experiments in this field of design.

Through edited interviews and personal contributions guided by a series of initial questions, the practitioners reflect upon their work, their conceptual and aesthetical choices and their methodologies. The agency of costume is clearly perceptible in these examples together with an underlying playfulness and a focus on materials and materiality. The practitioners were asked to describe their design ethos with particular reference to the projects where a performance develops from the costumes, or where the costumes are a fundamental part of the performance. The questionnaire included questions about whether they start working with a concept or an aesthetical choice or whether the costumes evolve from

■ Insubordinate Costume

experimenting with materials. Furthermore, they were asked to describe the collaboration between costume designer, costume and performer in their work and how their costumes instigate performance, whether play is an important part of their work method, whether they experiment with movement whilst building the costumes and how the constraints of the costume affect movement. Lastly, the practitioners were asked for their opinions on the role of costume as a powerful tool in theatre, dance, performance art and fashion.

MATERIAL IN MOTION

As noted in the introduction to the book, materiality is a prominent feature of Insubordinate Costume, as materials not usually associated with traditional tailoring techniques are often used in an experimental way to create interesting textures and shapes. Technological advancements such as three-dimensional printing, laser-cutting and led lighting, as well as innovative materials offer designers a wide range of creative possibilities. Designers such as Maria Blaisse, Daphne Karstens, Iris Woutera de Jong and Victorine Pasman investigate 'the inherent qualities of a material' (Blaisse), 'experimenting and developing ideas from seeing how it wants to be manipulated and connected, how it works on the body' (Karstens) in a 'kinetic interaction' (Woutera de Jong) where 'the design of the costumes dictates certain movements through constriction' (Pasman).

MARIA BLAISSE (NETHERLANDS)

https://mariablaisse.com/
Since the late 1960s, Dutch multidisciplinary designer Maria Blaisse's work has been, first and foremost, a study of form and material possibilities. Her artistic projects can be understood as sculptures or costumes where it is difficult to determine which is in control: the body or the form (Blaisse 2023). Her costume work includes Spheres 1987, Kuma Guna 1996 and mesmeric flexible bamboo structures 2007–12. The following text is taken from an interview with the artist.

One thing has always led to the next in my work. By cutting into the inner tube of an old car tyre to make fireman helmets for my daughters, I opened the way to something magical. The torus shape (which is like the inner tube of a car) is both an energetic form and a physical form: I tried a piece of a rubber inner tube with an incision on my head, and then something happened … the form of my head and the two different diameters of the inner tube interacted with each other … here the magic began.

So I started to investigate. It took me about a year to experiment with all the design possibilities for the rubber hats and to find exactly the right proportions – the thickness of the rubber, the size, the cuts to make. Sensing exactly when the form is right is intuitive. The final design for the *Flexicap* allows it to be worn in many different ways according to the wishes of the person wearing it, that's what I like. That also happens with my costumes. When these three-dimensional forms relate to the three-dimensionality of our bodies, amazing things happen.

The Practitioners' Voice ■

Issey Miyake saw me wearing my rubber hat in New York and invited me to design and make hats for his Spring/Summer 1988 collection. We wanted to make the hats in different colours in rubber but the production using moulds was expensive so I started to search for a material that could make the same shapes and I discovered EVA (Ethylene Vinyl Acetate) foam which comes as a block of foam that I cut into layers and profiles and vacuum shaped with heat. So that was a whole new story. The material is amazing as it is flexible and elastic, but it's very technical to work with, so I developed the possibilities together with engineers. It's important to understand the material you are working with and know how to deal with it. I learnt this because one very hot day in Tokyo we left the vacuum shaped hats for the show in the car whilst we were having lunch and … they all melted! Luckily, we could put them back in the vacuum machine and remould them. It was a wonderful experience to work with Issey Miyake but, at that time, I had small children and back home again, it was good to go back to silence and just focus on my own rhythm and way of working. Back in Amsterdam, I continued experimenting with EVA foam on a body scale and started performing and travelling with the costumes (Figures 9.1 and 9.2). I designed the costumes for Paula Abdul's 1992 world tour. The costumes needed to be transported easily so we made a 'Meccano' system which meant that the costume pieces could be taken apart and then screwed or clicked together – it's a simple solution and beautiful at the same time. The simpler you get, the more effective something is.

After a period of around seven years, I found a new dimension to my work with the form of the torus, and developed my way of researching further with materials that varied from rubber to foam and from gauze, glass and leather to

9.1
Maria Blaisse,
*Rolling Stripes
Kuma Guna* series,
1996. Photograph
by Anna Beeke ©
Maria Blaisse.

■ Insubordinate Costume

9.2
Maria Blaisse, *White Trousers, Kuma Guna* series, 1996. Photograph by Anna Beeke © Maria Blaisse.

bamboo. I discovered a flexible gauze material with a diagonal mesh, that made it possible to create the same forms that I had created with the torus inner tube. I have been interested in the flexibility of diagonal structures since my studies and travels in South America in the 1970s, researching pre-Inca textiles and their looping and plaiting techniques. That's how I could start working with bamboo: I know the structures and I can see the transformative potential. The bamboo resonates with the body. The richness comes when you go into the inherent qualities of a material, and once you really do that the possibilities never end. This is a way of working.

I was recently invited to a residency in Brussels at *TicTac* and took the bamboo structures with me. The performers, mainly improvisers, started playing and investigating the possibilities of the bamboo structures and it was totally magical. The work was new again, it came alive in a different way and exploded into possibilities. Things happen through curiosity and playing, and being open for much more than you could ever think of. That's a physical experience. Play and improvisation open the mind and body in interaction with the costumes. Even when there is no movement you sense the possibilities. A costume is connected to an energy which is not visible, but yet is full of potential. Improvising is important because when the body of the dancer is ready to meet the costume everything just happens by itself, it's almost effortless.

Because I work with form and structure, people think I'm very scientific but I'm not at all. I love geometry, and I understand it in my own way. I don't understand all the geometric forms I make; I just do them. That's really intuition. My body knows it, so that's enough. We should trust that more, perhaps. My work is always about the flexibility of a material or structure. I love the word insubordinate; nature is also insubordinate. Nature invents the most magical things all the time, it's important to get closer to our inherent connection with nature and focus on

9.3
Maria Blaisse, *Dance Improvisation with Bamboo Sphere Bamboo* series, 2007. © Maria Blaisse.

what's around us, learning to be careful with the materials we use, and finding creative solutions.

For thirty years I've been searching for the energy point that occurs when the body, form and music interact creating, something totally new. It rarely happens but I come closer and closer. I don't have any new projects now but I share my knowledge and my language of form through exhibitions and a series of workshops. I'm archiving my work and I am looking for a place where the costumes can be displayed with the intention that other people will see my way of working and continue with this richness, this abundance of possibilities.

DAPHNE KARSTENS (NETHERLANDS)

www.daphnekarstens.com

Daphne Karstens is a Dutch wearable sculpture artist based in Amsterdam. In her work she explores the concept of body sculptures in order to create experimental and innovative wearable art pieces. She often works with unconventional materials and combines the individual qualities of materials in experimentation with shape and structure. She wants to explore and redefine the boundaries and possibilities of wearable art and translate the outcome of this research into visual, experimental wearable sculptures and performances.

People who don't know much about costume often assume I make dresses or historical garments, but that's not what I do. I call my work wearable sculpture in order to describe what I do because it invites questions and opens up a conversation about the diversity of costume.

My work is a journey from idea to experiment to wearable artwork to performance. Although it's different for every project, I usually have a concept before I start construction, but in some cases I start with a blank canvas and develop

■ Insubordinate Costume

a direction as I go. This sometimes results in the most interesting wearable artworks as this creates the most open way of experimentation.

I often pick a material that intuitively feels like it makes sense for the piece I'm working on. The material directs my work, so the starting point is usually either the choice of material to use or deciding how to manipulate the material. Something that works on paper two-dimensionally will never be the same when translated into three-dimensions, the original ideas may not work. I prefer to start with the material, experimenting and developing ideas from that, seeing how it wants to be manipulated and connected, how it works on the body. The silhouettes develop from experimenting with the materials. The more sculptural the material, the more I can gain from it. The more freedom I have to experiment, the more surprises happen and the more interesting the designs become.

Discovering the sculptural essence of a material happens through experimentation, manipulation, and repetition. Repetition is very important; the strength of the material comes from finding a certain repetition in the material, which could mean either a lot of the same material or a certain structure that repeats itself. I find that repetition is usually stronger than combining a lot of different things together. For *'PANG'* (Figure 9.4), I had the overall concept of what I wanted to achieve, which was to start with something flat that could be manipulated to create different shapes. I experimented for a very long time before finding that the best technique for this was to use conjoined triangles. From this the ideas started to develop and I tried thick cardboard and different types of plastic before deciding on mirrors which play with light and open up the space around the costume.

I keep quite a lot of diverse materials in my studio and when I'm in the early stages of a design I will often open up a box and play around with this and that, just to find a direction. Sometimes I find an interesting material and start working with it. I originally made the black straw costume for an online theatre show for

9.4
Daphne Karstens, *'PANG'*, 2021. Photograph by Frank Wiersema. © Daphne Karstens.

children during COVID-19, because a friend of a friend had a cafe stockroom full of plastic straws and asked if I could do anything with half a million straws! (Figure 9.5). After that I made a variation on the straw costume for performance maker Lorraine Smith's *You Can Take Me Home Toni*[1], based on the *Hey Mickey* video by Toni Basil, which features cheerleaders and their pompoms. The straws recall the material of a pompom but the material choice originally developed from someone having leftover materials. Lorraine discusses and embraces female insecurity in this performance and the costumes are very playful, enlarging the subjects she focuses on. The concept for the hair costume which covers the body completely, for example, came from female insecurity about body hair.

The costume designer, costume and performer collaborate as one in my work. Even though I'm not the performer, I create something which invites the performer to experiment. For example, when I'm working with Lorraine Smith, I look at what the costume does from the outside, and Lorraine explores it from the inside. This mutual experimentation starts a conversation about possibilities which is where interesting things happen, because even though I don't put it on myself and I don't have the same experience of being inside, someone who's wearing it does not always know how things look from the outside. We both have our perspectives and sharing ideas is important.

Often when I start to make something, I put it on and play around with it to see how it moves, what shapes it creates, what noise it makes. Play is very important in developing the costumes, playing around with it myself, playing around with it with actors, performers, dancers, playing with the materials. My costumes invite movement. Movement guides the costumes and the costumes guide movement as the performer surrenders to the limitations of the costumes and is then inspired by the limitations to find alternative solutions. The development and the dramaturgy of the costumes come through performers playing and experimenting

9.5
Daphne Karstens, *STRAW*. A wearable sculpture-based performance, 2023. Performed by Maria Ribas and Sofie Kramer Photograph by Frank Wiersema. © Daphne Karstens.

■ Insubordinate Costume

9.6
Daphne Karstens, *'PING'*, 2014. Photograph by Alex Traylen. © Daphne Karstens.

with movement in order to develop ideas for the performance. Space is incorporated into the wearable sculpture, not only the shape that is created inside by the body, but also how the costume interacts with the outside space, creating the boundaries and the framework of the performance.

I am interested in how we define a wearable sculpture when it is not worn, does it have the same character as when a performer is still inside it? Do you always need a body for it to be called a costume? Without a body it is static but the negative space of the body remains. In *'PING'* (Figure 9.6) the performer wears a cocoon which she takes off. A shell is left behind but it had been worn so the audience continues to think of it as a costume. Had it been hanging on the set from the beginning of the performance it would probably not have been thought of in terms of a costume. Perhaps the idea of costume depends on how it is perceived by the audience.

The sooner costume is recognised as a powerful tool in a production, the more visually interesting it will become, as it has the ability to create unity and different depths of meaning. In the future I want to continue to explore how costumes and materials can direct or choreograph a production through movement and experimentation in order to arrive at a narrative.

IRIS WOUTERA (NETHERLANDS)

https://www.iriswoutera.com
Iris Woutera graduated from the Gerrit Rietveld Academy in Amsterdam and has been working as an independent artist since 2016. She received a Mondrian Fund Young Talent grant in 2020. Her work has been presented internationally, including a solo performance at the Palais de Tokyo in Paris. She is currently working in

The Practitioners' Voice

Rotterdam on Blob – Binary Large Object. The spatial work of Woutera focuses on all the senses, which leads to a synergy between sculpture and performance and inspires her drawings, photos and video work. Answering my questions, Iris explains her work ethos and inspiration.

Deform, 2019 (Figures 9.7, 9.8. and 9.9), is a performance in which a flexible cocoon envelops the human body. The combination of hard (plastic) and stretching (textile) provides a movable space, in which remarkable forms can be created. A performer plays with the material which in turn reacts to their movement. The organic flow refers to forms in nature, such as plants, fishes or a gently swaying sea anemone. With *Deform* the body can freely experiment on every sensory impulse. The person inside the cocoon is anonymous, but expressive through movement. The boundary between human, object and nature seems to blur.

The essence of my work is kinetic, an interaction between the movement of the human body and sculpture. The works are created around the human body and are worn by one person or form a connection between several people and their environment. The sculptures act as a tool for connection and influence the wearer's state of mind. Why? I think that is important for people to connect with themselves, with the community and with the landscape around them, especially the natural world as we are a part of nature. I find caring for and listening to each other, learning together, being inspired and being creative very important qualities in life. I would like society to be softer, more inclusive and adaptive. I like to experience the wonder of life together through art.

The process of making the sculptures is initially guided by chance: an intuitive play with objects from everyday life and found things from the environment. I experiment and 'let my hands' do the work, not overthinking it, but working intuitively in this first phase. I like to use materials that people know and to make

9.7
Iris Woutera,
Deform, 2019.
Photograph by
Leonor von Salisch.
© Iris Woutera de
Jong.

■ Insubordinate Costume

9.8
Iris Woutera, *Deform*, 2019. Photograph by Leonor von Salisch. © Iris Woutera de Jong.

9.9
Iris Woutera, *Deform*, 2019. Photograph by Leonor von Salisch. © Iris Woutera de Jong.

something unexpected, to give new meaning to everyday objects and find out what feelings are living under the surface, within ourselves. In a dream-like state perhaps. Contrasting material combinations arise, which together generate physical tension. The weight, colour, tension, movement, texture, etc. are all important and have a certain effect on the senses. When I find the final material for a project, the production process starts. Within the artisanal production process, there is then plenty of room for material innovation and new value attribution (circularity). This phase can take quite some time! Movement feedback is very important during the whole material creation process.

The sculptures are not just aesthetical or symbolic, they really provoke the senses of the wearer and the viewer in a relationship between body and mind. Watching the performance is also a creative process for the viewer. The abstract visual language creates space for personal interpretation and experiential exchange. The work is performed by performers or invites the spectator to participate. The audience determines its own time and place, and it is precisely in this uninhibited and improvised moment that the work acquires its meaning.

I mostly start working from personal experiences and take inspiration from society. Rather than my concepts having solely one theme, extensive research into literature/field/movement leads to the development of a set of ideas and feelings mixed together to create a new perspective. From this I start creating the wearable sculptures. During the making process, I firstly start experimenting with movement myself and then I experiment with the performers and the material together with the musician and sometimes with the lighting designer. To reach the 'right mindset' before every rehearsal and performance we warm up for forty-five minutes in a guided meditation and movement session with creative suggestions about the concept we are working on. I brainstorm and discuss the concept with the performers in order to generate a performance world together. The movement feedback is very useful to develop the concept further or to adjust the sculptures (like a tailor-made suit, gradually adjusted to the body and its environment). The process is like the growth of an ecosystem, everything interconnected. The work and the performance evolve together, the one cannot work without the other. I also make costumes for my performers, which are mostly inspired by daily wear which makes a nice combination with the sculptures and makes the performance more 'real', like it is happening in 'daily' life.

'Play' is the soul of the performance. The tension in the material constrains the body which initiates the play. In this constraint/tension, you can find the central emotion and visual concept of the work. You can't fix or set the choreography with the material because it goes its own way so it asks the performers to keep an open mind, being present in the moment. It's playful! It's about experiencing, feeling, guiding the material, and discovering, fun. I'm influenced by techniques like 'Body–Mind Centring' as a performance vision.[2] This is a creative language process between body, mind and material and which can be very personal for the performers. Even during a public performance, it's still a live experimental improvisation although there are naturally performance choices to make such as duration, tempo, placement, adaptions due to the location, number of performers, intention and perhaps audience participation.

I believe in creating a certain world for the performers, in which they can move freely. After the periphery of the performance is defined, the performers are free to explore. Improvisation is the basis of the performance but within the boundaries of the concept. It's like playing a game, there is no cohesion without rules, although the rules can be adjusted during the game. The performers and I experiment and the material always leads us to new things that we insert into the work. The more often we rehearse and perform, the richer the performance becomes. The work is always evolving and is never finished, it remains interesting and exciting to keep playing for years!

For me, the location determines the success of the performance. It's all about the management of the mindset of your audience. This has to do with an alternative way of choreographing. You need to have an open space to be experimental. Curators, programmers or makers themselves can create open spaces everywhere. But daylight spaces, visual art spaces, 'location-theatre' in nature or empty monumental spaces like factories attract me the most. I like it when the performance is on the same floor level with the audience as the expectations of the audience are also open because they can move around and determine their own time and place.

I find it very joyful to do my own performance productions from beginning to end because I like to create total concepts. For me, all the fun lies in this freedom of choice which I experience less when I take on the role of a traditional costume designer. But costume can be a powerful tool and today there are so many ways to collaborate. I see the material pieces I make as wearable sculptures as, in this way, I refer to the visual arts. It feels more open. I have learnt a lot, however, working in the theatre, especially the aspect of collaborating in a team that runs like a well-oiled machine.

VICTORINE PASMAN (NETHERLANDS)

https://victorinepasman.nl

Victorine Pasman's work is a crossover between theatre, art and fashion. She is an experienced designer of theatrical, interactive performances. In collaboration with other performers and musicians, she brings her designs to life and interacts with the audience, who are taken into her fabulous world. Her work can be seen in museums, at street theatre festivals and other cultural events, sometimes on stage, but mostly amongst the audience.

The extravagant and sometimes sculptural designs of my costumes determine the relationship of the performer to the environment and the audience. Concepts regularly arise from my fascination for archetypes and style elements from a certain culture or era, such as the seventeenth-century crinolines. The bizarre, exaggerated proportions I give my crinolines, in works such as *The Floating Diva* (Figure 9.10), reinforce their impact and meaning and evoke surrealistic images. In addition, some of the enormous dresses also function as a tent, where the audience is invited to become part of the performance, as in, for instance, *Under her Skirt*. Craftsmanship and special use of materials are characteristic of my designs and largely determine the value and character of the work. For example, *White*

9.10
Victorine Pasman, *The Floating Diva*, 2019. © Victorine Pasman.

Stranger is made up of almost 10,000 pipe cleaners, the costumes for *Black Eyed Susan Vine* consist of recycled scaffolding net and the *Floating Diva* dress is constructed with white umbrellas. I like to play with the different appearances and aspects of women as seductive, majestic, sinful or powerful beings (in a tongue-in-cheek way). I invite you to look at the world with an open mind and to dare to dream.

My work offers a theatrical experience in which you are asked to connect and surrender to the wonder. *Under her Skirt* was inspired by the huge seventeenth-century crinolines which fascinate me, because you could hide all kinds of things (or even people!) underneath such a big skirt. Although wearing a dress with a crinoline gave women more power and prestige, at the same time these things were a burden to wear, heavy and big, so women were practically imprisoned within the skirt. Crinolines also created a physical distance between the woman wearing one and the people around her, perhaps making her feel even more imprisoned and lonely. The idea for the performance came from this fascination. Someone from the audience gets 'swallowed' by this huge lady and finds another world underneath her gigantic skirt: https://victorinepasman.nl/en/under-her-skirt/. The spectacular costume made out of umbrellas worn by a soprano floating on water for *The Floating Diva* is more like a costume installation, an object. Only when there is someone inside it, on top, it becomes his/her costume. I wanted to make a dress with scales and came up with the idea of using umbrellas as scales. The shape of an umbrella reminds me of the blades of a windmill which is very Dutch – and an umbrella is also a very Dutch object since it rains a lot in Holland.

When I start a new work, I already think about the performance and the role of the performer. This is something that develops during the work process and keeps developing when we start doing the performance. Working with different performers who come from different backgrounds – mime, dance or theatre – is interesting because they find exciting new ideas or possibilities regarding the performance, the costume/s or both. I think about possible movements whilst designing the costumes, but the performers or dancers give back so much more. When I work with dancers the costume and the concept depend much more on their movements and the character they give to the costume whilst bringing it to life, for example in *Silent Transformation* (Figure 9.11). It would be interesting to be able to exchange experiences and ideas more with the performers/dancers during the creative process but often there is not enough time.

I love to experiment with materials and would like experiment further in the future. I often use materials other than fabric in many of my designs: like the umbrella's, pipe cleaners, foam and scaffolding net. I think in images and movement; the physical appearance and how to move, but also what actions could take place whilst wearing the costume and becoming part of the costume. The design of the costumes dictates certain movements through constriction. It is very interesting that costume is starting to be recognised as a powerful tool. I believe that costume can tell a strong visual story or become something in between a human performer and an object.

■ Insubordinate Costume

9.11
Victorine Pasman, *Silent Transformation*, 2023. © Victorine Pasman.

CHARACTER DEVELOPMENT

Costume can aid the audience's understanding of a performance or disorientate and upend their expectations and preconceptions. As with more traditional theatre productions, the development of character and characterisation can also be noted within the genre of experimental Insubordinate Costume. Picasso's French and American managers, for example, are exaggerated Cubist manifestations of the countries they represent. Contemporary designers are also interested in creating characters: Fruzsina Nagy, Simona Rybáková and Zuzu Hudek design costumes that 'tell stories by themselves' (Rybáková) and often 'transform or metamorphose during the performance' (Hudek), whilst Sandra Becker's work investigates recurring archetypes.

SANDRA HILLI BECKER (GERMANY)

www.sandrabecker.info
Sandra Hilli Becker is a costume and set designer based in Hamburg, Germany. With a background in Fine Art and Contemporary Dance, she studied art therapy and art pedagogy with a thesis entitled Force of Attraction: Clothing as Means and Objects of Change, followed by an MA in Costume Design for Performance at the London College of Fashion. Her work as a costume maker and designer has taken her to Russia, the United States, Rumania and the United Kingdom. She is a member of the theatre company TOBOSO which develops innovative theatre pieces for a young audience with a focus on physical theatre. Since 2012 she has worked for the theatre festival Gandersheimer Domfestspiele.

Within my studies of art therapy, I started to engage in fairytales, their narrative structure and psychological interpretation. I quickly became fascinated with their strong motif of repetition. On the one side, fairytales as folk tales were created by telling and retelling again and again, on the other side, these stories are based on a structure that is defined by recurring actions, words, figures and circumstances. And yet, despite their repetitive elements, fairytales are in fact stories about transformation. This fascination with repetition and its power became the starting point for my artistic practice. This is evident on a content level in the form of an investigation of archetypes (a constantly recurring symbol or motif in texts or images of any form), on an aesthetical level in researching ritual clothing, which is often the basis of my sculptural costumes, and on the level of making in choosing repetitive and minimalistic techniques as repetition and multiplication, which are my leading design principles. As I have learnt from fairytales, repetition can create transformation and is therefore a powerful tool to create the new.

My works *Goldesel*, *Interior* and *Peeled Shadows* demonstrate my approach. *Goldesel* (Figure 9.12) was inspired by the character of the donkey from the fairytale *The Wishing Table* by the Brothers Grimm. The piece is made from metallic yarn that I soaked in glue and placed randomly on a demountable form. The interminable repetition of cutting, dipping and placing the thin yarn led to an almost meditative making process, in which the shape of the costume slowly appeared just like a sketch that turned into a proper drawing with every stroke. *Goldesel* is a sculptural experiment that explores the costume genre of masking. Here the body and face of the performer remain visible under the costume. Performer and mask

9.12
Sandra Becker, *Goldesel*, 2012. Golden thread, starched with wood glue. Photograph by Petrov Ahner. © Sandra Becker.

are assembled to form a picture puzzle, in which the lighting reveals one layer or the other or both at the same time. *Interior I* (Figure 9.13) was one of a series of textile pieces created in my innovation lab, where I explore new techniques and the various possibilities of uncommon materials. Many materials I use are not found in a fabric shop, but in the pantry, the hardware store or in nature. In the lab I have the opportunity to play with a material in order to understand its character. For me a material is not only the matter I use to create but is also the basis of the meaning of the work itself in many of my pieces. For *Interior I*, I crocheted large organic formations out of tea-dyed jersey. The form itself was never calculated beforehand but was a result of coincidences and mistakes. The crocheted pieces then served as a nexus between the human body and a piece of furniture. The appearance of this irritating hybrid oscillates somewhere between a condensed home, a cursed creature, an alive prosthetic and a fatal cocoon.

Whilst in *Interior I* the specific performativity lies in the limitation of the performer's movements, it is the performer's movement that determines the costume of *Peeled Shadows*. *Peeled Shadows* (Figure 9.14) is my interpretation of the Danish fairytale *King Lindworm*, the story of a witch's curse which causes a prince to be born as a dragon and has to be liberated in order to become his true self. The structure of the costume is modelled on a pull-out garland, using the silhouette of a man as its basic form. Placed on the floor the costume is entirely flat and only gains volume and shape as the performer rises. When the performer picks up the loose end of the garland and starts to swirl, the costume turns into a rotating monster with numerous limbs. The costume of *Peeled Shadows* appears

9.13
Sandra Becker, *Interior I*, 2012. Photograph by Petrov Ahner. © Sandra Becker.

9.14
Sandra Becker,
Peeled Shadows,
2013. © Sandra
Becker.

almost like a body, the dragon's body itself. The performance turns into a dance between the prince (the performer) and the dragon (the costume). For this choreography the costume acts as a script and as such takes the leading role in telling the story.

Besides experimental and conceptual works like *Goldesel*, *Interior I* and *Peeled Shadows*, I also design for more traditional theatre productions. In my experience the audience and the reviewing journalists of such shows are in general very keen on the artistry of the costumes – but only as long as they comply with their expectations and level of prettiness. Beyond that, costumes often fall into a void of invisibility. Yet both traditional and experimental costume have something in common from my point of view: a missing vocabulary to reflect on costume and its design. Leaving aside the amount of decoration – the hours spent on beadwork, the metres of fabric in a baroque skirt, the precision of a Victorian corset – how can we talk about costumes? What skills do we need to be able to decipher costumes as symbols, as signs and as a language? How can developing a costume vocabulary influence my design for the better? These are questions that gain more and more importance in my current work especially whilst designing for theatre for a young audience.

FRUZSINA NAGY (HUNGARY)

https://www.nagyfruzsina.com/
As a costume designer, Fruzsina Nagy is interested in the relationship between the human body and its surrounding world in every aspect: costumes, masks, make-up, fashion or visuals. The lack of resources that defined the Eastern and Central European milieu that she grew up in, has pushed her to rely heavily on her creativity and to think outside the box in order to overcome obstacles and

■ Insubordinate Costume

bring to life costumes and masks that are both challenging and have a storytelling capacity. As a visual theatre director, she is co-founder and co-creator of Catwalk Concert Productions, a performing art genre that merges a choir concert experience with theatre and a fashion show where singing models move around a catwalk-like stage in extreme and abstract costumes. She is currently a lecturer at the University of Fine Arts in Budapest.

When I'm working with a director, I work as part of a team taking instructions and collaborating on the mood and visual ideas, but when I'm directing or co-directing, creating something that is visual theatre, that comes completely from me so it's a really different process. Sometimes I have the idea for a costume or something visual before the topic has even been chosen.

I know it sounds like such a cliché but the *Taboo Collection*, 2016 (Figures 9.15 and 9.16), was really like a dream come true (https://catwalkconcert.com/). One night I dreamt the form of the performance: there were singing models on a stage that looked like the catwalk of a fashion show, and they were singing individually not in a group. I met Dóra Halas, the co-director friend of mine who has an experimental choir, and when I told her about this dream, she thought it sounded so interesting that she suggested we should try to create such a performance. At that time, I had no idea that we were going to make the performance about different taboos, because all I had was the idea of a completely new form of presenting costumes, with singing models performing in my extreme designs. Her choir always works together as a team and uses collective composing techniques, so I also involved them in choosing the topic of the performance. After we discarded the ideas that didn't inspire us, or that we thought were too difficult, surprisingly ninety percent of those left were taboos, so we decided that the performance

9.15
Fruzsina Nagy,
*Taboo Collection,
Wicked Wicked
Wicked.*
Source: Author.

The Practitioners' Voice

9.16
Fruzsina Nagy,
Taboo Collection,
SEX, 2016.
Photograph by
Gergő Nagy. ©
Fruzsina Nagy and
Gergő Nagy.

would have different sections where each taboo section would be like a big collection. I was very happy with this decision, because I was looking for something abstract, as I think music is very abstract, and I wanted to create costumes that are not just something that you can wear.

My costumes have humour, they often tell a story and they often change on stage. I love costumes which can change or can surprise, so it's not something that you see and understand immediately, but has secrets or an afterlife. The taboo of death was one of the most fun to make, because it is something that everybody is afraid of, but it is something that none of us can avoid. Some people fear it, some people accept it completely and take it as the cycle of life and some people celebrate it. We all have different attitudes, but everybody has some attitude or some connection, some thoughts and feelings about this. Therefore, it's a really great topic because, whatever you do on stage, it will wake up some emotions and thoughts in the audience. We wanted to approach the topic with humour because we didn't want to be too serious, so we decided to present a party where it became a kind of a competition to see who could perform the craziest death. The costumes are a bit like three-dimensional illustrations which narrate the taboos. There is a plane crash costume which you can only recognise from a certain angle, a black costume which lights up to reveal the shape of a skeleton, a singing trio who poison each other with apples that turn to cider and a costume that can only be worn by two people that was created for a co-dependent relationship between jealous couples who cannot live without each other, but cannot live with each other. And the last death was a religious Brazilian sect, who committed mass suicide by zipping themselves into costumes created by body-bags.

When I create my own performances, I have greater freedom as there's no script and nobody to tell me what to do, so I can just play around like a child. I started to experiment with this kind of a method on stage in 2002, when The

■ Insubordinate Costume

House of Contemporary Arts in Hungary asked me to make a fashion show with my costumes, so I decided to make a fashion circus. I wanted every costume to perform some kind of magic on stage and to change. I managed to organise about fifty people, the performance was really strong visually and a big success but sometimes I had trouble with performers implementing my ideas. For example, one of the costumes was for an actress reciting an English sonnet about a woman who compares herself to a garden, so I designed and created a huge Baroque-style costume from fake grass, with flowers growing out of the dress. The actress was supposed to garden the dress with gardening gloves, secateurs and a watering can whilst she walked up and down the catwalk reciting the poem, but she said she couldn't do all these things together and how dare I have such a stupid idea, so she just wore the watering can like a handbag.

In another performance several years later, I tried working with a group of sixteen actors in a summer workshop, but I completely restricted them with the strength of my costumes. I created costumes of different vehicles for them: a trolley bus, a Mercedes, a Trabant (East German car), a Jaguar, a Porche, a Suzuki jeep, a street-car, a police-car and so on, but although they were normally really great improvisers, the experiment was a complete failure because they told me that the costume said everything and they didn't really have a space to act. That was a very good lesson for me.

Collaborating with dancers works well, as dancing is an abstract language. Obviously, my crazy costumes completely restrict their movements so we always have to make some compromises in order for them to create great choreography without destroying my costumes. The choir are not actors, they don't want to perform, just to sing the songs, so the costume works as the performative part. The singing adds an extra level to my costumes. The second performance undertaken with the choir was called *The Issue*, 2018 (Figure 9.17), which I think has been the most successful so far in Hungary. It was based on Hungarian folk music but

9.17 Fruzsina Nagy, *The Issue, Silence Regulation Costumes*, sound dimming sponges and egg-boxes, red Lego pieces. Photograph by Márton Kovács. © Fruzsina Nagy and Márton Kovács.

there weren't any folk motifs in the costumes, they were completely abstract. It was set in an imaginary mayor's office where people go to deal with their issues like maternity benefits, pensions, tax payments, all things bureaucratic, and the costumes reflected these. The Estate Agents for example had beer bellies which became huge skirts that had ground plans of buildings printed on them. They revealed their true selves when the singers started to turn in them like Dervishes.

In 2005 I worked with a film director and together we created a show called *Recycled*. It was a very interesting way to work because he created a short three-minute film, and I responded with my costumes on stage which then inspired him to create another short movie. We took the subject of recycled in a broad sense, which included, for example, recycling personalities, reincarnation and organ transplants, because in my mind these are kinds of recycling, too. I always love to stretch boundaries and try to experiment with things that are not possible. I'm really trying to get some funding to make a course, that I want to call Mission Impossible, where students have six months to create impossible ideas. I love experimenting with unusual techniques, like costumes inflating with ventilators, or sound sensitive lights. I think that, with my costumes, humour is even more important to me than aesthetics, which is quite a funny thing for a visual artist to say. I believe that if the costume is humorous or presents something more than what is seen at first glance, it's much more interesting than creating something really beautiful. I don't think I'm patient enough to do something really detailed, when I have an idea, I really want to see if it works straight away. I have to learn to be a bit more patient and give things time.

I'm very critical with myself sometimes and when a costume doesn't come out the way I want it, I want to cancel the whole scene. I also love to perfect ideas. I've used fans four or five different times to inflate costumes, I use a special fabric for them so the costumes don't burst. I always experiment to find the right fabric and the right shapes. I like to create costumes that don't exist, that aren't something you can buy. I'm trying to be as sustainable as possible but if I have a crazy idea, and I really want to do it, to be honest, I don't think much about sustainability I just go for it, but I don't know how much longer I can work with that attitude. Not just because I am judged by others, but because I judge myself.

SIMONA RYBÁKOVÁ (CZECH REPUBLIC)

Simona Rybáková is a Czech costume designer and independent researcher who studied at the University of Applied Arts in Prague, Helsinki and at the RISD in Providence, Rhode Island, United States. Her work includes designs for opera, drama, dance, film, TV, special events and multimedia. She was the head of the Costume Design sub-commission for OISTAT from 2015 to 2023 and is a member of the Czech and European film Academy. She curated the Extreme Costumes exhibition at PQ11. She was awarded the Swarovski Award 1996, PQ 1999 Golden Triga and prize for best costumes at World Stage Design in Cardiff 2013, Taipei 2017 and Calgary 2022. She works, lectures and exhibits internationally and in 2023 was appointed head of Fashion Design at the Academy of Arts, Architecture, and Design in Prague.

■ **Insubordinate Costume**

I strive to be an equal and creative partner to the directors I work with and all my creative collaborators. I never set self-censoring limits at the beginning of the creative process and aim for a sophisticatedly simple costume for the end result that helps the actor interact with the director to create a character that is understandable to all audiences. I have been fortunate in my creative life to have met directors for whom costume is an integral and important part of the stage expression. Thus, it very often happens that in the creative process of preparing a production, we search together for visual metaphors in the interaction between set and costume. My costumes are not subservient but autonomous, they try to be 'literary' in the sense that they tell stories by themselves, they are spectacles without any sense of ostentatiousness. Where the costume is the main driver and inspiration for the plot, its materiality, movement and shape transformations are guided by the physical action of the performer and always tend towards a non-verbal type of performance that communicates directly with the audience through image and sound. This is the case, for example, in the performances *Bon Appetit*, *Eastern Bloc*, the *Tribute to Rudolf II* or the opening and closing ceremonies at the *Karlovy Vary International Film Festival*.

When working with the directing duo Skutr (Martin Kukučka and Lukáš Trpišovský), on projects such as *Egon Schiele – Self Portrait* (Figures 9.18 and 9.19),

9.18
Simona Rybáková, *Egon Schiele – Self Portrait*, revolving stage in Český Krumlov, 2023. Photograph by Pavel Hejný. © Simona Rybáková.

9.19
Simona Rybáková, *Egon Schiele – Self Portrait*, revolving stage in Český Krumlov, 2023. Photograph by Pavel Hejný. © Simona Rybáková.

together with either Jakub Kopecký or Martin Chocholoušek as set designer, it is very intense at the beginning during the conceptual and spatial design phases of the production. This is where the decision is made as to whether the costume or the set or another element will play a bigger role. Often, we specify the function of the costume, or what we need from it first and finding a functional form is my creative task afterwards. If we want this interaction to work, it is essential to produce a working prototype for the whole rehearsal process. Only then is the costume integrated and accepted by the actor naturally as part of their means of expression. I have to build a sense of trust between me and the performer so that they know that my costume will help them to express themselves strongly on stage, even though it may not look like it at first. I will introduce them to the costume design and the intended material and we will discuss possible limits, pitfalls or their personal animosities together. I am open to any discussion as long as it is guided by the desire for a common understanding. If I feel some block on the part of the performer and I cannot remove it, I will call on the help of the director or choreographer who can explain certain situations more precisely or in more detail. For more complex costumes that have extra stage interaction, we work gradually with prototypes in the dressing room, and then on set. I am present for any adjustments that will lead to the intended result until the final rehearsals. I look for compromise and step back when I see that the costume brings complications and uncertainty for the performer. I will not back down if I see reluctance and laziness on their part.

I have always experimented with materials since the beginning of my costume career. Alternative and specific materials in costume design are also described in one chapter of my PhD dissertation. At first, the experiments were more of an economic necessity, now this approach has become part of my professional DNA. I find that enthusiasm and the willingness to play and explore are important characteristics to have in order to keep moving creatively and not to burn out. Sometimes I have a concept before I start making costumes and sometimes the costumes evolve from experimentation. Both ways go hand in hand in my creative process, the degree of which depends on the type of show as a grand opera, where you need to be very prepared beforehand, is different to an experimental original dance show where costume experimentation is part of the concept. With the dramatic form, the conceptual decision always comes first. I need to know who and what my character is, what their relationship is to the other characters, the environment they are in, what they express, what social bubble they belong to, what drama they bring, and many other aspects. Aesthetic form is what I look for secondarily. But, if I am creating a unique costume-object or an installation, the aesthetic consideration of form is usually primary and the deeper meaning is defined by subsequent interpretations. For dance performances and installations, the collaboration with the choreographer and dancer is very intense and the result is a team effort. If the performers are to express movement on stage, we always call on a choreographer to collaborate. I solve the construction and shape of the costume together with them, rather than with the director, and together we discuss the limitations of the costume and the performer. We know from experience how far we can go with actors and dancers who have different technical skills.

Dancers often perform very demanding physical performances and it is important that the costume does not hinder them or lead to injury.

Costume has always been a very important and significant artistic discipline but, until recently, it has never had as much social attention as scenography or architecture, for example. This is probably partly related to the gender issue, as traditionally costume has been a predominantly female profession. Costume is a significant phenomenon of contemporary society.

ZUZU HUDEK (SLOVAKIA)

www.zuzuhudek.com

Zuzu Hudek is a freelance stage and costume designer as well as teaching art classes and leading creative workshops for professionals, young people and children. She is a member of the OISTAT costume design group and is a general manager for Slovak OISTAT centre PRO SCENA. During her career as writer, director and artist, she has won several grants to create small independent projects and art installations.

During my career I have always tried to design costumes which do not only function as decoration and garment, but also include meanings and character transformation. My costume designs oscillate between sculpture, objects and performative installation. My intention is to create costumes which transform or metamorphose during the performance. They change their shape and function together with the performers' movement. The body is hidden inside the costume and looks like an inanimate object. The body starts to appear when the performer moves inside. Frequently my costumes interact with the space and, together with the body of the performer, create scenography.

The main aim of the funded research project *METAMORPHOSE*, 2021–23, was to create costumes that would change their appearance and form whilst on

9.20
Zuzu Hudek, *METAMORPHOSIS*.
Photograph by Simona Babjaková.
© Zuzu Hudek and Simona Babjaková.

stage through the movement of the performer's body and the use of lighting and sound. The costumes and objects were created first and then the performers were given the freedom to experiment and to find the boundaries and limitations of each piece. The costumes and objects, together with the expressive movements of the body, depicted different human states such as illness, depression and ageing.

The costumes for the *METAMORPHOSIS* dance performance shaped Barbora Janáková's choreography and the whole concept of the performance (Figures 9.20 and 9.21). The process of transformation in adolescence offered a huge number of subtopics including changes in the body, self-evaluation, the search for identity, an unclear future, social events and the uncontrolled influence of social networks. The creative team drew on their memories, feelings, sensations and thoughts about the period in which they were shaped into adulthood, and seventy young respondents filled out a questionnaire, the results of which documented a variety of fashion styles, musical genres and world views. The costumes were made from various recycled materials, pieces of clothing, forms and shapes.

The collaboration with the performer is a very important aspect of my work. The costume is built together with the body and the choreography as I 'sculpt' the costume together with the performer and choreographer. Often in my work the performer is asked to operate some parts of the costume which means that these movements must be integrated into the choreography. I love to experiment with materials. It is always a big challenge for me to create a costume from a material other than a textile. I have already experimented with recycled plastic bags, plastic bottles, paper, various upholstery materials, metal and wood. For one costume in the *Eastern Bloc* production, I decided to create a costume out of

9.21
Zuzu Hudek,
METAMORPHOSIS.
Photograph by
Natália Zajačiková.
© Zuzu Hudek and
Natália Zajačiková.

wood veneer. It was a long process to find the most suitable technology to sew the parts together but the costume representing a wooden Slovakian weekend cottage worked much better on stage than if it had been made from ordinary textiles. The performer was somehow trapped in the shelter.

My costumes are not purely aesthetical, they always have a deeper meaning. Rather than just designing garments, I prefer to go deeper into the role, characterisation and vision, to experiment and give the costume another meaning. I start with a concept, but, as I always create prototypes and use unconventional materials, I often have to make changes and customise the costume during the process because I cannot predict how the material will behave. I continually experiment with movement whilst I am building the costumes as my costumes are mainly based on the idea of transformation through movement. It is therefore important to have time to play together with the performer. During the process of developing a costume, I produce models and sketches in order to try out different variations, material possibilities and construction methods before I create the final costume. My designs always constrain the performer and dictate their style of movement; very often the costumes generate the choreography. The wooden costume in the *Eastern Bloc* project only allowed the performer to walk sideways, which inspired the choreography and made the character more interesting.

In Slovakia, many directors and choreographers are still scared to experiment with costume and prefer the traditional 'afterthought' costume design. They do not like the costumes to constrain the performer and do not want to use the costume as inspiration. Mostly, it is a matter of time and money as rehearsal times are very short and there is no time left for experimentation. The budget and management do not allow us to fail and try again. I like to have free space to play and sculpt the costumes in collaboration with dancers, actors, choreographers and directors, however this does not happen very often. The *Eastern Bloc* project, led by costume designer Fruzsina Nagy, was an ideal collaboration as the costumes and their inspirations were discussed much earlier than any other parts of the performance. Suddenly I had a feeling that all my crazy thoughts, sketches and designs were supported and taken up with pleasure. The collaboration gave me the opportunity to bring all my ideas onto the stage. I think all costume designers should have the opportunity to experience creative freedom and to be able to push themselves beyond their limits, even at the risk of failure.

THE *EASTERN BLOC* CATWALK PROJECT

Fruzsina Nagy, Simona Rybáková, Zuzu Hudek and Dorota Kuzniarska
https://catwalkconcert.com/eastern-bloc/
The Eastern Bloc Catwalk Project was based on the collective memories of four Eastern Bloc designers who took inspiration from the ex-communist-socialist era. Designers Fruzsina Nagy from Hungary, Simona Rybáková from the Czech Republic, Zuzu Hudek from Slovakia and Dorota Kuzniarska from Poland, together with composer Dóra Halas and the Soharóza Choir, created a catwalk concert, a performing arts genre somewhere between theatre, a choral concert and an

extreme fashion show. The performances are themed and feature a group of performers who present vibrant, innovative, storytelling costumes on a thrust stage, whilst singing contemporary compositions. In this way, the music and the costumes themselves become the two main protagonists.

The first step in our creative process was for the four costume designers to talk about our collective memory living in the ex-communist system. Although we all come from different backgrounds and experience, we set up our creative process together with given priorities. What was important was absolute artistic freedom, brainstorming without self-censorship, accepting each other's ideas without interference or limitations, building on and connecting with each other's ideas, perceiving ideas and comments that reflected our different historical, generational and territorial experiences. We did not set up any hierarchy and worked in a democratic system where each of us had an equal say. An important aspect of the whole collaboration was our mutual trust, generosity and non-competitiveness, with everyone working towards the best possible final result. The costumes were developed after several meetings, discussions and workshops as well as collecting references, memories and visual materials. At the same time the choir members discussed the topics and rehearsed sound and music ideas. After several weeks we made a final decision on the collections and single costumes. Some of the collections were designed by a single designer, others as a collaboration between designers.

Because we wanted to perform *Eastern Bloc* in all four countries with a local singer, each designer had the special task of designing and creating a costume for their local singer playing the *Red Demon*. Fruzsina Nagy's costume was inspired by the communist badges you receive if you are a good worker. These metal badges were attached to a red velvet dress and made the costume very heavy, symbolising the restrictions of the communist era. Other costumes included some that were printed with panel housing inspired by the 'Kádár-cube' concrete blocks of flats, typical of the 1960s, that Fruzsina passed on her way to school every day for eight years. Her funniest costume was a Meteorology costume which inflated with a built-in ventilator and had magnetic attachments on it.

The *Spartakiada* pompom costumes (Figure 9.22) were inspired by a big event in the former Czechoslovakia which served as communist propaganda to show how happy and healthy people were. First Simona collected visual references from 1980 from her personal experience, as she took part in the event as a seventeen-year-old girl. She designed the costume and made a prototype of the skirt which did not work at first because the rope she used was too soft and tangled together. She tried several different methods before finding that the best solution was to use cable ties and nylon thread. It was a frustrating situation, but this often happen with experimenting. The costumes were then photographed in the studio as preparation for a video which was used as a projection onstage. Simona and Fruzsina collaborated on the costume designs for *Lalaton* (Figure 9.23) that were inspired by summer holidays on the Balaton, the Hungarian lake – inflatable toys, tents, rubber rings, knee-high water.

Zuzu Hudek's *Factory Costumes* (Figure 9.24) were a big challenge as she had the idea to create a skirt that transformed into a conveyor belt but had never

■ Insubordinate Costume

9.22
Simona Rybáková, *Eastern Bloc Spartakiada* pom-pom costumes. Photograph by István Juhász. © István Juhász.

created such complicated and demanding costumes in her native Slovakia before. The factory workers wore the conveyor belt costumes for the other actors to use. The fact that the conveyor belts really worked and made sounds brought a stronger industrial atmosphere into the scene. Working on these costumes inspired Zuzu in her subsequent practice research into costumes that can function as moving object and scenography.

Although the *Eastern Bloc* project bought a lot of challenges, such as coordinating the production of several complicated costumes remotely, financial limitations and little rehearsal time as the choir is non-professional and everyone has other jobs, it was an absolutely unique experience for all of us. Despite its large

9.23
Fruzsina Nagy and Simona Rybáková, *Eastern Bloc Lalaton* costumes. Photograph by István Juhász. © István Juhász.

9.24
Zuzu Hudek,
*Eastern Bloc,
Factory Costume*.
Photograph by
István Juhász. ©
Zuzu Hudek and
István Juhász.

scale, we managed to create a unique atmosphere rooted in mutual respect and openness to new ideas, regardless of experience, background or age.

SENSE AND SENSATION

The phenomenological philosopher Merleau-Ponty theorised that, since experience consists of both mental and bodily experience, thought and perception are embodied and the body is fundamental to our understanding as 'we perceive the world with our body' (Merleau-Ponty 2013: 206). Our senses are crucial in helping us to understand the world around us. Whilst costumes naturally have a visual aspect, they can also activate other senses, both for the performer and for the audience. Several contemporary designers aim to activate the senses by incorporating touch, sound and even smell into their work whilst others investigate the difference between hearing and listening or the pervasive but less tangible sense of grief.

Performance artist and researcher Madaleine Trigg works closely with natural materials, such as dough and unprocessed wool, directly on her body in order to 'uncover a more intimate understanding of the material by moving with(in) it' (Trigg). Laura Marnezti's costumes 'generate a soundscape by interacting with the performers' bodies' (Marnezti) whilst Charlotte Østergaard's work explores the 'performative potentialities of costume materialities' through listening and co-creativity (Østergaard). Saudi Arabian designer Shahd Albahwash's work 'enhances the olfactory senses by emitting the smell of burning oud ... a dark, oily, wood-scented resin' (Albahwash) whereas designer and director Daniela Portillo Cisterna's sonorous costume for *ALMA Y MUERTOS* leads the audience in a silent and emotional, processional 'mortuary rite [to] connect us with those loved ones who are no longer with us' (Portillo Cisterna).

■ Insubordinate Costume

MADALEINE TRIGG (UK)

Madaleine Trigg is a performance artist, photographer, researcher and lecturer. Her solo, Sutre, featured a dress that disintegrated throughout the performance. Created with costume designers, Francisca Rios and Cristina Valls, Sutre was exhibited at Extreme Costume (2011 Prague Quadrennial), longlisted for the Aesthetica Art Prize (2013) and transformed into a hologram with Musion (Kinetica Art Fair, 2011). Madaleine has performed at the Southbank Centre, Institute of Contemporary Arts, V & A museum, The Roundhouse, National Theatre Studios, Royal College of Art and The Place. Her practice has been presented internationally in Brussels, Cologne, Helsinki, Prague, Porto, Vitoria-Gasteiz, Wellington and Zagreb. Madaleine completed her practice-based PhD in 2023 at the College of Creative Arts, Massey University, with a thesis entitled 'From Dough to Wheat: A Posthuman Performance Practice with Companion Species'.

Materials. Their characteristics and interactions with other bodies fascinate me, leading me to an embodied approach to costuming within performance. Starting in the studio, I bring big bundles of the material to work with. I spend time touching, smelling, listening and wearing. As a performer my instincts are to move within the material, discovering its subtleties and idiosyncrasies. The costume is formed out of physical frictions between my body and the various materials I have explored.

I am naked. During these improvisations my whole body comes into close contact with the material. It becomes a sensuous second skin that I move in. The aesthetic of these works is stripped back. Focusing on the moving materials and bodies foregrounds the encounter. These works stretch conceptions of costuming as the materials that cover my body are continually in flux and alive. Resisting completion and dwelling in acts of costuming focuses on the agency of these materials.

The materials I collaborate with are often modest, malleable and unprocessed, such as wool and dough. The palpable associations these materials have to 'women's work', domesticity and labour are important threads within these performances. Scaling up the quantity of material so that it is not manageable by my hands alone, means that it is necessary to engage my whole body or invite others to help me in the making process. Felting and kneading these massive amounts magnifies the material's agency. I persist with the process of making rather than completing a costume. I have never wanted to create a resolved garment.

Felt Me (Figure 9.25) evolved during a residency in Freising (Germany, 2013). Living at the Europäisches Kunstforum Oberbayern, affectionately known as 'Schafhof' ('Sheep House') I was struck by the absence of these animals. I learnt to felt from a local female artist, spending an afternoon transforming white wool, warm water and a bar of olive oil soap into textiles.

'Would you like to felt me?'

In *Felt Me*, I wrapped 2 kilos of white wool around my body and invited the audience to felt a garment onto me. This ambiguous question drew audiences to me and I conversed with them to create a convivial atmosphere where they felt comfortable working so closely with me. Circulating, rubbing, caressing and pressing,

9.25
Madaleine Trigg, *Felt Me*, 2013. Photograph by Inès Dümig.

the different directions, intensities and qualities of the audiences' movements were captured within the fabric(ation) of the costume. Over several hours the felted dress traced encounters between multiple bodies and materials, becoming a tangible record of those interactions. The performance was a collaborative process of costuming.

Felt Me was an opportunity for audiences to immerse themselves in a material encounter, co-creating with other human and non-human bodies. Felting on my body created ambiguities as to what was being touched. Were the audiences touching my skin, the wool or felt? Skins and bodies became confused and entangled through feeling and felting. This shifted experiences of costuming in performance from the visual to the visceral. In these embodied encounters, the dual definition of felt, as both past sensations and fabric, merge.

Whilst the initial performance was site-specific, subsequent performances in Wellington (Aotearoa/New Zealand) and London have focused more on the distinctive qualities that different breeds of local sheep and their wool bring.

Participants have been respectful, playful, curious and absorbed in the work. Diverse demographics participated in this dialogic process, with lots of conversation and laughter as they fumbled through, learning together. Felt is the oldest handmade textile and is unique as the wool fibres don't need to directly touch to form into a whole. However, touch is essential for the fabric to materialise. Indeed, friction and agitation make the felt stronger. Moving bodies are integral to this process of co-creation. Multiple human and non-human bodies become deeply entangled in the making of new memories and materialities through felting.

■ Insubordinate Costume

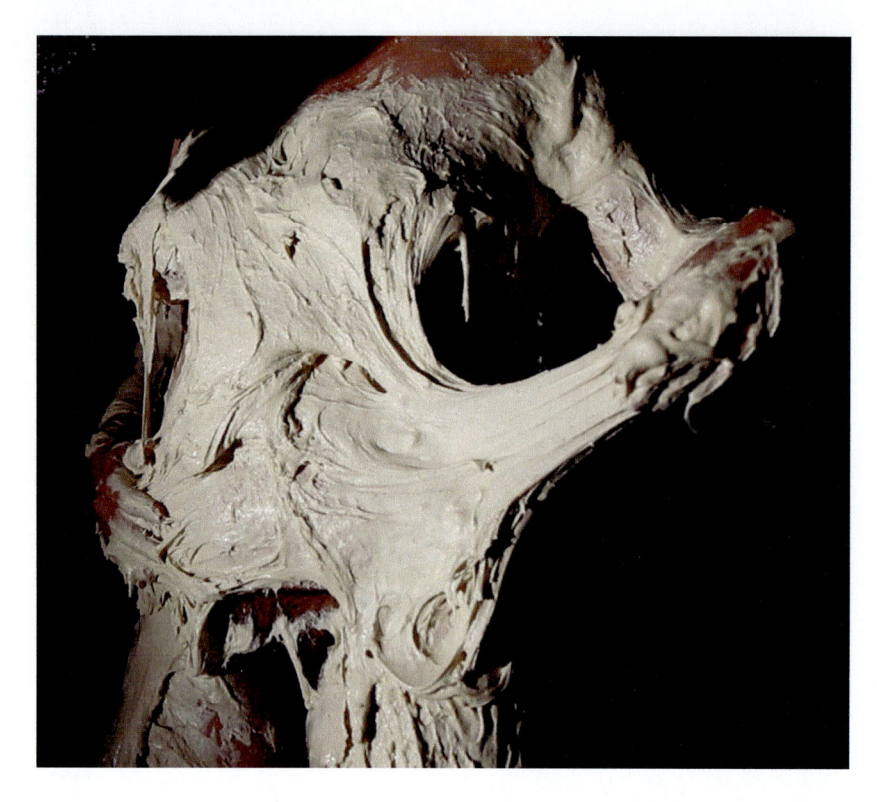

9.26
Madaleine Trigg and Simon Donger, *Knead (Still)*, 2018–19.

Recently my practice and research have dwelt on dough (Figure 9.26). Dough appealed to me as it resembled another body, growing over time and moving of its own accord. In a black box studio, I poured litres of warm water onto a pile of white flour, watching the liquid ooze before being absorbed. I spent an hour kneading fifteen kilos of dough, rolling it into thick sheets that were ready to wear. My collaborator, Simon Donger would quickly manoeuvre the dough onto my bare shoulders. The camera was on. I felt the weight press down on me as soon as it came into contact with my body. As I tried to move, my balance was destabilised by the dough and it brought me closer to the ground as it covered me. In other experiments the gluten was so strong my hands were stuck to my body. It was difficult to clean my body too, bits of dough stubbornly clung onto me, hiding in the creases of my skin.

I consider this an act of costuming as the dough was covering my body and I was wearing it; indeed the dough wasn't static, it moved with me, like a second skin. However, the dough forced me to move in surprising ways, as if it was wearing me as much as I was wearing it. Whilst dough is a domestic material, it isn't subordinate. Dough isn't easily modelled or moulded onto my body, instead it reconfigured my movements. The tactility of the encounter was also more pronounced than with other textiles as it kept reminding me of its heavy and sticky presence.

In these explorations the inability to separate myself easily from the dough led to a more porous understanding of intersections between bodies, skin and costuming. This practice is connected by a conviction that material bodies aren't separate entities but instead co-constitute each other. As such, an embodied approach to costuming can touch us deeply by revealing the intricate interactions between materials and bodies that invariably shape us.

LAURA MARNEZTI (MEXICO)

http://www.marnezti.design

Laura Marnezti is a theatre designer and visual artist, interested in interdisciplinary projects focused on the research, design and creation of stage costumes which are based on the exploration of materials and the integration of sculptural values. She participated in the Prague Quadrennial in 2011, 2019 and 2023 and in Critical Costume 2020 and 2022 and her work won third place at World Stage Design 2022. She is part of the independent association for stage costume artists, Vestuario A Escena, in Mexico.

For me, designing costumes means creating a space that will stimulate a dialogue between the body and the environment. It is common that, to create a costume, the designer must be guided by a character or dramatic text; however, I believe that there is always a different way to create. In my case, I begin to explore other methods by integrating sculptural values into the design, in order to find other discursive possibilities in form, matter and space. An example of this is the costume design entitled *Inhabiting Noise and Silence*. This is a personal project that was inspired by the desire to create the costumes without resorting to a dramatic text or character analysis, and from there to develop the stage piece.

The concept arose after studying 'soundscape', a notion developed by R. Murray Schafer, who describes a 'soundscape [as something that] consists of events heard, not objects seen'.[3] I began to reflect on how the sounds of the environment affect my mood and my behaviour. Spaces change and with them the sounds we hear, there are sounds that take us to another space and time. For the concept of the *Inhabiting Noise and Silence* costumes (Figures 9.27 and 9.28), I focused on the idea of creating a design which could generate a soundscape by interacting with the performers' bodies. I began to investigate projects and sound sculptures by the Baschet brothers, Max Eastley, Reinhold Marxhausen and Etienne Krähenbühl, but my greatest inspiration was the percussionist Evelyn Glennie who perceives sound through the vibrations that reach her body since she lost her sense of hearing.

After extensive research on space and sound, I began to make sketches, which was useless, since sound is impossible to illustrate on paper. Later I resorted to making express pieces, quick prototypes of an idea, or some activity such as object art or installation inspired by the concepts behind the project. I explored different forms and materials; but, whilst looking for possible materials I was given some plastic bags and, in the end, this was the material that I decided to explore in sound and form for the development of the costumes. The costume was built using recycled plastic bags to form structured panels that functioned as resonators, as the circulation of air caused a sound landscape similar to the sound of the sea to be generated.

■ **Insubordinate Costume**

9.27
Laura Marnezti sketches for *Inhabiting Noise and Silence*, 2018. © Laura Marnezti.

The Practitioners' Voice

9.28
Laura Marnezti, *Inhabiting Noise and Silence*, 2019. © Laura Marnezti.

177

■ Insubordinate Costume

I integrate sculptural values into my costume designs, mainly form, matter, space and time. I'm interested in exploring the interrelation between the costume, the body and the space/environment. In the research I did for my master's degree, I named my pieces proxemic devices. that is, through them, movement can be controlled and the relationship between the person wearing the costume and what surrounds them can be established.

Some of the premises for designing proxemic devices are:

- Thinking of the costume as a proxemic device where artistic themes can arise from any nature or field.
- Reflecting on the creation of a living space
- Analysing the behaviour of the material and assigning it an intention
- Thinking 'activation' instead of 'acting'
- Considering sculptural values as guides for action
- Conceiving costume as a dramatic motor for the scenic piece

When collaborating with the performers, it was important to share knowledge from our different areas. Carol Cervantes, who is a dancer, choreographer and poet, joined the project together with musician, performer and writer, Diego Cristian Saldaña. The work sessions were very precise and we explored movement, sound and the construction of the sculptures as we shared the vital elements of our disciplines. In this way, the costumes developed beyond an aesthetic purpose, as the concept and meaning grew deeper.

The interaction of the performers' bodies with the costumes led to the creation of ephemeral sculptures. At times the choreography creates a soundscape similar to the sound of the sea, at other times the costumes become sound sculptures where more sounds are explored. After the performance, the costumes are shared with the public so that they can explore, inhabit and create a unique and unrepeatable sound landscape for themselves. The movement of the costumes, in addition to the soundscapes, allows us to create different visual landscapes, the material of the costumes invites us to move in a certain way, as if the costumes become the director or choreographer.

With this project I have observed how a costume can become a space to be inhabited as well as a meeting point. When we presented the work at the Prague Quadrennial in 2019, it was not necessary to speak the same language since the costume served as a guide to our interactions. Costumes can arise from any topic that is of interest to us and I believe that costume is a very powerful means of expression. By involving the body, the costume invites us to think about movement, about space, about matter, about different contexts. For me, the costume is an artistic piece since it is built from specific references, it dialogues with the public and can change paradigms in addition to disrupting the body of those who inhabit it and those who observe it.

The Practitioners' Voice ■

9.29
Shahd Albahwash,
sketch for *The Wind
of Good*, 2023. ©
Shahd Albahwash.

9.30
Shahd Albahwash,
The Wind of Good,
2023. © Shahd
Albahwash.

179

■ Insubordinate Costume

SHAHD ALBAWASH (SAUDI ARABIA)

Shahd Albahwash is from Jeddah in Saudi Arabia. She holds a Master's Degree in Art and Fashion and is undertaking a PhD programme in Fashion Design, studying parade costumes. In 2023, she took part in a Costume Design course organised by the Saudi Fashion Commission, Dar Al-Hekma University in Jeddah and Fashion Academies ITS Cosmo and AFOL Moda in Milan. Students created their own characters that reflected their interests and incorporated various aspects of Saudi culture.

All my ideas come from conceptual notions and thinking deeply about a subject in order to find and show different aesthetic paths of meaning. Usually, I start with a concept in my mind and develop it with many sketches, then I experiment during construction with both techniques and movement which is a very important aspect of my costumes. My design for the costume *The Wind of Good* (Figures 9.29 and 9.30) was inspired by Saudi Arabian culture and the generosity and the warmth of the welcome we offer to guests and visitors. Giving a gift of Oud perfume is a tradition deeply rooted in Arab culture and one of the warmest welcomes we offer in Saudi Arabia as it shows a person how much they mean to us. Oud is a dark, oily, wood-scented resin which forms in the heartwood of the agar tree when it becomes infected with mould and it is one of the most expensive raw fragrance ingredients in the world. In Saudi Arabia we burn the resin as incense on a *bakhoor* or use it as an ingredient for perfume. My costume symbolises the burning of oud.

    The base of the costume is a welded-metal spiral structure on wheels and an air conditioner vent hose, on top of which I attached fabric to simulate flames and smoke and coloured lights for effect. I worked with lots of elements and tried many experiments in order to find the right fabric to achieve the shape and colour shades I was looking for. In the end the flames were created with lurex organza and recycled fabrics and constructed with manipulation techniques made with glue and paint. The costume enhances the olfactory senses by emitting the smell of burning oud through the hose which I pierced with small holes. The performer is an integral part of the artwork. Dressed in a pale pink sheath dress, she is elevated in the centre of the costume with the fabric flames and smoke swirling around her as she dances. The audience can move around and view the performance from all sides. The costume for *The Wind of Good* is central to the performance. Nowadays costume is acknowledged as fundamentally important in all areas of performance … this acknowledgement should have happened before!

CHARLOTTE ØSTERGAARD (DENMARK)

https://www.charlotteostergaardcopenhagen.dk/
Charlotte Østergaard is a Danish costume/textile/fashion designer/artist, educator, and researcher. She has designed costumes for more than sixty-five performances including contemporary dance companies like Dansk Dance Theater (DK), Skånes Dansteater (SE) and Rambert Dance Theatre (UK) and received several grants from the Danish Art Foundation. Her artworks have been exhibited at curated exhibitions

in Canada, China, Denmark, Germany, Norway, Russia, Ukraine and United States, and her designs are in the museum collections of the Design Museum Denmark and The National Gallery of Denmark. Charlotte's independent costume-driven performances have been shown, among others, at the 15th Prague Quadrennial for Performance space and Design, CZ (2023), SWOP – international dance festival, DK (2022) and at the Metropolis festival Wa(l)king Copenhagen, DK (2020). Her costumed performance-project AweAre was nominated for the biennale prize at The Biennale for Craft & Design, DK (2019) and received an Excellence Award at From Lausanne to Beijing – 11th International Fiber Art Biennale, CN (2020).

In my artistic research and pedagogical practice, I search for co-creative spaces where our (me and whomever I collaborate or entangle with; human or non-human) 'mode of production' can contain tangible and intangible 'things' that might be surprising and/or lead in unexpected directions. In creative, performative, and/or pedagogical situations, for example, I 'play' with different ways that we, as designers, performers, audiences, students, teachers and others, can participate and explore ways of creating temporal communities, where we co-creatively explore performative potentialities of costume materialities. I have no intention of directing the participants to embody or inhabit a costume or a situation according to my own predefined vision or to position myself hierarchically above those human and non-human elements that participate.

Over the years I have crafted multiple versions of costume that physically connect people. (Here, I use the word craft to suggest that design and making are entangled.) The subjective experience of wearing these connecting costumes is affected by the movements of the fellow wearers. I intentionally use the noun *wearers* to suggest that everyone, whether performer, designer, audience or other, is invited to explore the impact of being connected to one or more wearer. The *Community Walk* project is an example of how I use these connecting costumes. In this project, I play with the roles that designers, performers, and audiences have in 'traditional' costume and performance settings. For example, as a costume designer I am often placed outside as a witness that watches how someone else is affected by the costume that I have crafted. Hence, in the first version of the *Community Walk* (2020), I decided to place myself in the centre of the wearing experience. For twelve hours I walked in the centre of Copenhagen, Denmark, dressed in a bright yellow costume that I had crafted in stretchable textiles (Figures 9.31 and 9.32), which connected me to the twelve guests that I had invited to participate, one hour with each guest. Prior to the walk I planned a detailed route and created five simple rituals that I would repeat with each guest. These I shared with my guests, but I had no idea what we would experience.

In the first instance of entering the costume most of my guests expressed that they had an unpleasant sensation, an 'extreme' self-awareness of being exposed in public. Even though they and I were extremely exposed in the urban environment (and some people that passed us at a distance felt it was ok to yell insults), the connectedness of the costume somehow created a shared space between us. During the twelve hours, and with all twelve guests, I experienced situations where urban/nature elements caught their/our attention. Thus, trees,

■ Insubordinate Costume

9.31
Charlotte Østergaard, *Community Walk,* Metropolis festival Wa(l)king Copenhagen, DK, 2020. Still of video by Benjamin Skop. © Charlotte Østergaard.

9.32
Charlotte Østergaard, *Community Walk, Metropolis Festival Wa(l)king* Copenhagen, DK, 2020. Photograph by Benjamin Skop. © Charlotte Østergaard.

street signs, lampposts, building columns, different kind of roadblocks, and other urban/nature elements became sites of shared exploration. In these situations, we explored how the elements 'invited' us to stretch the connection and/or we tried to include the elements by moving around, tangling, hanging, or leaning on them. Other elements, like the wind, were sometimes present momentarily, which made us explore how we could catch the wind and transform the connection to create a parachute. In these moments, it felt as though the wind directed our orientation and movements. Several of my guests had an urge to invite people passing by into our costumed connection, therefore, in various situations, we explored ways in which passersby could be invited to join, for example, to jump over or crawl between the connection. The most successful interactions between

182

us and people passing by were situations when we focused on capturing their attention by making eye contact whilst we were standing still.

These are just a few of the embodied experiences that the first version of the *Community Walk* fostered. With this experience I met the costume that I had crafted on new terms. The costume also allowed my guest and I to explore the environment in a new way or on other terms than in our daily life. Even though the costume exposed us and prevented us from 'hiding' or 'blending in' to the urban environment, I am still amazed by the openness and playfulness of my guests. As a costume designer, I gained deeper understanding for other perspectives through this experience, for example I now understand what dancers mean when they talk about 'an embodied archive' – when I close my eyes, the experience is still vivid in my body.

Since the first version of *Community Walk*, I have hosted multiple walks on multiple occasions: at conferences, at performance festivals, in educational situations or with groups of friends. What amazes me is that none of the situations are alike. Each event forms a new constellation that allows me to learn with and from those that are present. As such the *Community Walk* project has taught me that costume is never static. Costume is a site for shared exploration. It is a privilege to have practiced my profession for more than thirty years and to discover that costume practice can still be new and fresh and that there are multiple things to explore together with human and non-human others. This excites me.

DANIELA PORTILLO CISTERNA (CHILE)

https://www.instagram.com/portafolio.portillocisterna

Daniela Portillo Cisterna is a Latin American artist from Northern Chile. She is a Performance Designer and Professor of Arts, with an MA in Theory and History of Arts and MA in Performance Design. Daniela runs the Regional Training Program of Scenic Design in Chile and is the coordinator of the Scenic Design Diploma at the University of Chile.

My design ethos is based on seeing design as a narrative in itself. I passionately believe in its power beyond imposed hierarchies. We are in an era where we can push boundaries and blur disciplinary lines and verticalities. Along with this, we must work towards democratising the knowledge of our profession, decentralising our work, and extending it to other territories that have not had access to learn or practice design from an authorial and more horizontal logic.

My performance *ALMA Y MUERTOS* (SOUL AND DEATH) was a challenge to break away from those rigid structures. For a very long time, I desired to extend my practices beyond tradition and the notion of roles that are so fixed. In that sense, in this project, the costume plays a fundamental part in the performance, as it directly connects with the audience to create an experience without an associated text, where the costume and its materials act as the narrative conductor. *ALMA Y MUERTOS* (Figures 9.33 and 9.34) is a ritual performance exploring the funeral rites of Northern Chile as a way of connecting with those we've lost. This performance was created in honour of Germán Droghetti, a great master professor and theatrical designer from Chile, who died of COVID-19 in 2020.

■ **Insubordinate Costume**

9.33
Daniela Portillo
Cisterna, *ALMA Y MUERTOS*, 2022.
Photograph by Jois
Ann. © Daniela
Portillo Cisterna.

9.34
Daniela Portillo
Cisterna, *ALMA Y MUERTOS* Prague
Quadrennial, 2023.
Photograph by
Susan Marshall.
© Daniela Portillo
Cisterna.

The purpose of the production was to involve the audience in the idea of a journey and, through it, to construct a mortuary rite that would connect us with those loved ones who are no longer with us. Since the ultimate goal was to elevate this experience in the audiences through the costume, my role as director and designer directly intersected with the costume. The costume instigated the performance through the concept of the procession as well as through its materialities that are not only visual but also sonorous. The costume was entirely sewn and dyed by hand by me in collaboration with my mother, Alba Cisterna, a craftswoman from Northern Chile, as part of the creation process. For me, it was not just a textile piece; it was a vehicle for experiences. That was the signal I gave to my performer, Margarita Gómez, so that her body would activate *ALMA* and thus, the sculptural costume would come to life as well. A life that, from the textile material, invites reflection on death, memory, and the journey.

This particular costume is a fusion of materials. Each of the fabrics that make up the costume is a leftover piece reused from another project I designed in the past. Along with that, the tin flowers were also constructed by my mother, applying the principle of reuse. The experimentation with the material was crucial because it was the material-costume that would communicate with the audiences. I took a deliberate step back for *ALMA Y MUERTOS*, not fully designing the idea, but allowing the materials to speak and guide me in a compositional direction. I did this consciously because I wanted to break away from the more linear creation methodology I usually follow. In other words, I adopted a reverse approach that involved an exploratory laboratory process where the materials themselves were connected, composed, and shaped to create the costume. Within the visual aspect, the concept of the textile artefact and empowering materials was tremendously important to me. The final result of the costume is largely associated with the experimentation of those materials, even though I had a previous idea in my mind. This freedom also speaks to me about how the costume itself has an evolutionary and communicative capacity.

The costume is a link to a greater experience. In that sense, there is a deeper meaning behind the costume that goes beyond its form and visual appearance. In fact, I spent many nights wondering how I could connect the audience to a different state, one that wasn't just about contemplation but also invited them to embark on the journey. I believe that the interplay between considering the costume as a vehicle, and also the atmosphere it creates, completes the journey. For me, it was crucial not to focus solely on the aesthetic aspect. During the creation of the costume for *ALMA Y MUERTOS*, I myself sought its initial movements, then a specific artistic residency was dedicated to discovering the mobility of the costume and what it could offer in choreographic terms. I explored its extensions, its rhythms, how it interacted with the performer's body, and how these movements communicated with the audience without relying on words. I wanted the costume to lead the movement, not the performer's body. Since this work is essentially a methodological challenge, an exploration of what we traditionally don't do, the performer was at the service of the costume. The limitations, extensions, and possibilities had to be discovered to uncover the costume's unique rhythm.

I feel part of an Expanded Vision that considers design as a channel of communication in itself. I believe we are experiencing a shift towards greater autonomy, where it is possible to live experiences and create works through new formats and methodologies that offer a more open and expanded landscape. In this context, design can engage with the audience, creating performative experiences without necessarily adhering to a predefined dramaturgical script, without having to translate someone else's ideas. The tool of connection becomes the material, the form, and the meaning that lies behind it.

EMOTION AND BODILY AWARENESS

Emotion and bodily awareness, internal sensations and psychological well-being are being explored by some contemporary designers through the use of costume. Sally E. Dean employs somatic movement practices, using her Somatic Costumes to elicit a mindful response from active participants. She notes that by becoming 'conscious of the impact of the costume, through its touch, on our bodies', design or performance-based choices can be made (Dean). Linnea Bågander uses 'textures that suggest and inspire motions and emotions [and] generate choreographic processes that are based on the somatic experience of the material' (Bågander). 'The costume's physical form and materiality [drove] the devising process' in Kate Lane and Valentina Ceschi's performance *Confinement* which was 'a sensorial and emotive reading of ... collective memories [of] motherhood and birth over lockdown' (Lane). Yuka Oyama 'investigate[s] physical and psychological inter-dependence, inter-action, collaboration, and inter-affectional relationships between persons and (worn) things [in order to understand] people's skills to maintain well-being when their sense of belonging is eroded' (Oyama). Debashish Paul envisages his costumes as landscapes 'beyond the concepts of body and gender' where he can 'shout about [his] identity through [his] body and attire' (Paul).

SALLY E. DEAN (NORWAY/UK/USA)

http://www.sallyedean.com / www.betwixtduo.com

Sally E Dean is a PhD Research Fellow at Oslo National Academy of the Arts. Her artistic research investigates choreographing attention through the touch of Somatic Costumes. Sally leads (2011–22) the collaborative SMCP Project, co-designing Somatic Costumes that generate psychophysical awareness in wearers and immersive sensorial performances. She has been a professional artist and teacher for over 25 years throughout Europe, United States and Asia between the fields of costume design, dance and somatic practices. Her performances have been supported by the Arts Council England and the British Council.

My design ethos comes from my background/training in 'somatic movement practices', my training as a dancer/choreographer and my ongoing research on how costume's touch impacts bodies. I start with the sense of touch or 'haptic' (including the tactile, the kinaesthetic or kinaesthetic body consciousness and proprioceptive senses) as opposed to the visual. I aim to rebalance the sensorial hierarchy in modern culture where vision often dominates in design and performance practices. Such an approach has led me to prioritising 'wearing' the costume over 'viewing' the costume. Often the costume is not worn during the process of making/designing and can be absent in the dance/ choreography process until the end just before the performance. This has led me to inviting design and performance practices into the practice of 'Aware Wearing' – where we become conscious of the impact of the costume, through its touch, on our bodies and then can make choices (design or performance based) from the touch impact.

I have been creating *Somatic Costumes*, personally and in collaboration with Sandra Arroniz Lacunza and Carolina Rieckhof, as part of the *Somatic Movement Costume Performance Project* since 2011. The *Somatic Costumes* were originally designed to generate a specific psycho-physical awareness in the wearer – for example, a *Balloon Hat* to sense the buoyancy and volume of the skull or the *Furry Heart Protector* to sense the front, back and space in between of the torso, along with sensing the 'feet of the heart' – connecting the heart through weight, to the ground. Some of the *Somatic Costumes* designed have become costumes not only for the performers, but also for the audience to wear. Wearers of costume can become 'performers' in my immersive performative work. Because costume designers, performers, audiences are all wearers in my process, there is less hierarchy or division between them.

This practice continues in my current performance in progress for my PhD called *Give Them Wings & We Shall See Their Faces*. The Feather fingers include wool-elastic finger sleeves (co-designed with Lydia Hann) that create slight compression but also help attach the feathers to the fingers in a way that allow the fingers to sense lengthening (extension) in the space. The audience is invited into many different rituals of dressing and wearing specific *Somatic Costumes*. In this case, the costume as a form is not as important in the performance as the experience of dressing/undressing and wearing it and sensing its impact on the body. The touch of the costume becomes the portal to activating the wearer's poetic imagination. The costume then not only extends the body but extends the imagination of the wearer. And additionally, this extension has also included the *Somatic Costumes* extending into the environment itself to become part of the scenography. For example, the paper costumes are not only worn as costumes, but they also become nests to rest in and also a hanging installation at the end of the piece (Figure 9.35).

My artistic research has grown into a practice called *The Somatic Costume Dressing Room* (Figure 9.36). This has shifted the design intension and process further and widened the definition of what a Somatic Costume can be and is. In the *Somatic Costume Dressing Room*, the costume design is created for one wearer and their specific psychophysical needs that arise through simple acts of touching materials, and a dressing and making process than unfolds between us (with myself in the role of guide). We co-create the *Somatic Costume* together. The *Somatic Costume Dressing Room* becomes an intimate performance based on listening to the specific tactile needs of one wearer.

I have developed a *Somatic Costume Wardrobe* which is a collection of *Somatic Costume* elements or materials that can be put together in different combinations.

■ **Insubordinate Costume**

9.35
Sally E. Dean, *Carrying Paper Costume, Give Them Wings & See their Faces*, with Katrine Kirsebom, KHIO, 2023. Photo by Elin Osjord. © Sally E. Dean.

9.36
Sally E. Dean, *Somatic Costume Dressing Room* – Kristina Gjems & Sally E. Dean, KHIO, 2023. Photograph by Elin Osjord. © Sally E. Dean.

The tactile library includes touch impacts such as weight, temperature, location, direction, texture, time, movement and more. Materials include balloons, lentils, different kinds of paper, fake and real fur, potatoes, stones, hula hoops, an assortment of elastics, tights, water bags, braille, fake grass, to an array of different tactile fabrics. The process usually begins by making touch aesthetic choices rather than visual aesthetic choices. For example, in *Give Them Wings & See their Faces* I chose how I wanted to choreograph the wearer's attention through the sense of touch by deciding which *Somatic Costume* they should wear first. In the *Somatic Costume Dressing Room*, the choreography of attention is not pre-planned, but is an improvisation in response to the individual wearer. The costumes instigate performance through the sense of touch and through the act of wearing, dressing/undressing and moving. This is a relational act, a different process than activating the imagination starting with the visual. The pathway is sensation, often with movement, that moves into feeling and last thinking, the meeting of touch, materials, my body and the wearer's body guide the process. Costumes and wearers are choreographing each other. No one is leading, no one is following.

Haptic touch includes movement, in its definition. Movement is often needed to sense how the costume impacts the body through touch. The touch impact also changes as the body and costume move – so it is key to understanding tactile effects. In the *Somatic Costume Dressing Room*, I will sometimes move materials to create sound or even wind, and also move my own body to embody the movement of the wearer. The physical constraints or boundaries of the costume are the directors of the experience. Costumes generate specific possibilities of movement and limit others which influence the physicality of the wearer or engender a specific emotional and physical response. A jacket worn that brings the shoulders forward and creates a sinking in the chest will translate emotionally and physically more as an emotional quality of sadness or exhaustion than elation or energy.

LINNEA BÅGANDER (SWEDEN)

http://www.linneabagander.se/
Linnea Bågander is a senior lecturer in Fashion Design Artistic Research at the Swedish School of Textiles. Through collaborations within the field of dance, she explores dress as a performative element, working with movement, materials, and bodies and how they co-exist and create expressions and experiences together. Her work ranges from how material can interpret and express the body's movements to how materials affect and inspire the movements of the body and how this enables new bodies entwined with materials to appear. She sets out to define practical methods, teaching modules, and innovative artistic research that aims to provide an understanding of the field of dance costume and to expand on its artistic fields. Both her stage-based work and artistic projects have been performed and exhibited internationally, including Copenhagen, Berlin, Budapest, Tel Aviv and Hong Kong.

My artistic practice approaches costume as a second skin which links the somatic experiences of a wearer to the way they express themselves in terms of both form and kinesthetics. Through the costumes the performers encounter living textures that suggest and inspire motions and emotions, by tacitly and kinaesthetically speaking to the wearer. Experimenting with these costumes allows, and sometimes demands, new ways of working from a choreographic perspective. Consequently, this inspires non-traditional choreographic methods that are based on somatic experience rather than imaginative or visual triggers. The restrictions that 'complex' costumes entail appear constrictive at first, but after some sessions of improvisation, dancers express that these limitations are helpful in the artistic process. When designed to do so, the material suggests a logical framework that assists in creating space to explore and improvise.

The notion of 'temporal form' is central to my artistic research both in its definition and in my methodology. Temporal form is a term that I use to bring attention to the temporality of garments which are activated through acts of wearing and motion. In particular, it refers to a design method where movement is fundamental; a costume designed as a temporal form is a costume that is designed to link the system of the body's movements to the possibilities offered by the material properties. Designing costume as a temporal form involves designing a form with an 'inherent capability to undergo changes in expression between more or less defined states. Designing material systems with an inherent logic of a series of expressions in one design, a temporal expression and a temporal form-thinking' (Bågander 2021: 168). Hence, the link between body and garment has the body at its origin and, for that reason, similar kinaesthetic and visual characteristics link the costume and body. Traces of the body might be noted in the proportions of limbs, in the symmetry or in the characteristics of movement. This type of costume however deviates notably from typical garment forms which are usually designed around body parts, with the purpose of being comfortable and interfering as little as possible with the natural movement of the body.

Through my practice, I have developed design methods for artistic movement-based processes. *Cuttlefish*, 2017 (Figure 9.37), and *Homo(Sapiens)*, 2021, demonstrate part of the development of my design method. In *Cuttlefish* the design process was based on the dancers' individual movement characteristics.

9.37
Linnea Bågander, *Cuttlefish*, 2017. Still image from video recording by Joakin Envik Karlsson. © Linnea Bågander.

9.38
Linnea Bågander, *Homo(Sapiens)*, 2021. Photograph by Donovan Von Martens. © Linnea Bågander.

We started with a workshop where small 1 metre square samples of a great variety of materials were explored in relation to the dancer's individual movement language and material preferences, as well as training and abilities (Bågander 2020a: 259–64). What followed was a process where the chosen material sample for each dancer underwent individual development of both an artistic and a technical nature, resulting in three costumes worn throughout the greater part of the performance. A design process can also be based on the more general structural abilities of the body, meaning that a more mechanical approach to the body's abilities leads the process rather than individual abilities and movement preferences. Structural abilities can, for example, be implemented by arranging materials on the body so that a specific motion is enhanced. An example of this is the stick costume for *Homo(Sapiens)* (Figure 9.38) where the material was arranged so that spiralling and twisting motions would be enhanced and enabled. Both these methods use a design process that depart from the body's perspective, where materials are chosen to support that and to generate choreographic processes that are based on the somatic experience of the material. The material is explored through its physical properties, it can be arranged on the body as textures taking the form of the body, in relation to the body's movements, as the example of *Homo(Sapiens)* shows, or through their ability to take on a geometric form that the body enters as some of the costumes of *Cuttlefish* demonstrate (Bågander 2020).

KATE LANE (UK)

https://www.katelane.co.uk/
Kate Lane is an artist, scenographer and academic with a practice led research into scenography and costume. She is one half of performance collective Ceschi + Lane, the other half is director and movement specialist Valentina Ceschi. After

■ Insubordinate Costume

9.39
Ceschi + Lane, *Confinement*: A project exploring motherhood in the pandemic, 2022. © Ceschi + Lane.

initially studying Sculpture at Camberwell College of Arts she undertook a Master's in Costume for Performance at London College of Fashion. She also has a background in dance being part of a contemporary dance group as a teenager and later as a cabaret performer in her twenties.

My practice is developed through a design-led methodology, where the costume's physical form and materiality drive the devising process, both in the design of the costumes and in directing the development of a visual dramaturgy within the performance. The project *Confinement* was a Ceschi and Lane collaboration with Japanese choreographer Masumi Saito and Nigerian Composer Helen Epega from 2021–23. *Confinement* (Figures 9.39 and 9.40) was a testament to motherhood and birth over lockdown. It interrogated the representation and the positioning of the act of mothering and birth in society during COVID-19 using costume as prothesis, body scenography and wearable sculptures that distorted and manipulated the human form. It drew on our own experiences of mothering during Covid and presented a dystopian alternate world of the maternal, looking towards the fantastical and myth-making as way to raise political and social awareness. This piece spoke of a Surrealist staging post trauma, a vision of a dystopian nightmare of abstracted ante-natal scenes and through this we aimed to give critical voices to our collective experiences.

    I started with a material palate, informed from a sensorial and emotive reading of our collective memories and referencing British pagan tradition of costumes constructed from natural materials drawn from the landscape. Collectively we

9.40
Ceschi + Lane, *Confinement*: A project exploring motherhood in the pandemic, 2022. © Ceschi + Lane.

then started the devising process alongside the development of the design. This material palate was a combination of costumes from my archive, structural forms and often non-traditional materials such as sticks/ twigs and paper. We explored the materials together, experimenting with their inherent movement qualities and creating a fluid interchange between the design process and the movement development of each costume. This allowed the agency within the materiality of the forms to direct the development of the visual dramaturgy and inform the individual choreography of each costume. It became a borderless process between physical form, materiality of matter and its relationship with the body, drawing heavily on sensory perception and working with and through the materials to drive form and choreographic movement.

My work is often a combination of both aesthetic and conceptual choices. With *Confinement*, we had broad concepts to explore within the piece. Some costumes have their own conceptual meaning, whilst others are more about an emotive, sensorial response, driven by the reading of the inherent movement qualities in the material. For example, the costume that became our symbol of both the mother and the witch was inspired by my personal experience of having pre-eclampsia and looked at the maternal transformation that happens between birth and the subsequent formation of the child's otherness. This costume had its own conceptual reasoning from the start whereas others were driven from material exploration, for example the costume made from paper wrapped round the performer was more symbolic than conceptual.

Play is essential in my design and devising methodology, which is formed through an understanding of materiality, sensorial perception, and curiosity. I don't always know what direction the work will lead, whether in the rehearsal devising process or in the construction of the pieces in the studio. When making something, it is totally fluid between design, construction, and movement. I'll always wear and explore how a costume feels to move in whilst constructing it and this will often drive the decisions of its final design.

With *Confinement*, as well as other work by Ceschi + Lane, costume is the instigator in both the direction and the choreography. We start with the costume which might then evolve and transform as we explore its movement potential. Each costume form has its own movement language and from that we start to weave a dramaturgy and narrative arc. This style of working will often produce an abstracted story-arc. In *Confinement* we had a central story pulling the audience through but the abstracted visuals of the costumes allowed the audience to create their own meaning and narrative. It was more about an emotive experience for the audience than a literal story.

Costume-led performance has a long and deep tradition globally within folklore, community celebrations and religious events, from west African masquerades to British traditions such as Jack of the Green and the Whittlesea Straw Bear. These costume-focused celebrations are often site-specific in their location or seasonal. I think there is something so human about transforming to the other through costume in order to create our myths and bring us together. It's exciting to see this now being recognised within wider cultural sectors such as dance, theatre, performance art and fashion. The act of adornment and physical transformation through our clothes is how we read people and how we are read within society, therefore, from my perspective costume, is central to performance whether this is through more realistic clothing or fantastical, abstracted costume forms. I wonder if it's what makes us human?

YUKA OYAMA (JAPAN/GERMANY)

www.yukaoyama.com

Yuka Oyama's artistic practice incorporates sculpture, jewellery, video, public interventions, and performance. Her transnational backgrounds (Japan, Malaysia, Indonesia, United States, Germany) has led to her interest in the implications of clothing, adornments, and carried things to (re)construct a sense of self and identity. Oyama has participated in international exhibitions since 2003 and is currently professor of Jewellery Art/Sculpture at Burg Giebichenstein University of Art and Design Halle.

Whilst moving and uprooting frequently during my childhood and early adulthood, I gradually developed skills to make me feel stronger by making a collection of clothes, jewellery, and items that I carried with me from place to place. Sometimes I tried to integrate by mimicking other people, sometimes I tried to hold onto my previous self and other times, I deliberately tried to stand out. It was my solution to negotiate with the changes and the new contexts. Over time, the façade often shaped my inner self but sometimes there was a clear discrepancy between my façade and who I was inside. These experiences are essential to describe why I have turned to wearable and carriable media to build my artistic expressions. In my practice-based artistic research, I work with wearable sculptures in various sizes that range from 3 cm to ca. 200 cm and investigate physical and psychological inter-dependence, inter-action, collaboration, and inter-affectional relationships between persons and (worn) things. My life-sized costumes, that I call person-thing-hybrids, are props to access subjective realms and memories through experiencing the mental, physical, and emotional imprints that are made by things.[4] My main focus is on understanding people's skills to maintain well-being when their sense of belonging is eroded.

With *The Stubborn Life of Objects*, 2012–17, I investigated why certain personal possessions that we own instigate a strong emotional impact on their owners. What makes them embody inherent power that affects us (owners/users), makes us behave and feel differently? As a research method, I employed an auto-ethnographical approach, where I examined my own relationships to my personal possessions. I chose five objects that I felt had power over me: a bundle of keys, a piano, a bag of flour, a cap and a handbag. I then sought to become them through constructing life-sized thing-costumes, where I could enter their internal space. Whilst wearing and documenting each costume, I investigated the associations and memories that each thing evoked, biographies of these items, physical constraints and sensations. Additionally, I tested all kinds of body movement and developed motions, where the person–thing-hybrid sculpture and I would appear as one mysterious living entity. Different personae emerged through my choreographic experimentations, and I recognised that becoming and moving in my personal possessions made me revisit and reflect upon my life based on the memories that the objects evoked. These sets of memories were different from how I remembered the past, events that my conscious had considered unimportant to keep as memories that had however stayed in my unconscious.

Giving up my Japanese citizenship to become German in 2017 I believed that the decision was a sensible one until I experienced sadness on entering Japan as a foreigner. I had underestimated my emotional ties to Japan and questioned where do I belong? Where am I native? I belonged nowhere and everywhere. I then decided to collaborate with people who shared similar personal experiences. Over the years, I have developed my own object-based methodology, where I investigate emotionally charged objects, personal experiences and associative thoughts that are facilitated by them, creating an archive of objects, interview transcripts, images, drawings, construction notes and theoretical discourses. In *Power of Small Things* I aimed to identify how small things that individuals wear and carry with them can contribute to generate stability and a sense of continuity as their lives unfold between multiple homes, constantly travelling, going through transitions, and uprooting. How do they deal with the vastly changing living situations? What kind of skills are learnt, rituals are practiced, space and other arrangements are made to stay anchored?

Power of Small Things consisted of three artistic projects: *Helpers Changing Homes*, 2018 (Figure 9.41), *A Home is a Home is a Home*, 2019, and *SurvivaBall Home Suits*, 2021 (Figure 9.42). In the first, my research collaborators had experienced at least thirty relocations and were mostly voluntarily (and some involuntarily) migrants. In the second, I approached persons who had commuted between multiple places for many years due to work. In the third, my participants were children and young adults, who lived between their mom and dad's households where there was 50:50 joint custody. For each artwork, I conducted twenty

Insubordinate Costume

qualitative object-based interviews and constructed wearable sculptures for five to seven interviewees who then wore and enacted in the sculptures, unfolding their personal stories. I aimed to depict something in the sculptures that captured an important essence of the interviewees, establishing an emotional closeness between the wearers and the costumes. The non-human appearance of my sculptures creates a physical and psychological disconnection to the wearers' sense of self but, by starting to play and experiment, an enormous creative freedom and potential is released.

During our feedback sessions, many participants mentioned how surprised they were to discover unexpected memories and feelings related to their experiences. I have discovered that a space called 'home', for people who move frequently, relies on recreating the feelings of home: the feelings of being relaxed, secure, familiar, protected, free, loved and comforted. It is important to note that home can offer the complete opposite of these feelings to many individuals. Mobile tangible personal possessions help assure emotional security by keeping memories that remind the owners who they are. Many people have also developed strategies to maintain almost identical body sensations and experiences using things as 'jigs' to create the illusion that home has never shifted. For example, perfumes, candles, a ticking clock, recreate the same conditions, ambient, atmospheres, and multisensorial experiences that surround the body. With running shoes, a book, a football, a bicycle, the same activities can be practiced. Consequently, these items, specific senses, sensations, activities, experiences, and rituals enhance an individual's sense of anchoring and continuity in the moments of rootlessness. I am convinced that problems caused by rootlessness – an eroded sense of emotional and physical ties to a singular home(-base) – may affect future generations, whose sense of being present in one place shifts between physical and digital worlds. I believe that costume design that supports

9.41
Yuka Oyama, *Helpers Changing Homes, Motorbike*, 2018, cardboard, bamboo, 320 x 150 x 150 cm. ©Yuka Oyama and Alex Efimoff.

The Practitioners' Voice ■

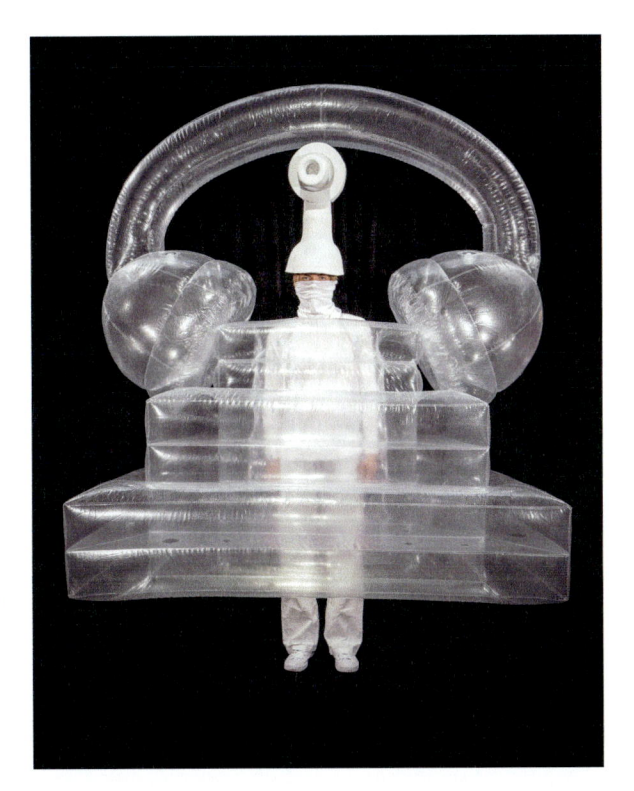

9.42
Yuka Oyama,
White – SurvivaBall Home Suits (white),
2020, plastic, PE sponge, textile,
190 x 181 x 129 cm.
Photograph by Zoe Tempest.

self-making and identity-designing through garments and adornments can play an indispensable role in fostering a sense of stability.

DEBASHISH PAUL (INDIA)

https://www.debashishpaul.com/
Debashish Paul is a contemporary Indian artist known for his unique performance style in elaborately designed attire. Alluring and haunting at the same time, his performance revolves around gender and identity, following a multi-expressionist methodology that involves various mediums – drawing, sculpture, craft and even dance. Made of paper pasted on cloth and filled with drawings intimately connected to his personal memories, the enormous sculptural attire Paul wears during his performances simultaneously reveals and conceals the body's movements inside it. Through this, he addresses the multiplicity of form and meaning beyond the standard codes of social behaviour. Although his performances have no connection to any rituals, there is a distinctive 'ritual quality or effect' – the onlookers have an elevated experience of time that separates them, for a moment, from the mundane everydayness of their lives. Through his work, Paul navigates landscapes as he perceives them – as queer ecologies. What he finds within himself, and in nature, reflects the complexities that lie within – he describes these as conversational exchanges. The artist believes that his body is not separate from the river, which has been his companion since childhood, always forming the periphery of

his home. He carries this river within him on every journey. In this interview, Paul talks about the inspiration behind his work.

I have been passionate about women's clothes ever since I was a child. People in my native village weave saris, one of the traditional garments for women in India. Life in my village is therefore always vibrant, with women wearing saris of various colours wherever you go. As a child, I used to collect scraps of the homespun woven saris and make clothes for my dolls.

When I started pursuing art academically, I wanted to use my body in my work. However, I could not speak about my identity whilst doing my degree, as homosexuality and queerness were not accepted by my society, and I was far too scared to be honest about myself. Things changed when I went to study for my Master's in Varanasi – a beautiful, spiritual, and culturally rich city, one of the seven sacred cities of Hinduism. The colourful costumes of the goddesses in the temples of Varanasi inspired my work during my Master's as well as during the lockdown in 2020, and I started to make costumes linked to my body and our cultural fashion. What the costumes did was help me hide my body. I was very uncomfortable with my physical appearance because I had been teased about being effeminate throughout my childhood and high school. I was also very lonely, but my costumes helped me perform and break down barriers. At the moment, I am in Paris as part of the residency programme of the Institut Français at the Cité Internationale des Arts. My multimedia project *Kas – To Shine/Enlightenment* will bring together the two cultures of Varanasi and Paris and their rivers, the Ganges and the Seine. Both cities are known as 'the City of Light', and I will explore the notion of enlightenment. According to Hindu philosophy, this quest for enlightenment is the ultimate journey for a man.

I usually prepare the surface of the costumes by pasting fragile rice paper onto the fabric. I draw on it with charcoal, sometimes with watercolour or even acrylic, after which I paste other natural materials, such as roots and flowers, onto it. Drawing, for me, is like writing – like writing poems (Figure 9.43). I fold the costume and then unfold it to create a landscape of my queer body. Through this process of folding, unfolding, and trying the costume on, as I build it, I discover its shape and get to know myself. The costume for *Beyond the Body and Gender II*, however, was made with shells. One day, whilst walking along the banks of the river Ganga with my friends, I started collecting shells, which inspired me for this project. Shells hide and protect the body of the creature inside, so I decided to use them to create a costume which would protect me. It took two months to make the costume as it required a lot of shells. I made a video performance with this costume which is quite heavy and painful to wear – the shells are so sharp that I ended up with cuts all over my body! When I perform, I perform with my mind, so I do not notice the physical pain, but after it is over, I am exhausted.

Every costume has its personality or character. Working with a larger costume gives me more fluidity to move and helps with the performance. The sound of the costume is also essential. The shell costume makes a fantastic tinkling sound. During my projects, I collect lots of sounds from my surroundings and edit them

9.43
Debashish Paul, *Me with My Pet*, 2022–23. Photograph by Anil Kushwaha. © Debashish Paul.

to make new ones which I use in my live performances. Sometimes I work with musicians. Sometimes my costumes are very loud, and it feels like I am shouting about my identity through my body and attire. Sound is how I protest, making me more confident in myself. When I draw many things on the costume and feel the outfit around me, it is as if the universe has become a part of my body. My work combines the costume and the body with nature and the landscape. It gives me a sense of freedom (Figure 9.43).

I experiment with the body in space. My costumes are beyond the concepts of body and gender; when I am in them, my body becomes a landscape (Figure 9.44). I like to perform in a natural space like a river or a mountain because the costume and the landscape become one – there are no boundaries, no social structures, no one telling you how to behave or how to move. In a landscape, you are alone – you have body language and more movement. You can follow the slowness of the river flowing in your body and feel the sound of the mountain. It inspires me to move as I desire. Being in a theatre space with an audience is very different.

My work is both conceptual as well as organic. My costumes are alive – they develop and grow. Each costume carries a new identity or tells a new story. The costumes allow me to reveal my internal desires, for my inner body has no boundaries – it transcends gender. I feel more powerful when I wear my costumes, for although I hate my physical body, my art helps me reveal my innermost self. Costumes are a powerful medium and can be very playful and colourful – this is why I prefer feminine clothes over the more masculine severe garments. My costumes are extraordinary gender-neutral characters born out of a new world concept or a dream. I dream about a world where everyone can live together, with love and sans boundaries. I believe nothing in this world is more valuable than love – it makes us more powerful.

■ Insubordinate Costume

9.44
Debashish Paul, *Body as a Landscape; Body in a Landscape*, 2021. Photograph by Anil Kushwaha. © Debashish Paul.

POETIC LANDSCAPES

Costumes can generate poetic landscapes that narrate their own stories. For her performance *DONAULLSDONAULLS (womaneyeswomaneyes)*, Mariaelena Roqué creates 'a visual poetic manifestation' of herself by interacting with archival images of her past work projected onto the translucent *Primitive Venus* costume she wears. She notes that the constantly changing mapped images of the costumes 'have something to tell, about me, about other people who were with me, about landscape, about space, about time and are 'an indication of how costume design can be powerful and empowering' (Roqué). Fredrik Floen's work explores the 'storytelling and fictional potential of costumes'. He believes that 'we must rekindle the art of reading costumes, venturing beyond surface aesthetics to understand the narratives, historical references, and artistic depth they carry' (Floen). Naseem Albahwash's costume and design work illustrates different aspects of Saudi Arabian culture. For her costume *The Line* she was inspired by the futuristic city in construction within the new urban development of Neom. My own design practice, uses modular forms to build different landscapes for the body and create costumes that can weave tales and spin a yarn.

MARIAELENA ROQUÉ (SPAIN)

www.mariaelenaroque.com

Mariaelena Roqué is a Catalan-Venezuelan multidisciplinary artist, performer and costume designer. In the 1970s she started working as a photographic model and as a contemporary dancer under Martha Graham, Merce Cunningham, Alwin Nikolais and Lindsey Kemp and was influenced by Isadora Duncan. At the same time, she began researching visual-performing arts, experimental music and ethnic and oriental traditional performing techniques, in order to widen her artistic vocabulary. Since 1980 she has focused on costume as her main inner to out/ out to in, pushing-pulling external tool to create and develop her own and others' artistic language. In the 1990s she created a theatre company to generate and develop shared visual performances. Her journey has been a trajectory of conceptual and accumulative self-portraits interacting with other artists and using many different techniques. Since 2010 she performs solo and lectures around the world exploring the possibilities of visually poetic costume.

My costume designs are a visual poetic manifestation of myself because I am the first person I work with. I started designing costumes when I was a dancer and fashion model. Little by little, I explored how I could create characters in whatever I had to do – advertising, movies or daily life. I started to play and experiment and learnt how to work with costumes, depending on the intention and the purpose. As a dancer I studied under Cunningham, Graham, Nikolais, Kemp but then I decided to leave everything else behind to be a free dancer and make my own costumes. I am always fighting! I've fought with every theatre because there is always someone trying to make you submit to their ideas. I've always been very radical. I have to do my own work so I work for myself, I never work for others. I always did my own thing, trying to find my own language. I don't work in an ephemeral way. I work in a cumulative way, I like how things, costumes, ideas mutate through time. I trained in psychology and am interested in anthropology and these are both aspects of my work.

My first experiments were with flat pieces of fabric on the floor, moving on top of them with my body and thinking about movement. I started to develop costumes that could be seen by the birds in the sky, flat landscapes where you could enter with your body. I always experiment with movement whilst I'm building the costumes because I am a dancer. Movement has always inspired my artistic designing. The movement of the body, the movement of the performance and the movement of the costume have to go together, it's definitely a collaboration. My work flows between making myself through the costume and feeling the costume through the performance. The movement in the costume is very important as if the costume is a dancer by itself. I consider the costume as another being, not a human being, but another being. Things happen that you never imagined when you are working with costume, they bring movements and concepts to you. This is because you're working with all of yourself, it's not magical, it's a matter of being very aware.

In the past, when I experimented with historical costumes, I always looked at them through a contemporary filter, exploring materials and finding very simple ways of putting things together, even using industrial things. The costumes became sculptures with visual and mechanical functions before the computerised age. My costumes develop both from a conceptual idea and from working with materials, from trying everything together. I like that freedom of not restricting yourself to working only in one way but I don't like to disguise anybody. Fantasy is one thing, a conceptual idea is another, although you can work with both of them on superficial and deep levels. We have many brains working at the same time, some of which we're not aware of. Whilst you work with your hands you

■ **Insubordinate Costume**

are connected to your brain, you are watching, thinking, simulating performance ideas, making decisions. Everything works together whether you start from a concept or a material, from a mechanical thing, a landscape or a scientific investigation. We are a clever machine. a very clever machine, putting together and associating everything in order to build an artistic element. I speak during my performances but I have always worked more with onomatopoeic sounds rather than language, although I iterate some words in the language of the country I am performing in.

After forty years as a costume designer, I have a large stock of materials which I now share with my students. It is interesting to see how they use the materials very differently. When I teach, I make the students become aware of themselves and their own bodies because they usually work for something which is outside of themselves. I get them to put themselves in the centre of the creation and to explore with materials. The costume designer needs to be involved in the making and to feel it as well, then you have to learn how to be out of yourself again in order to build the costume. One of the main things I do in my workshops is to help the students rediscover the playfulness of children without being afraid of what others think. But, of course, we are adults and we have a something to say so the conceptual thing must come before or after. If you play first, you must play freely and put the concept aside, but at a certain point you must stop playing and make decisions, otherwise, you only have an experiment you don't have a performance. I think we need a lot of other knowledge besides costume experimentation otherwise it is only an investigation of the material or of the performer's body, we need that further step.

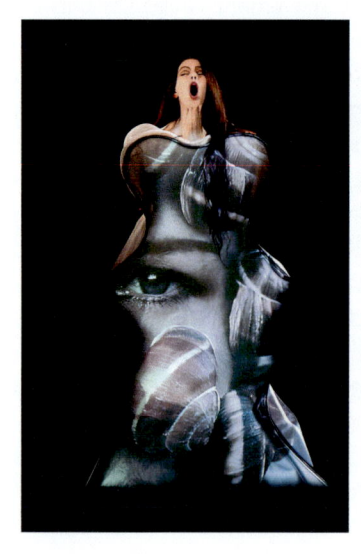

9.45
Mariaelena Roqué, performance, mapping and costume for *DONAULLS-DONAULLS (womaneyeswomaneyes)*, 2009–2011–2024. © Mariaelena Roqué/ MER (1975–2023)/MER-CCS (1985–2010).

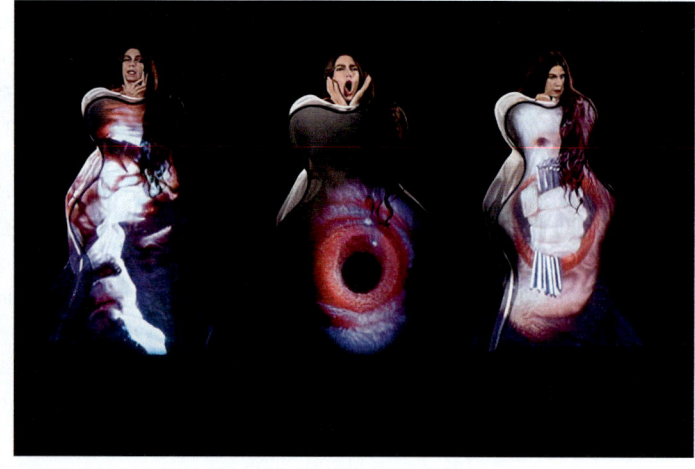

9.46
Mariaelena Roqué, performance, mapping and costume for *DONAULLS-DONAULLS (womaneyeswomaneyes)*, 2009–2011–2024. © Mariaelena Roqué/ MER (1975–2023)/MER-CCS (1985–2010).

My last costume, and I do think it is my last costume, is a *Primitive Venus*, shaped like a three-dimensional guitar, that forms part of my ongoing performance *DONAULLSDONAULLS* (Figures 9.45 and 9.46). After making so many crazy costumes, amazing costumes with sounds, with lights, with voices inside, with liquids, with explosive things, with fire, inflatable, I found myself using a primitive shape made from nylon crinoline fabric which is translucent. I have a big archive of images of myself and other characters I created together with my performers in different costumes so I made a mapping which is projected onto the *Primitive Venus* costume and I perform in relation to the images, my expressions just flow. All of the costumes have something to tell, about me, about other people who were with me, about landscape, about space, about time. I am the generator and a boomerang acting as medium. It is again an indication of how costume design can be powerful and empowering.

Recently scientists discovered a new organ, the *interstitium*, a network of fluid-filled cavities that connect all parts of the body. For me, costume is another organ, the *extertitium* that external thing that communicates with the organic, spiritual side and intellectual parts of ourselves. Costume is the main artistic tool on stage because it can narrate exactly what you want to it to narrate. Perhaps we need to find a new word for costume, to describe all the possibilities it can produce.

FREDRIK FLOEN (NORWAY)

http://www.friedrichfloen.com
Fredrik Floen is a Norwegian costume designer and visual artist who presents his work in a range of different theatrical contexts. He has been assistant professor in fashion and costume at Oslo Academy of the Arts since 2024. His artistic practice circles around the theatrical, the challenging, the unfinished, fantasy and maximalism and he works with new ways of approaching identity, fiction, future, body(culture) and co-existence.

As I reflect upon my role as an Insubordinate Costume designer, I find myself constantly navigating a delicate balance between enhancing the creative process and occasionally acting as the wrench in the performance machine, disrupting the flow of work in ways that challenge and redefine expectations. In the world of costume design, my mission is clear: to breathe life into characters through dressing that not only looks interesting on paper but also during the performance when worn by performers. It's a challenging task that often requires me to step out of my comfort zone, pushing the boundaries of my creative abilities and sometimes placing myself in direct conflict with collaborating practitioners. One of the lessons I've learnt on this journey is the importance of looking beyond the costume drawing itself. Early on, I encountered the disheartening reality that many costumes that appeared magnificent on paper lost some of their allure and practicality when translated into the real world. This realisation served as a wake-up call, compelling me to redefine my primary goal as a costume designer. No longer was it enough to create aesthetically pleasing drawings, I needed to ensure that my ideas integrated into the bodies of the performers who would wear them. It became a matter of functionality and practicality – a quest to make costumes that are both visually stunning and carriers of meaning but which also sometimes challenge comfort and function for the performers.

In *What Gender Is, What Gender Does*, Judith Roof writes 'Genders are neither binary nor essential. Nor are they singular, unchanging, invariable, inherent, or flatly definitive. Genders are not names, labels, or identities; they are neither nouns nor adjectives. Gender is a verb, a process. Genderings constantly change' (Roof 2016: 1). This demonstrates the complexity of the human experience, one that transcends simple categorisations. In my work, gender, like costume design, exists in a realm that defies easy definition. It's a nuanced and ever-evolving landscape, much like a black hole that absorbs all light, constantly shifting and challenging our perceptions. It leans more toward the Dionysian than the Apollonian, reminiscent of the Dionysian mysteries where intoxicants and trance-inducing techniques liberated individuals from inhibitions and social constraints.

Together with playwright Runa Borch Skolsegg, I created *The Dionysian Corporation*. In recent years, we have both had the sensation that the world feels as if it is at a breaking point and vibrating and so it has been a natural reflex for us to look back and try to think about the tools we need to create a better world than we have now. Through re-discovering old myths, texts and ideas we have felt more invested in the idea of developing an iteration of something, like politics, and how, in certain contexts, it has a liberating and transformative power. With our hybrid opera project, *Disorder of Desire*, we want to create a work that opens up and helps us to become brave, vulnerable, strange and messy. The work starts from a rewriting and resewing of Greek classical dramas and myths. We are making an opera from costumes and text, with no composer or director. We are cutting off heads, and new ones pop up like on the mythological monster Hydra. We will resist the urge to 'progress' and 'innovate', but also 'regress' and 'repeat'; we will be mutant, porous and sentient, creating irrational spaces that do not resemble geographical ones, but exist in time and are always in motion.

The last years I have been working on a project based on the cultural traditions of the *Dance Macabre* or *Totentanz*. This motive became a central interest whilst researching different historical artworks where costume plays an important role. The *Tanz Macabre* is a representation of dance to/with death which had its origins in poetry from the end of the thirteenth century that combined the essential ideas of the inevitability and impartiality of death. The portrayal of this in art is recognisable by the long line of people, representing all the different layers of the society of the time, dancing with skeletons in a straight line like on a modern-day catwalk.

The carnivalesque is of particular interest to me and my practice. I work on the essence of costume design and have studied Bakhtin's conception of the carnivalesque as a social and literary trope, translating this into my costume design methods. The key elements of the carnivalesque that I have incorporated into my work are:

- The exaggeration of Proportions,
- Parody and Satire,
- The inversion of Hierarchy,

The Practitioners' Voice ■

9.47
Fredrik Floen,
On the Lips of Living Men, 2023.
Photograph by
Julie Hrnčířová.
© Fredrik Floen.

9.48
Fredrik Floen, *On the Lips of Living Men*, Prague Quadrennial, 2023.
Photograph by
Julie Hrnčířová.
© Fredrik Floen.

- Grotesque Elements,
- Masking and Disguise,
- The mixing of Styles and Eras.

The project *We Shall Not Even Know That We Have Met, Yet Meet We Shall, and Pass and Meet Again. Where Dead Men Meet; On the Lips of Living Men* (Figures 9.47 and 9.48), was first presented as a ten-day long open rehearsal at the Prague Quadrennial 2023, and turned into a twenty-five-minute-long catwalk performance with eighty-eight costumes, premiering November 2023 at the Blackbox Theater in Oslo.

205 □

■ Insubordinate Costume

In my work as a costume designer, I find it intriguing to create costume drawings that serve as riddles, not only for myself but also for the skilled costume workers who bring my visions to life. These enigmatic designs add an extra layer of complexity to the creative process, inviting collaboration and exploration of symbolism and metaphor. In today's fashion and costume landscape there seems to be a crisis – a struggle to grasp the essence of costumes and infuse a sense of genuine enjoyment into the way fashion is approached. The industry has increasingly gravitated toward utilitarianism and short-lived trends, often overlooking the storytelling and fictional potential of costume. This departure from the joyous and imaginative spirit, that for me defines fashion and costume appreciation, calls for a re-evaluation. We must rekindle the art of reading costumes, venturing beyond surface aesthetics to understand the narratives, historical references and artistic depth they carry. It's a call to embrace risk, diversity and experimentation, reclaiming the sense of wonder and excitement that fashion and costume design should bring.

The world is complex and dynamic. Through costume, I research what and how the body can/could be always in relation to and in the world, and how this affects how we dress (or do not dress). For me, the insubordination of the costume designer's praxis extends beyond aesthetics; it is also about taking responsibility for understanding the broader context in which our work exists. This involves educating ourselves about the whole world of the production, a role that might traditionally belong to choreographers or directors, and is a profound commitment to align our designs with the narrative essence, bridging the gap between visual artistry and storytelling. This signifies embracing roles that extend beyond aesthetics and delve into the philosophical underpinnings of the production. Like philosophers contemplating the essence of existence, we contemplate the essence of characters through our costumes, a blend of body and garment, and explore their psychological depths and societal roles.

I find solace in the philosophical potential of my role. I create, not just costumes but vessels of expression, carrying the weight of cultural, social, and psychological significance. It's a journey that transcends the superficial, enriching the narrative and leaving an indelible mark on the world of theatre and performance. In the era of complexity and nuance, where identities defy categorisation, and creativity knows no bounds, the insubordination of my praxis serves as a testament to the limitless possibilities of collaboration between artistic vision and skilled craftsmanship. We could be philosophers of aesthetics, storytellers through materials, the nerdy cousins of the fashion designer or custodians of the human experience.

NASEEM ALBAWASH (SAUDI ARABIA)

Nassem Albahwash is a Saudi fashion designer and researcher in international and traditional fashions who aims to highlight the beauty and authenticity of Saudi heritage. She holds an MA in Fashion Design and Cultural Heritage Design. In 2023, she took part in a Costume Design course organised by the Saudi Fashion Commission, Dar Al-Hekma University in Jeddah and Fashion Academies ITS Cosmo and AFOL Moda in Milan. Students created their own characters that reflected their interests and incorporated various aspects of Saudi culture.

The Practitioners' Voice

9.49
Naseem Albahwash,
The Line, 2023. ©
Naseem Albahwash.

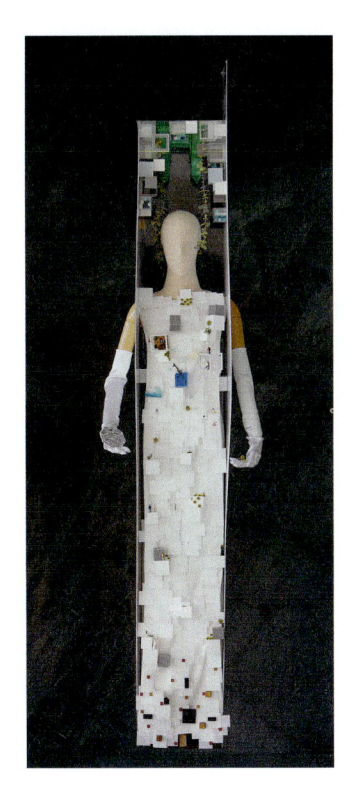

9.50
Naseem Albahwash,
The Line, 2023. ©
Naseem Albahwash.

207

■ Insubordinate Costume

Performance costume is part of a wide genre that includes many cultural, visual and historical aspects. Typically, the garment must combine the function of comfort for the wearer with the ideas and concepts being clear to the viewer. This is a somewhat difficult equation! The Costume Design course opened up horizons and gave me the opportunity to experiment and find unusual solutions. I am interested in Saudi Arabian culture both from a historical and a contemporary point of view. My last projects were inspired by the early Islamic inscriptions at al-Ula and traditional textiles but for the costume design project I chose the new urban development of Neom in the Tabuk province as my inspiration, specifically, *The Line* a futuristic city designed by architects Thom Mayne, Peter Cook and Reinier de Graaf. Enclosed between mirrored walls, *The Line* was designed to stretch from the Red Sea, across the desert to the mountains: one 170 kilometres long, 500 metres high and 200 metres wide. Plans show the architects envisaged a city with no cars and no emissions running on 100% renewable energy with a high-speed rail system taking you from one end to the other in twenty minutes (https://www.neom.com/en-us/regions/theline).

The idea of this, almost science-fiction, city of the future, intrigued me and I started by researching different aspects and architectural details of the project that could be used on the costume. I am a very methodical researcher! The basis of the costume is a sheath dress made from heavy polyester satin. To this simple, elegant shape I attached flat squares and rectangles of plastic and small cubes of white, mirrored or transparent plexiglass. Inside the transparent cubes I added miniature trees, waves, people and desert scenes that recall *The Line* project, as well as tiny lights and some humoristic details such as a shark, skiers and mountaineers. A tall plexiglass box, towering above the performer's head with extra cube details, is worn like a rigid, elongated coat and symbolises the mirrored walls of the urban design (Figures 9.49 and 9.50).

SUSAN MARSHALL (UK/ITALY)

www.susanmarshall.info

I first developed the idea of using modular costume pieces during my doctoral research into Insubordinate Costume and have since elaborated on the concept in two further projects: the *White Lady of Liselund* and *Performative Pockets*. As part of my practice, it was necessary to find a way to resolve specific practical prerequisites as the costumes needed to be light-weight and easily transportable whilst still retaining their three-dimensional nature. In response, I looked to origami techniques and modular structures more typical in architecture, industrial design or children's toys such as building bricks, Lego, Meccano, Stickle Bricks and GeoMag as possible solutions to the problem. From playing with small repetitive shapes in paper and fabric, the idea of flat-pack modular scenographic costumes evolved and were then refined and simplified as my research progressed (Marshall 2021a: 107). The modules in se are completely neutral and can be used in innumerable ways to create representational or abstract forms and, as such, are versatile, enabling multifaceted, creative interpretations and offering numerous dramaturgical possibilities. Recycling and upcycling are fundamental aspects of my design ethos and the modules fulfil this criterion in a playful and creative way.

The original modules were made from recycled paper, unbleached cotton calico and washable stone paper, which is made from calcium carbonate powder blended with a small amount of recyclable high-density polyethylene resin that renders it waterproof and tear resistant (Marshall 2021b: 284). Modules included simple geometric shapes – triangles, squares, circles, crosses – as well as cocoons, flexible tubes and crinolines. The modules are punched with holes to allow the pieces to be joined in different ways through twisting, folding and connecting with split pins, string or elastic. The crinoline modules, in unbleached calico, continued with the flat-pack modular theme and are based on the idea of the Victorian crinoline which uses boning to form a three-dimensional shape when held up, but which collapses upon itself to lie flat. The 'crinolines' are different sizes and shapes, ranging from a giant 4-metre tubular structure to a tiny version that fits on two fingers. Most have open-ended zips so they can be zipped together or to each other.

9.51
Susan Marshall, *Caterpillar*, 2020. Photograph by Emile Carlsen. © Susan Marshall and Tilde Knudsen.

In a series of short workshops participants were invited to play and improvise with the modules in order to create a costume or costumes before developing their ideas and giving a final brief performance. Looking at the diverse creative results of the workshops, the overriding impression is of the originality of each performance, with very few patterns arising. The modular costume pieces led to a

■ Insubordinate Costume

seemingly endless amount of creative and unique solutions, both in the costumes and the performances the participants produced.

A non-verbal production of *Alice in Wonderland* (Figures 9.51, 9.52 and 9.53) developed from workshops with Danish actress and dancer Tilde Knudsen of Asterions Hus, a Danish physical and experimental theatre company. The production has been performed both online and in venues across Europe, proving that the modules have the ability to extend beyond the experimental workshop context. Tilde's inventive and versatile approach to performance form a perfect synergy with my experimental modular costumes, which are enhanced by her training as a dancer.

9.52
Susan Marshall, *Walrus*, 2020. Photograph by Emile Carlsen. © Susan Marshall & Tilde Knudsen.

9.53
Susan Marshall, *The Queen of Hearts*, 2020. Photograph by Emile Carlsen. © Susan Marshall & Tilde Knudsen.

Although the forms and types of materials have changed from one performance to another, two further projects with Tilde and Asterions Hus have also involved modules. More symbolic than realistic, the modules for the production of *The White Lady*, made from strong waterproof blind fabric and corset boning, were inspired by natural elements such as the shapes and structures of leaves, mushrooms, seeds and the wrinkled bark of a tree. Instead of following a plot, the performance involved a series of moving sculptural figures who created tableaux in different areas of the park, the white modular pieces standing out against the black worn by the performers and the luscious greenery. There was no set way to wear the modular pieces and the performers were encouraged to play and experiment with the costumes and to find actions that reflected their given theme.

Continuing with the modular theme, *Performative Pockets* (Figure 9.54) is currently in the early experimental stages. For hundreds of years women wore a separate pocket or pair of pockets tied around their waists, hidden under their skirts. These were often beautifully embroidered and held all kind of objects from sewing kits to money and jewellery, from keys to love letters. Pockets contained intimate secrets and personal stories and it is here that the idea for a performance began. Inspired by eighteenth-century pannier pockets and flat tie-on pockets, the modules are made from stiff, translucent crinoline fabric which can be attached to each other and the body.

Modular costumes unfold new worlds. The costumes open up, become three dimensional, join together, bend, move, metamorphose and unfold new possibilities, shifting human centrality towards a co-creativity between object and body. The modules activate, and like a character can be played in different ways. They are multifaceted, offering numerous possibilities to performers as the modules can be used to generate and regenerate multiple costumes. They could be considered to be 'phoenix' costumes, as described by theatre researcher and theorist Patrice Pavis, in the 1998 *Dictionary of the Theatre: Terms, Concepts, and Analysis*, 'a true intermediary between body and the object' (Pavis 1998: 82).

9.54
Susan Marshall, *Performative Pockets*, 2024. Photograph by Susan Marshall.

NOTES

1. https://www.instagram.com/youcantakemehometoni/
2. https://www.bodymindcentering.com/about/
3. Murray Schafer, Raymond.: *El Paisaje Sonoro y la afinación del mundo*. Cazorla, Vanesa G. (Trad.), Barcelona, Intermedio, 2013: 153.
4. In her reflections on contemporary dramaturgy, Camilla Eeg-Tverbakk expresses her preference to speak of 'things' rather than 'objects' (Eeg-Tverbakk 2021) as things are 'free' whereas objects are 'captured'. I refer to 'things' when objects impact on their users.

REFERENCES

Bågander, Linnea. 2020a. 'Cuttlefish – performing body', *Studies in Costume & Performance*, 5:2, pp. 255–271. https://doi.org/10.1386/scp_00028_7

Bågander, Linnea. 2020b. BODY FRAGMENTED – Temporal expressions. *VIS* #4, *Affecting Material and Technique*. https://doi.org/10.22501/vis.710802

Bågander, Linnea (2021). Body movement as material: designing temporalexpressions. Borås: University of Borås, Faculty of Textiles, Engineering and Business

Bågander, Linnea. 2023. 'homo(sapiens): Designing raw and defined material opportunities in studies', *Costume & Performance,* 8:2, pp. 263–278. https://doi.org/10.1386/scp_00100_1

Eeg-Tverbakk, Camilla. 2021. Dramaturgies of Reality - shaping and being shaped by things. 24 p. *Nordic Journal of Art and Research* (A & R). Vol. 10.https://doi.org/10.7577/information.4659

Marshall, Susan. 2021a. Insubordinate Costume. Doctoral thesis, Goldsmiths, University of London [Thesis]

Marshall, Susan. 2021b. 'Insubordinate Costume', *Studies in Costume & Performance*, Volume 6, Issue 2, Dec 2021, p. 283-304 DOI: https://doi.org/10.1386/scp_00052_3

McLuhan, Marshall & Quentin Fiore. 1967. *The Medium is the Massage: An Inventory of Effects*. New York: Bantam Books.

Merleau-Ponty, Maurice. 2013. *Phenomenology of Perception*. Abingdon: Taylor & Francis.

Pavis, P. 1998. *Dictionary of the Theatre: Terms, Concepts, and Analysis*. Toronto: University of Toronto Press. https://doi.org/10.3138/9781442673908

Roof, Judith. 2016. *What Gender Is, What Gender Does*. Minnesota: University of Minnesota Press. https://doi.org/10.5749/minnesota/9780816698578.001.0001

Afterword – Can Bad Costumes Do Good Things?

Rachel Hann

This book offers a thesis on costume as insubordinate; as a denial of the prevailing authorities of costume, performance and fashion. By way of an afterword, I ask whether bad costumes do good things. Any notion of 'bad' (as unwelcome, incorrect, harmful) is of course conceptualised in relationship to a judgement criterion. Bad is always bound to scales of good. Good is a success, the planned or a desirable outcome. Good costumes behave well. Bad costumes enable behaviours that are unwelcome, undesirable or outside of quality standards. Costumes can behave badly when they either perform in unexpected manners or solicit actions from the wearer that are read as ill-advised or even criminal. Badly assembled costumes result from a perceived failure of technique or selection of materials, which may even result in collapse, breakage or malfunction. Any discussion of bad costume is therefore a discussion on how costumes are judged to behave in line with expectations, whether agreed or implicit. Yet, I want to suggest that bad costumes can reveal the work of costume that may have otherwise been unseen or dismissed as frivolous. Bad costumes can offer a method for investigating how costumes are judged, understood and politicised.

Marshall's focus on Modernist costume and performance practices provides an apt frame for assessing whether bad costumes do good things. Modernist experiments were devoted to examining the elemental qualities or traits of an artistic medium. Costume, while often collapsed into the gestures and politics of 'the body', offered a critical medium for performance makers to rethink and re-articulate the purpose and function of costume in performance. As Marshall outlines, both Schlemmer's compositional playforms or Graham's tube dress resisted the expected rules of costume judgement. For instance, Graham's costume was neither constructed from ornate materials nor communicated a particular character (a representational symbol). It was a tube of purple elasticated material. In comparison to the ornate construction of other dancewear such as a tutu, Graham's costume could have been judged to be crude or unrefined. Yet, the simplicity of a costume's material form can reveal potentially new approaches to the judgement of costume practices. More directly, Graham's costume explicitly argued how costume performs in collaboration with a human performer. Likewise, Schlemmer's clown-inspired costumes similarly explored how simple structural forms can be a starting point for performance. What is clear from both experiments, is that insubordinate costumes perform in ways that often resist the criteria for 'good' within their own time period. Bad costumes can change the history of costume practice.

Failures of costumes to perform often reveal an innate tension between appearance and risk. Janet Jackson's 'wardrobe malfunction' at the 2004 Super Bowl XXXVIII in Houston is possibly one of the most infamous examples of a costume failure. Another might be Madonna's Armani designed cape getting caught and pulling her over at the 2015 Brit Awards at the O2 Arena in London. While these failures were not productively 'good' in artistic terms, they did reveal the wearing of costume as bound to a level of risk. Costumes are risky. Anyone who has staged a theatre show knows that dress rehearsals reveal the mis-performances of costumes as much as affirming the significant role costumes play in making a performance come together. The riskiness of costume can be assigned as a quality of a bad costume. But I am keen to stress that the riskiness of costume signals broader politics on the risks of 'being visible'. Costume is, for the most part, a highly visible mode of appearance. Outside of the naturalistic criteria of popular film or the notion that a good costume is 'invisible', in cultural terms costumes often increase the visibility of the wearer. This brings with it power and risk. The insubordination of costume, therefore, also gestures to an element of risk: asking a performer to move differently, or wearing an item or material in an uncustomary manner. Insubordinate costumes want to move performers in ways that feel risky. Yet, at the same time the potential for failure is also a quality of insubordination. Costume failures always reveal.

Badly constructed costumes also perform, albeit with their own register. In the summer of 2016, Rio de Janeiro in Brazil was preparing for the Olympic Games and the World Cup in quick succession. The construction of new stadiums and infrastructure was a momentous investment by the government authorities and, on this global stage, was aimed at presenting Rio as a well-functioning city. However, Rio is a city of significant wealth inequality. Protests arose in certain quarters of the city by inhabitants who questioned the expenditure on facilities that many of Rio's citizens were either too poor or disinterested to benefit from. From these protests emerged the story of Rich Batman and Poor Batman. Dressed in a shop-bought plastic modelled Batman cowl, painted unitard with muscular outlines, detailed gold belt and a thick flowing black cape, Rich Batman was performed by a protester after the governor of Rio had been depicted as The Joker character in news articles and the Guy Fawkes masks (associated with the political movement Anonymous) were banned at protests. Rich Batman was quickly adopted as a media interest story, especially after images emerged of their arrest by the local police. However, it was the emergence of Poor Batman that revealed the full political power of costumed protest. With all the items constructed from black bin bags, Poor Batman emerged as a counter narrative to Rich Batman and underlined, whether intentionally or not, that Rio's politics were not best served by a representation of a billionaire (Bruce Wayne/Rich Batman). The materialities of Poor Batman's costume spoke to the social and economic inequalities of Rio. The 'bad' costume of a binbag-wrought Batman performed in a way that the shop-bought counterpart could not. The performance of costume is also bound to an audiences' familiarity with construction techniques, material or the cultural framing of naïveté. The bad costume of Poor Batman as a naïve (childlike) interpretation of the superhero crafted from a highly familiar material (binbags) was fundamental to politics performed. Bad materials can speak in good ways.

In conclusion, costumes perform through multiple registers and with multiple intentionalities. Bad costumes can perform in different ways to good costumes. Beyond a value or quality judgement, the work of bad costumes can reveal and inspire new lines of thinking and practice that the parameters of good costume (at any historical moment) struggle to fully account for. To describe costume as insubordinate is to recognise the urge to experiment, to identify and break some rules. Bad costumes break rules. Make some bad costumes!

Index

Abstract 11, 35, 44, 77–8, 152, 160–3; art 8; figure 25, 116; forms 34, 36, 194, 208; sculpture 32; space 25; stage 16, 25
Abstraction 25–6, 34, 37, 74–5, 84
Aelita 17, *18*
agency *see costume agency*
Albahwash, Naseem 200, 206, *207*, 208
Albahwash, Shahd 171, *179*, 180
Alice in Wonderland 209–10, 210
ALMA Y MUERTOS 171,183, *184*, 185
Anderson, Jonathan xv, 78, 84, 87, 92
Architecture xiii, 23, 57, 77, 163, 166, 206; for the body 34, 55, 67
Architetture per i Corpi 56
artistic research 15, 23, 119, 129, 131, 134, 186–7 189,190, 194; Costume Agency artistic research 106–7
avant-garde: art 11,17, 38; artists xv, 9, 31,78; art movements xii, 3, 6, 11; 27, 31, 41, 48; fashion xiii, 69, 75
Avenza 44, 44

Bågander, Linnea 117, 186, 189, 190–1, *190–1*
Bakst, Léon xiv, 6, 8, 23
Ball, Hugo xv, 20, *20*
Balla, Giacomo xv
Ballets Russes xiv, 6–10, 21, 23, 33
Ballets Suédois 9–12
Bamboo 144, 146, *147*
Barbieri, Donatella xi, xiv, 133
Bartenev, Andrey 65, *66*, 66–7, 69
Barthes, Roland 53, 61, 84
Bauhaus xv, 4, 12, 23, *24*, 25–7, 34, 36–7, 66, 99,116
beauty 61, 99, 206; ideals 71, 77, 100; norms 23, 57, 69, 73, 79; pageant 45
Bech, Sidsel xvi
Becker, Sandra Hilli 156, 157–9, *157–9*
Becker, Signe xvi, 108–10, *110*, 111–17
Bennett, Jane 100

Biacchi, Sonia 55-6, *56*
Björk 69
Blaisse, Maria 144, 145–7, *145–7*
Body as a Landscape; Body in a Landscape 200
BodyMap xv, 54, 71, *72*
Botanic Ballet 65, *66*
Bourgeois, Louise xv, 43–44, *44*, 45
Bovan, Matty xv, 84, 87–8, *88*, 89–90, 92
Bowery, Leigh x–xii, xv, 23, 54,59, 62, *63–64*, 64–65

Cabaret Voltaire 20, *20*, 21, 41
carnival 61, 71, 89, 99, 204
Carrying Paper Costume, Give Them Wings & See their Faces 188
Casati, Marchesa Luisa 22, 23, *24*, 62
catwalk *see* runway
Cave, Nick 59, *60*, 61, *61*, 64
Chalayan, Hussein
Characterisation xii, xv, 106, 113, 156
Choong, Felix xv, 83
Chrysalis 37, *38*
Chopinot, Régine 54, 73,
Clark, Michael xii, 54, 62, 71, *72*, 73
Collaboration 106, 119, 168–9, 185–6, 192, 195, 201, 205; creative xiv, 137, dance 39–40, 54, 165, 189; fashion 21, 54; performer 108, 130, 133, 136, 154, 167, 213
Comme des Garçons, *see also* Rei Kawakubo 69, 73
Community 77, 151, 194
Community Walk 181, *182*, 183,
Compression Carpet 58, *58*
Conceptual xi–xii, 22, 54–5, 57, 69, 159, 199; 201–2; art xiii, 42, 75; choice 143, 193; development 122, 132–3, 165, 180; fashion xv, 65, 70, 75–7, 83–4, 85, 91
confinement 34, 47
Confinement 186,192, *192*, 193–4
Confrontation 44, *45*

Index

Constriction 3, 31–32, 40, 46–48, 144, 156
constructivism 4, 15,17, 34, 66
costume agency xvi, 106–9, 113, 117, 134
costume research x, xiii, 102, 116, 120, 129–132, 138
Craig, Edward Gordon 18, 99
Critical Costume xiv, xvii, 99, 107, 120, 175
Cubism 7–8, 10–11, 17
Cuttlefish 190, *190*, 191
Cunningham, Merce 31, 38–41, 48, 54, 73–74, *74*, 200–1

Dada xv, 4, 9, 11–12, 19–21, 39, 41, 76
Dalí, Salvador xv, 21–23
Delaunay, Sonia xiv, 8–9
Deform xvi, 56, 151-2 *151–2*
Depero, Fortunato xii–xiii, xv, 6, 18–19, 23
Diaghilev 6–7, 19
DONAULLSDONAULLS 200, *202*
Dragon Zoo 110–111, *112*, 113
dramaturgy xiv, 97, 106, 108, 111–12, 114, 116, 134, 149, 192–4
Dean, Sally E. 98,186–7, *188*, 189
Do You Me? I Did 72

Eastern Bloc 164, 167–170, *170–1*
Electric Dress 42, *43*
Egon Schiele – Self Portrait 164, *164*
embodiment xiv, 23, 33, 42, 53, 89, 97–8, 102
emotion 8, 31–2, 33, 44, 55, 67, 86, 90, 110, 116–17, 153, 161, 186, 190
emotional 32, 35, 58, 113, 135, 171, 189, 195–6
Entanglements 125
Ermakov, Roman 67, 69
Expressionism 15,
extension 10, 34, *36*, 46–7, 97, 100, 187,
Exter, Alexandra xv, 17, *18*,

Felt Me 172, *173*
The Floating Diva 154, *154*, 155
Floen, Fredrik 200, 203–204, *205*, 206
Fressato, Leo 134, *135*
folk xii, 6, 11, 75, 157, 162–3, 194
Fontes Amoris. Pink 67–8, *68*,
Frolova, Sasha 67, *68*, 69
Fuller, Loïe x, xii, xiv, 3–5, *5*, 6, 19
Futurism/Futurist xii, xiii, xv,4, 6, 9, 15–19, 21, 27, 34, 41, 88

Gaultier, Jean Paul 54, 73
gender xii–xiv, xvi, 23, 25, 42, 44–5, 69, 99, 109, 134, 166, 186, 197–9, 204

General Idea 45, *46*
gesture 26, 32, 53, 55, 86–7, 89, 91–2, 213–4
Gillot, Marie-Agnès 75,
Goldesel 157, *157*, 159
Graham, Martha xii, xv, 32–3, *33*
Granata, Francesca 71, 99
Green, Craig xv, 64, 70, 84, 90, *90*, 92
grotesque 12, 17, 19, 27, 46, 56, 73, 91, 99, 109, 111, 205
Gutai Art Association 42, *43*

Hallstrom, Gunnar 12
Hann, Rachel xvii, 32, 99, 213
Haraway, Donna 119–120, 123
Helpers Changing Homes, Motorbike xvi, 195, *196*
hierarchy 115–6,169, 186, 205
Holdt, Walter 12, *13–14*, 15
Homo(Sapiens) 190, *190*, 191
Horn, Rebecca 46–47, *47*, 48, 77, 99
Hudek, Zuzu 156, 166–7, *166–7*, 168–9, 170–1, *171*
Humour 71, 73, 161, 163

Identity xv–xvi, 26, 39, 42–3, 45,48, 53–4, 59, 61, 69, 71, 78, 84, 89, 97, 134, 136, 167, 186, 194, 197–9, 199
Imago (The City Curious) 36, *37*
Inhabiting Noise and Silence xvi, 175, *176–7*
Improvisation 21, 101, 111, 113–14,147, 153, 172, 189, 190
inspiration 6, 45, 65, 74, 97, 109, 97, 151–2, 164, 168, 175, 198, 208
Interior 157–8, *158*, 159
intuition 101, 130, 146
The Issue 162, *162*

Jalet, Damien 76–7
Judson Dance Theater 40–1

Karstens, Daphne xvi, 144, 147–8, *148*, 149–50, *149–50*
Kawakuba, Rei xv, 39, 54, 69, 73–4, *74*, 89
kinetic 19, 55, 73, 86, 144, 151
Knead 172, 174, *174*
Knotting Connections 124
knowledge xiii, 77, 79, 90, 101, 107, 108, 119–20, 127, 130–4, 143, 147, 178, 183, 202
Kuma Guna 144, *145–6*

Lady Gaga 23, 64, 69–70
Lamentation xii, xv, 32, *33*, 35
landscape 106, 151, 192, 202–4; body 197–200, *200*, 201; costume 138,

Index

186, 205; sound xvi, 175, 178; textile xvi
Lane, Kate 186, 191–2, *192*, 193, *193*
Larionov, Mikhail 7, 9–10
Léger, Fernand 9–11
lighting xii, 5–6, 10, 32, 36, 39, 83, 107, 112, 138, 144, 153, 158, 167
limitations 25, 32, 39, 41, 99, 111, 149, 165, 167, 169, 185, 190
Lindgren, Christina xvi, 106–8, 110–12, *112*, 113–17, 134,
The Line 200, *207*, 208
Lismore, Daniel 62, 65
Loewe xv, 78, 84, *85*, 86, 92
Lotker, Sodja Zupanc 106–7, 110

Malevich, Kazimir xv, 8, *13*, 15, 16, *16*, 17, 20, 32
Margiela, Martin 70, 89
Marnezti, Laura xvi, 171, 175, *176–7*, 178
Marvin, Gena 69
MASK #32 137
masks 11, 12, 15, 16, 19, 21, 34, 67, 76–7, 111, 136, *137*, 157, 159–61, 205, 214
materiality xi, xvi, 4, 7, 34, 42, 54–5, 79, 90, 100, 107, 117, 119, 122–3, 127, 134, 136, 143–4, 164, 186, 192–3
Matisse, Henri xiv, 6, 19
McQueen, Alexander 64, 77
McRae, Lucy 57–9, *58–9*
Me with My Pet 199
mechanical 18–19, 25, 27, 46–7, *47*, 69, 78, 85–6, 114, 191, 201–2
Mechanical Bodyfan 47
memory 32, 97–8, 119, 121–2, 169, 185
Merleau-Ponty, Maurice 98, 171
METAMORPHOSIS 166–7, *166–7*
methodology 102, 130, 134, 185, 190, 192–3, 195, 197
Miss General Idea Pageant 45, *46*,
Miyake, Issey xv, 54, 145
Modernism xi, 3, 27, 78, 87
modules 127, 207, 209–10
Monks, Aoife xii, xv, 53, 61, 79
music 6, 10–12, 15–16, 26, 35–6, 39, 41, 55, 67, 74, 83, 106, 121, 147, 153–4, 161–2, 167, 169, 178, 199–200

Nagy, Fruzsina xvi, 156, 159–160, *160*, 161–2, *161–2*, 163, 168–9, *170*
narrative xii–xiii, 17, 39, 54–5, 62, 77, 86, 97, 102, 110, 126, 136, 150, 157, 183, 194, 200, 206, 214
Netherlands Dance Theater 75

New Materialism xiv, xvi, 97, 100, 106–7
New Puritans 71, *72*
Nikolais, Alwin xii, xv, 35–6, *36*, 37–38, *38*, 39, 48, 99, 200–1
Noguchi, Isamu 32, 34–5, 38
non-human 100, 107, 110, 117, 119–23, 125–7, 173, 181, 183, 196
norms x–xiii, xvii, 15, 23, 27, 54, 57, 71, 78, 89, 98–9

On the Lips of Living Men 205, *206*
Osipova, Polina 67, 69
Østergaard, Charlotte xvi, 119, *124–5*, 136, *137*, 171, 180, 182, *182*, 183
Oyama, Yuka xvi, 186, 194–6, *196–7*

Page, Ruth 33–5
Paladini, Vinicio 18
'PANG' 148, *148*
Pannaggi, Ivo xv, 18,
Pantouvaki, Sofia x, xiii–xiv, xvi–xvii, 54, 120, 129
Parade 7, *7*, 8, 11, 21, 34, 62, 73, 75
Pasman, Victorine 144, 154, *154*, 155, *156*
Paul, Debashish xvi, 186,197–9, *199–200*
Pavis, Patrice xi, 211
Peeled Shadows 157–9, *159*
Pelican xii, xv, 40–1, *41*
Penetrating Costume – The Girl and the Autumn 135
perception 26, 39, 91, 98, 100, 121, 130, 133–4, 136–7, 171, 193, 204
Perceptive Fragility 134, *135*
Performative Pockets 208, 211,, *211*
performativity xvi, 54, 83–4, 87, 90, 99, 107, 158
phenomenology xiv, 98
philosophy of costume xiii–xiv, 54
Picabia, Francis 10–11
Picasso, Pablo xii, xiv, 6–7, *7*, 8, 11, 34, 156
'PING' 150, *150*
playfulness xiv, 4, 7, 21, 23, 54, 64, 97, 100, 102, 143, 183, 202
Poiret, Paul xiv, 6, 23, *24*
political xii–xiv, xvi, 3–4, 17, 19, 27, 48, 69, 90, 98, 100, 102, 106, 131, 143, 192, 214
Portillo Cisterna, Daniela 171, 183 *184*, 185–6
Postdramatic 54, 106, 133–4
Prague Quadrennial xvii, 106, 143, 175, 178, 181, *184*, *205*, 205
props 22, 34, 37, 39, 73, 195
prosthetic 39, 46–7, 57, 99–100, 158
protagonist xi, 3, 54, 123, 169,

protect 58–9, 61, 69–70, 77, 91, 187, 196, 198
protest xi, 20, 54, 69–70, 199, 214
Pugh, Gareth xv, 64, 99
Pyuupiru 64, 69, 99

queer xiii, 45, 69, 127, 197–8

Rauschenberg, Robert xii, xv, 38–41, *41*,
recycling xvii, 69, 89, 102, 163, 209
Roqué, Mariaelena 200–3, *202*
runway xiii, xv, 54, 62, 65, 70–1, 75, 77, 78–9, 83–6, 160, 161, 168, 204–5
Rybáková, Simona xvii, 156, 163–4, *164*, 165–6, 168, *170*

Scenario 39, 73–4, *74*,
scenography x–xi, 16, 19, 97, 100, 106, 112, 114, 116, 166, 170, 187, 191
Schiaparelli, Elsa xv, 21,
Schlemmer, Oskar xi–xii, xv, 8, 12, 15, 23, *24*, 25–7, 32, 34–7, 55, 99–100, 116, 213
Schulz, Lavinia 12, *13–14*, 15
semiotic x, 53–4, 130, 133
sensation 91, 98, 113, 116, 121–2, 167
Silent Transformation 155, *156*
Skeleton Woman 109, *110*, 111, 113–5
The Snow Queen 65, *66*
Solitary Survival Raft 58, *59*
somatic xiv, 91, 98, 186–7, *188*, 189–91
Somatic Costume Dressing Room 187, *188*, 189
soundscape 171, 175, 178
Soundsuits 59, *60–1*, 61
storytelling 78, 160, 169, 200, 206
STRAW 148–9, *149*
subvert 20, 27, 92, 98–9
Summerlin, Dawn 134, *135*
Suprematism 15, 17
Surrealism xv, 4, 8, 21
SurvivaBall Home Suits 195, *197*

symbol 25, 33, 91, 152, 157, 159, 169, 180, 193, 208, 210, 213

Taboo Collection 160–161, *160–161*
Taeuber-Arp, Sophie xv, 20–1
Tanaka, Atsuko 42–3, *43*
technology 3, 15,17, 25, 57, 76, 87, 168
theory xi, xiv, 23, 25, 37, 97, 100, 107, 119, 127, 138
tool: creative 39, 112, 117, 203; powerful 144, 150, 154–5, 157; research xii, xiv, 3, 102, 129, 133, 137
transformation 18, 76, 89, 155, 157, 167–8, 193–4
Triadic Ballet (Das Triadische Ballett) xii, xv, 8, 15, 23, *24*, 25–7, 32, 34–6, 55, 99, 100
Trigg, Madeleine 171, 172–3, *173*, 174, *174*

Ulargui Escalona, Paula 78
unconventional material xvi, 89, 134, 137, 147

Van Beirendonck, Walter xv, 75–6
van Herpen, Iris xv, 70, 77
Victory over the Sun 8, 15, 16–17, 20, 32
Viktor & Rolf xv, 75

Waltz, Sasha 77,
Watanabe, Junya xv, 69
wearable art xiv, xvii, 75, 147
wearable sculpture xiv, 55, 67, *147*, 149, 153–4, 192, 194, 196
The Wind of Good 179, 180
Worning, Jeppe 136, *137*
Woutera de Jong, Iris xvi, 144, 150, 151–2, *151–2*

Zhou, Terrence 78
Zofia Jakubiec xvi, 108, *109*, 110–11, 113–17